DATE DUE			

Margaret Michaelis

Margaret Michaelis
love, loss and photography

Helen Ennis

■ national gallery of **australia**

Produced by the Publications Department
of the National Gallery of Australia

nga.gov.au

The National Gallery of Australia is an Australian Government Agency.

Editor: Paige Amor
Designer: Sarah Robinson
Printer: The Craftsman Press

Cataloguing-in-Publication data

Ennis, Helen.

    Margaret Michaelis: love, loss and photography.

    ISBN 0 642 54120 5.

    1. Michaelis, Margaret. 2. Photographers - Australia -

    Biography. 3. Photography - Australia. I. National

    Gallery of Australia. II. Title.

    770.92

Distributed in Australia by
Thames and Hudson
11 Central Boulevard Business Park
Port Melbourne, Victoria 3207

Distributed in the United Kingdom by
Thames and Hudson
181A High Holborn
London WC1V 7QX, UK

Distributed in the United States of America by
University of Washington Press
1326 Fifth Avenue, Ste 555
Seattle, WA 98101-2604

Front cover: 14 June 1948, Parramatta River, Sydney (self-portrait) (detail)
29.5 × 36.8 cm
Page vi: Christmas 1931 (detail) 11.8 × 8.8 cm

Contents

Names used in this book

Margaret Michaelis was born Margarethe Gross and was known as Grete to her friends and family. Her first husband Rudolf Michaelis (also spelt Rudolph), whom she married in 1933, called her Gretl and Gretele. Rudolf was known as Michel and occasionally as Michele. In Spain, where Margaret Michaelis lived from 1933 to 1937, she was known as Margarete or Grete. After moving to Australia in 1939 her first name was anglicised to Margaret. In 1960 she married Albert Sachs and became Margaret Sachs.

In this book I have used the names depending on the context.

The full names for some of the most commonly used abbreviations in the book are as follows:

A.C.	*A.C. Documentos de Actividad Contemporánea (A.C. Documents of Contemporary Activity)*
ARXIU	Arxiu Històric del Col.legi d'Arquitectes de Catalunya, in Barcelona
CNT	Confederación Nacional de Trabajo (Federation of Anarcho-Syndicalist Trades Union)
DAS	Deutsche Anarcho-Syndikalisten (Group of German Anarcho-Syndicalists)
FAI	Federación Anarquista Ibérica (Federation of Anarchist Groups)
FAUD	Freien Arbeiter-Union Deutschlands (Free Workers Union of Germany)
GATCPAC	Grup d'Arquitectes i Tècnics Catalans per al Progrés de l'Arquitectura Contemporània (Group of Catalan Architects and Technicians for the Progress of Contemporary Architecture)
GATEPAC	Grupo de Arquitectos y Técnicos Españoles para el Progreso de la Arquitectura Contemporánea (Group of Spanish Architects and Technicians for the Progress of Contemporary Architecture)
IAA	Internationale ArbeiterInnen Assoziation (International Workers Association)
UGT	Union General de Trabajadores (Socialist Trades Union)

1 MRS SACHS

I did not know Mrs Sachs well. I met her only a few times in 1985, the year of her death. Our relationship was a professional one based on a shared involvement in photography. She had been a photographer in Sydney in the 1940s and I was Curator of Photography at the National Gallery of Australia. My reason for approaching her was pragmatic: her photographs had been recommended to the Gallery by two independent researchers in Melbourne and I hoped to acquire a small group for the collection of Australian photography.

The arrangements for our meetings were very formal. I would write to Mrs Sachs from Canberra to make an appointment and ring her once I was in Melbourne to confirm the time. When I arrived at the Montefiore Homes for the Aged where she lived, I would stop first at the reception desk, confirm my appointment and then walk up to her room on the first floor of the main building overlooking St Kilda Road. There she would be waiting for me, quietly, with everything in order around her. No music playing, no open book in her lap, no half-written letters on the table nearby.

On my first visit I realised that negotiations were not going to be concluded quickly. This wasn't unusual. In my experience people needed time to decide what, if anything, they could part with. Only once have I met a photographer who wanted no time at all; with great cheerfulness he had urged me to take away, at once, everything he had kept for the last five decades. Mrs Sachs was much more cautious. She showed me only one photograph – a relatively unexciting portrait of a man – and made only one commitment: to see me again. I was happy with the outcome. I assumed Mrs Sachs saw me clearly as the stranger I was and wanted to be sure of me, and my motives, before proceeding further. I remained interested in her work and was impressed by her manner, especially her seriousness and alertness. I also remember being struck by her European-ness: her accent was quite pronounced and her expression was sometimes awkward.

Our subsequent meetings took shape as long conversations. To tape them would have been far too intrusive and so I have since had to return to my recollections of them over and over again. My questions revolved around photography – her training in Vienna, her work in Berlin, Barcelona and Sydney, and her sources and influences. I was curious about the two photographs on the bench in her room; one was a portrait of Albert Schweitzer, by Austrian photographer Lotte Meitner-Graf, whose work she said she admired, the other was her own photograph of Bertrand Russell, taken while watching a television program on the philosopher.

Every now and then Mrs Sachs would ask questions of me. What did I think of the quality of photographic reproductions in books she showed me? What were my views on feminism? Did I know who Saccho and Vanzetti were? I felt that she was watching me closely as I replied, as if these were tests that I had to pass. I never knew whether or not I had responded satisfactorily.

Sometimes Mrs Sachs spoke of matters other than photography: her upbringing by liberally minded and supportive parents, and the wonderful opportunities she had enjoyed as a teenager studying photography in Vienna. She told me a little about her life in the early 1930s with her first husband Rudolf Michaelis, whom she called Michel, referring to the difficulties they experienced after Hitler came to power – the Nazi's raid on their Berlin flat and their hasty departure for Barcelona. Whenever she mentioned Michel it was with a tenderness I can still recall. From her account of their relationship I was convinced that theirs had been a great love defeated only by circumstances completely outside their control. She told me, for instance, that when she fled Spain at the height of the Civil War it was with the understanding that Michel would soon join her. It was some years before I discovered that this wasn't the case. She never mentioned her second husband, Albert Sachs, whom she married in 1960 and who died five years later. She did, however, allude to recent disappointments in friendships, betrayals and exploitation, and described her impatience with the people around her who were old and frail. Nevertheless, she remained active, telling me of her interests in music and the visual arts, and her voluntary work repairing books in the Home's library.

As our meetings continued I realised that no conclusion to our negotiations was in sight. On each visit Mrs Sachs would show me only a very small number of photographs, which she selected in advance and laid out ready inside their bright orange Agfa envelopes. Any that I expressed interest in she wanted to have copied, despite my explanations that the Gallery's preference was for 'vintage' prints (made around the time of the negatives). To convince me that modern prints were equally desirable she commissioned a photographer in St Kilda to make a copy of the very first portrait she showed me, declaring that she was very pleased with the result. She was right. The copy was good. And yet, while the process of duplication enabled us each to have copies of the same images, it didn't resolve the question of ownership of the shared object of our desire: the vintage print. Obviously Mrs Sachs was greatly attached to her photographs and didn't want to be parted from them. But there was more to it than that. Slowly I became aware that she was deliberately drawing out our negotiations for the simple reason that she didn't want them to end.

It became clear that Mrs Sachs and I had different expectations of our relationship. She wanted me to spend time with her. She was lonely, 'incredibly lonely' a friend was later to say, though she was 'surrounded by an army of people'. I felt her loneliness there behind all of our conversations, heavy and immovable. She wanted companionship. She never said so in words but I knew she wanted me to become her friend. I didn't want that. The terms seemed too intense and too exclusive for me. I couldn't respond to what I saw as the sharp, demanding aspects of her personality, which I have since discovered various friends had experienced more directly. Amidst the loving and positive comments they made after her death – she was 'astute, alert, charming', 'attractive and sharp', 'interesting ... to be with', 'a very vivid person' – came the refrain that she was 'difficult'. They said that she was 'difficult to get on with', 'egotistical', 'melancholic', 'intense, demanding', that she had 'no patience' and was 'manipulative, often unconsciously so'. One former friend, who had broken with her some years earlier, told me that she 'needed love and affection but wrecked all possible relationships'.

Only once did I see Mrs Sachs outside the Home. She came to hear a paper I was giving at the University of Melbourne, at a conference organised by the Art Association of Australia. I was touched to see her in the audience; I had mentioned the event to her only in passing and she had gone to great lengths to find out where and when it was on. At the end of the day my partner and I accompanied her on the tram ride down Swanston Street and along St Kilda Road to the Home where she lived. She was full of conversation, engaging and lively. When we came to her stop she declined our offers of help and climbed down from the tram herself. As she walked away I remember noticing how smartly she dressed and how small she was: five feet two inches, I later read in her passport.

The next time I saw Mrs Sachs was the last. The visit began like the others. I made my appointment in advance, went to the reception desk as before and was referred to her room. When I knocked on the door there was silence. I knocked again, Mrs Sachs called out and I went inside. The blinds were down, it was dark and she was lying very still on her back in bed, her arms outstretched on the blankets. There was an unopened block of chocolate on her bedside table and a book by James Michener lying next to her. She didn't know who I was to begin with. I told her my name and after a pause she said 'Take the photographs'. I explained that I couldn't possibly take them, not now, not while she was ill. I would come back some other time, soon, when she was better and we would talk more about it then. She didn't respond. I stayed standing beside her bed not sure what to do. She asked me to fill her hot-water bottle, giving me quiet, careful instructions about how hot and how full she wanted it. She told me that she was losing the words for things, she couldn't give them their names in either English or German. She asked me whether I had read the Michener book. I hadn't, and she told me she liked it because of its references to Buddhism. Some time later an elderly woman came into the room. We exchanged a few words, she took the hot-water bottle from Mrs Sachs, filled it again, wrapped a handtowel around it and helped Mrs Sachs get comfortable as she handed it back.

I cannot remember whether I kissed Mrs Sachs goodbye. Thinking back, I hope I did. I do remember touching her hand and telling her that I would come to see her again in a few days' time. I hoped that she would be feeling better by then.

I was angry and upset when I left her room. It was the image of her suffering alone that most distressed me; the sickbed scenes I imagined were generously peopled with loved ones, or at least with caring professional staff. Downstairs, in response to my questions about Mrs Sachs's condition the receptionist directed me to a medical attendant on duty nearby. He calmly heard me out. 'Had I had many dealings with old people?' No, I had not. 'Was I aware that Mrs Sachs was not the easiest person to get along with?' Yes, I knew that. 'Could it be that she was exaggerating her illness?' Possibly, I didn't know.

A few days later, without phoning ahead, I returned to the Home, a get-well bunch of flowers from Prahran Market in my arms. As always, I paused at the desk to say I had come to see Mrs Sachs. The receptionist looked at me matter-of-factly and said that she was sorry but Mrs Sachs had died two days earlier. If I wanted further information she suggested I approach the social worker whose name I remember as Yvette and who at that moment was organising Mrs Sachs's affairs. On my way to her office on the first floor I walked past

Mrs Sachs's room: the door was open and it was empty and clean. Yvette told me that Mrs Sachs had died from cancer of the liver, which had been diagnosed only a few weeks before. Everyone had been surprised at the rapidity of her deterioration – in what was seen as a characteristically uncooperative, obstinate act Mrs Sachs had chosen not to eat, thereby hastening her death.

On the social worker's advice I contacted Mrs Sachs's lawyers and declared the National Gallery of Australia's interest in her photographs and personal papers. The lawyers granted me permission to retrieve any relevant material from Mrs Sachs's possessions, which had been packed up and temporarily stored in the Home's shed prior to auction. The few items of furniture, including the bed, television and refrigerator had been stacked to one side, the more personal belongings piled up next to them. In their bright orange boxes and envelopes the photographs were easy to find, but there were many more than I expected. Not the handful Mrs Sachs had shown me over the last few months, but hundreds of photographs in envelope after envelope. Not just portraits, but architectural shots, still lifes, street photographs, landscapes and experimental works taken in Europe and Australia over a thirty-year period. There were also personal photographs, mostly snapshots stored loose inside an old shoebox; others were arranged in two photograph albums.

Amongst the personal papers I gathered up were official documents – a birth certificate, two marriage certificates, a Spanish divorce decree, a death notice for Albert Sachs – and an assortment of semi-official items. The latter included certificates of study; employment references from Vienna, Prague, Berlin and Sydney; and membership certificates for Australian photographic societies. Especially significant for the turn this story has taken were the most personal items Mrs Sachs had chosen to keep with her throughout her life. These were the notes and letters – to 'Grete' as she was known by those closest to her – from her beloved Michel. As is to be expected from the remnants of an exchange between lovers, the dialogue was mostly one-sided: the majority of letters Mrs Sachs had kept were those she received, not those she sent. More than thirty of them, in Michel's distinctive small, tight script were tucked inside a large white envelope with his name written in large black letters on the outside. Mrs Sachs also had a few copies of her own letters to Michel, a fact I still find curious.

For a long time after Mrs Sachs's belongings entered the National Gallery of Australia's collection – 'Gift of the Margaret Michaelis-Sachs estate 1986' – I was interested only in the photographs, and then only from the perspectives of art history and museology. The first priority, from a curatorial point of view, was to sort through the collection, dividing the photographs into exhibition-quality prints and archive prints. This involved the consideration of a whole

range of factors. Were the prints vintage or non-vintage? Were they signed or
mounted, both of which indicated a state of completion? Did they carry any
inscriptions, stamps or labels? For what purpose had they been taken? What was
the significance of their imagery in terms of subject matter and style?

Art historical methodology offered me a useful way of defining Mrs Sachs's life
through her work; for example, by establishing a chronology of the photographs,
and by considering their stylistic origins, influences and connections to broader
photographic movements. At the time, scholarship on European modernist
photography of the 1920s and 1930s was flourishing and there was a plethora of
exhibitions and publications in the United States and Europe. A particular focus
was Germany, which had been central to the development of the so-called New
Photography movement. The work of Albert Renger-Patzsch, August Sander and
László Moholy-Nagy was ubiquitous but work by women, including Germaine
Krull, Lucia Moholy and Florence Henri, was also beginning to appear. The
common shadow behind all these photographers' careers was the rise of fascism
in Europe and the diaspora following Hitler's ascendancy to power.

Mrs Sachs's photographs, especially those produced in Spain between 1934
and 1937, had all the hallmarks of the New Photography movement – disorienting
viewpoints, sharp focus and bold compositions. In addition, her approach in the
early 1930s could be aligned with a particular strand of modernist photographic
practice, one that had a social activist or reformist base, as exemplified in the
much-published work of Tina Modotti. There was also an Australian context for
Mrs Sachs's practice – that of modernist Australian photography, which was re-
invigorated by the contribution of European refugees, like her, who had arrived
in the late 1930s and early 1940s. In Sydney, where between 1940 and 1952 she

ran a studio specialising in portraiture and dance photography, she was one of the few independent female practitioners of the period.

In the late 1980s I laid aside my research. I felt dissatisfied with what I had done, though I don't think I could have articulated the exact reasons for my dissatisfaction. I do remember having a suspicion that I had rendered the material lifeless and had somehow failed to do it justice. Around this time I decided to leave the Gallery and change my career.

A few years later I often found myself thinking about Mrs Sachs, usually at night-time when I was patting my youngest son to sleep. In what became an extended reverie I went over and over our conversations; I felt that I hadn't properly heard what she was saying to me and that I had been asking the wrong questions. But it was our final exchange that I kept returning to because it perplexed me the most. Did she tell me to take the photographs because she was attached to them and wanted to ensure their safekeeping? Or did she, like the other photographer I had met, tell me to take them because she had already shed her attachment to them? Either way I wished I had responded differently to her request and said, with a Molly Bloomish kind of affirmation, 'Yes, yes of course I'll take them. Don't worry, they'll be safe with me'.

Then my aunt died. She too had left behind an unfulfilled request that bothered me. In the last few years of her life she had kept a notebook in which she invited members of our family to list any of her belongings we wanted after her death. I couldn't write anything down, even though she asked me to on two or three occasions. To have done so, I thought, would have solicited her not-at-all desired death and, in light of that, declared my own flourishing connectedness to things. As far as I know the notebook stayed empty, though after my aunt's death the distribution of her belongings was attended to with great care by her siblings.

When I returned to the Margaret Michaelis-Sachs Archive it was with the desire to begin another kind of conversation with the material she had left behind. Not just with the photographs but with all those other things that I either hadn't noticed before or didn't know how to deal with: dried rose petals, envelopes, maps, postcards, inscriptions on photographs, the looseness or tightness of a handwritten script. But, above all else, I now found that it was the notes and letters that drew me in. No longer simply an adjunct to the photographs, interesting only where they spoke about photography, they had assumed a power of their own. It is a peculiar kind of power that comes, in part from the insistency and immediacy of their present tense. 'Darling,' Grete wrote in a note to Michel a few months after they met,

All day I have been cheered by your letter, by your love for the two of us, for our life. How exciting life is now, dearest.

Well, you make fun of dancing, that's okay, but in this respect you are blind. I love your well-meaning mockery.

I am writing in a bit of a hurry, can you see? I was just rung by the studio and they want me to come immediately. Temporary help until Christmas. I have to accept it, naturally, but for us, my darling, this is not good.

I won't be able to meet you after work tomorrow and don't know at all how things will turn out in the next few days. There will be a lot of overtime, till late at night. The nice Christmas stroll through the streets is gone, we will hardly see each other until Christmas, my dearest, and all that overturned for a lousy few Marks. You will have to ring here tomorrow and I will leave a message about when I will be free. Will you come to meet me, even if it's 10 o'clock at night?

I have to rush, excuse my haste.

I embrace you, wholly your Grete.

These notes and letters began to shake open a past – a messy, ordinary yet extraordinary past that had a multitude of missing threads. Tantalisingly they offered the possibility of a narrative that the photographs alone could not. There's no saying that the story they have since become part of is the only one that could have been written, but this is the version that insisted on being written, the others did not.

A few weeks ago I gathered together my copies of all the photographs Mrs Sachs had kept of herself and laid them out on my writing table at home. Most are snapshots taken by unknown people but a few may have been taken by Mrs Sachs herself. One snapshot from a sightseeing trip to Uberlingen in 1967 (the year she visited her first husband, Michel, in East Berlin) has an inscription: 'that's what they do to me if I at last get a foto of myself. One leg – and although I said: Hold the camera straight, the house is falling over!!' This is an exception; hardly any others have details about the time or place in which they were taken. After all, why write on the photographs you know best, those that are most secure in your memory?

While looking at them all again I was struck by their similarities to other groups of photographs that have been cut loose from their moorings, the kind you come across in second-hand shops, rubbish tips and archives. Like these other bundles of an unwanted past, Mrs Sachs's photographs are generally very quiet in the presence of strangers. There are, however, two portraits that have begun to speak to me. In them I can see something of the person I knew, especially those eyes – like an eagle's, as one of her friends said of them – that so dominated her face. And yet it is something that I don't actually recognise that draws me into the images, inviting my scrutiny. It is the look on Mrs Sachs's face and the fact that it is the same in each image, even though they were taken more than thirty years apart. In the earlier photograph she appears as a stylishly dressed and obviously European woman posing for a moment in downtown Sydney, possibly Castlereagh Street where she had her photographic studio. Three decades later she is standing in front of the Home in Melbourne,

Unknown photographer
Mrs Sachs at Montefiore
Homes for the Aged,
Melbourne 1985
7.0 × 9.2 cm

where I met her the year she died. So close is the likeness between the two faces that it would be easy to merge them together in a slow filmic dissolve or digital transformation.

In itself this seamless transposition isn't very remarkable; indeed, it has become commonplace in a digital age. What is more intriguing is that these portraits of Mrs Sachs don't merge with any that have survived from her early years in Europe. If you lay all of the portraits side by side, a mismatch becomes apparent. The young and old, pre and postwar, and European and Australian faces don't properly mesh together. Certainly the facial features remain consistent (so one can feel confident that the photographs are of the same person), but the expression or the 'look' of the faces is altogether different. In the European portraits the face is still in the process of becoming, whereas in the Australian versions it is fixed, having already decided on itself. This latter face knows how it looks when photographed and wears one of those telltale expressions you settle on as being an adequate or sufficient representation of yourself (it doesn't reveal too much, it isn't unflattering). It's the kind of face you come to know from looking at photographs others have taken of you, the one you effortlessly summon up in the instant before the shutter is released.

What I like most about these two portraits of Mrs Sachs is something different again. It's the way her watchfulness charges the photographic transaction: even in the process of being photographed hers is a face that is actively looking.

2   DUSK

Dzieditz, Margarethe Gross's hometown, is not easy to find as it doesn't appear in contemporary atlases. It was in the nearby, much better known town of Bielitz, now Bielsko-Biala, that Gross's birth was registered, her birth certificate carrying the stamp of the local Registry Office of the Jewish Cultural Community. In Gross's early childhood Dzieditz and Bielitz were part of Austria and, as her birth certificate affirmed, she was an Austrian national. In 1919, however, these towns were included in the territory returned to Poland in the re-drawing of boundaries that followed the end of World War I. Twenty years later, after the Germans invaded Poland, they became part of the greater Reich.

When Gross returned to Europe in 1967, as an Australian citizen, she chose not to revisit the territory of her childhood. Her older sister, Lotte, and younger brother, Erich, had lived in South America since the late 1930s and their parents, Dr Henryk and Fanny Gross, had apparently died in the Holocaust. Margarethe Gross's images of home, of the centre of her world, had therefore long been frozen in a small group of photographs taken in the years before the outbreak of World War II. These were among Mrs Sachs's possessions when she died.

Most of these images are snapshots of her closest family and their maid Terezia. In a few instances Gross appears herself – a striking, dark-haired and rather intense-looking young woman. However, even when not physically present in the photographs, she is there as an implied viewer, one who has been immersed in these intimate and highly sensory family moments. Looking at them it is easy to imagine her joining her mother and Terezia in the kitchen, or walking outside to the spot where her parents are resting in the sun – her mother in a hammock and her father, book in hand, seated beside her.

One of these photographs stands out from the others. It is a landscape, or more precisely a rural scene, showing gently sloping hills criss-crossed with paths, tracks and trees, and in the distance some buildings that are probably

Mama ... midday, July
1925, Dzieditz. Terezia
in background Poland
1925 8.2 × 5.8 cm

Foto-Atelier Weintraub
Henryk and Fanny
Gross c. 1925
8.2 × 5.8 cm

Henryk Gross in deckchair
c. 1921–27 11.1 × 8.2 cm

Unknown photographer
Margarethe Gross and
her father, Henryk Gross
c. 1925 7.2 × 6.2 cm

farmhouses. A much larger print than the others, it has a relatively long inscription on the reverse, handwritten in German by Gross:

> This is our favourite walk to the convent in Dzieditz. When I was three or four years old our blonde Anna always took me with her when she went to the farmers to get butter and eggs. And she made a big detour in order to go to the convent. And there she knelt a long time by herself deep in prayer. And I was with her. The impression is still alive today. Anna left us and became a nun.

What confounds me about this image is the exclusivity of its terms, the fact that it can say so little to me. The scene it depicts is not special in any way that I can see; its attributes are not enhanced by the choice of an advantageous viewpoint, as in conventional tourist views, or the kinds of artful representations that characterise so much landscape photography. This is a photograph of a different order, resolute in its ordinariness, its muteness or what could even be called its dumbness.

By taking up a position within the landscape itself, rather than a viewpoint outside it Gross, as the photographer, is able to convey a sense of the continuity of the scene. What lies beyond the trees and hills in the distance, to either side or even behind her can be assumed to be similarly unspectacular. This, it seems, is a photograph that can make sense only to those familiar with this part of the world, those who have walked through it, known it and who remember what is there. In effect, Gross's landscape is a field for memories, not the generalised memories that the artist Christian Boltanksi mobilises in his photographic work but those that are highly specific. From her inscription on the back of the photograph it isn't possible to tell whether Gross is remembering for herself, out loud as it were, or whether she is addressing her memories to someone else. However, what is clear from the sure, firm handwriting is that this inscription was not written by the elderly Mrs Sachs; she would engage in a different way with the process of remembering her childhood years.

The town where Margarethe Gross grew up was situated on an important railway junction. This was Dzieditz's most noteworthy feature, and one can imagine that the movement of the freight trains carrying coal from the rich deposits in Silesia to Vienna gave rhythm to the town's life. In Australia such a close association with the railway would be relatively benign, signifying

Scene near Dzieditz, Poland c. 1921–27 12.1 × 17.0 cm

progress, expansion and mobility, but Dzieditz was located at the hub of an efficient rail system linking Austria, Poland and Germany. By the end of World War II this rail network had carried millions of Jews to their deaths; Gross's parents, two of Dzieditz's former residents, were probably among them.

Photographs of the railway – tracks, trains, sidings and stations – are common enough in the sprawling archive of imagery from World War II. They may have been part of the group of photographs from Bergen-Belsen and Dachau that triggered Susan Sontag's negative epiphany in July 1945 when, as a child of twelve browsing in a Santa Monica bookstore, she encountered 'the photographic inventory of ultimate horror'. Of this 'prototypically modern revelation' she later wrote in her book *On photography* that

> Nothing I have seen – in photographs or in real life – ever cut me as sharply, deeply, instantaneously ... When I looked at those photographs, something broke. Some limit had been reached, and not only that of horror; I felt irrevocably grieved, wounded, but a part of my feelings started to tighten; something went dead; something is still crying.[1]

Since their initial appearance in the last days of the war in magazines, including *Life*, *Vogue* and *Picture Post*, photographs related to the Holocaust have been widely circulated in publications dealing with aspects of modern German and Jewish history. I have some of the images in front of me now: *Jews being loaded into railway trucks, Seidlce Station, 22 August 1945*; *Germans cramming Jewish women and children of Miedzyrzec into freight cars 1943*; and *Train at Dachau: prisoners have died on the short march to camp 1945*. The latter image, by Lee Miller, so devastating in its banality, lodged itself in my mind years ago. Its composition is split into two so that a small township with a cluster of houses appears on the left and a railway track, with a huge stationary train, is on the right. In between the two spaces is a long, straight road with two, possibly three corpses lying, with awful casualness, where they have fallen.

Lee Miller's photograph was one of many taken with the express purpose of bringing to public attention the unbelievable atrocities that had taken place under Hitler's regime. 'I IMPLORE YOU TO BELIEVE THIS IS TRUE' Miller wrote in the cable accompanying the dispatch of her Dachau photographs to her employers at *Vogue* magazine in the United States. Photographs of railway associated imagery have functioned as evidence of the mass transportation and extermination of the Jews for decades, but in recent years the railway has emerged as a more general visual symbol for the route to unspeakable horror and destruction. And in the ceremony that marked the fiftieth anniversary of the liberation of the concentration camp in Auschwitz, people lit thousands of candles along the railway lines leading to and from the station that fed the camp.

Towards the end of her life Mrs Sachs chose the railway as a central image in a story about her childhood, which she wrote as an assignment for a creative writing class. Called 'Dusk', it begins:

> There was one long road in our village and we moved into the last house when I was five. Ten minutes walk away was the railway station. It was quite a big one for such a small village. As we were near the border of three countries, meeting all in a corner so to say, it was the meeting and shunting ground for trains coming from Prague, Warsaw, Berlin and our own capital, Vienna.
>
> I liked to look down from our verandah window. There were cornfields and poplars. And the sun set over the fields there, big and red.
>
> But at the front and seen through my window there was something fascinating going on almost every afternoon. When a train arrived from Vienna, the engine came right out to the waterpipes and filled its thirsty belly. After that, it returned to the train but came back again in a funny way. In front of it, it was pushing a carriage which was locked and had no windows. The engine puffed and coughed and far out on the network of rails gave the closed box on wheels a gentle push and let it run all the way by itself ...
>
> The far side of our road was fenced in, hiding all these rails and the engine-houses where all the noise and steam came from. But from my window, of course, I could see everything. Just opposite our house were sheds leaning inside behind the fence; men must have used their tools there. I always saw men coming out with hammers and screwbars [sic] and returning with them later. Normally there was no sound coming from the sheds but, one day, coming home from school ... I heard squeaking and squealing and grunting behind the fence; it must have been pigs. When I came closer I heard a terribly desperate squeaking just at that moment. Had somebody killed a pig? There was silence. I had never seen a pig or any other animal on the shunting-ground. Perhaps I imagined it. But there were pigs there. I heard the fearful squealing quite often after that ...
>
> One day in autumn I came home by myself. I must have played longer than usual with Eva. She had a wonderful cubby-house far back in the garden. One could almost live there.

Dusk is long and quiet in autumn where I come from. Light treads softly and takes a long time to follow the setting sun.

When I came closer to our house, there was silence in the shed. But something was standing there across the street. I could not see much in the half-light. Some strange fear was creeping over me from there. Thin, short legs, a bulky body, a big head, it was leaning awkwardly, stiffly against the fence. It wasn't a man; this over there was dead, quite dead. So they did kill the pig. I didn't know they could make a dead pig stand up on its hind legs. I ran home and banged the gate. But I could not tell anybody about such a horrible thing.

Next morning the day was bright, the fence empty and the shed quiet. I forgot about it altogether.

With this disturbing episode behind her Mrs Sachs continues her story in a more positive vein, describing her time in Vienna where she went to study photography at the Gräphische Lehr und Versuchsanstalt (Institute of Graphic Arts and Research) at the age of sixteen. This was one of the most buoyant phases of her life, when 'Life was colourful, new, fascinating; there was so much to learn, to see, to discuss'. Her day was divided into

College in the morning, piano study in the afternoon and museums; and sometimes I sneaked into the University with my two friends who were studying philosophy and art; in the evenings there were ... many lectures and discussions, Karl Kraus, Sigmund Freud, Alfred Adler, lectures in politics and then chamber-music and Gustav Mahler with Furtwangler.

However, even recollections of this memorable, relatively happy period are underpinned with anxiety. As she strolls along the Schottenring on her way to meet friends at a café near the University, the delight in her surroundings proves short-lived. The arcades, the quiet green quadrangle, the lime trees and acacias define her favourite area of Vienna, but in their midst she comes across the same horrific vision that struck her at home in Dzieditz. What she assumes is a dead pig – with its thin, short legs, bulky body and big head – is thankfully nothing more than the shadow cast by an upright wheelbarrow.

Mrs Sachs was not able to finish her story. She kept the copy that her teacher had returned; attached to it, on the back of an envelope, was the draft of a letter she had written thanking him and explaining that she was unable 'to do any more writing':

Unfortunately I have been ill since October 83 ... my age also caught up with me and I am in an Old People's Home, I think for good.

I didn't go back home and now everything will be sold or given away.

A complete collapse, physically and mentally.

I thank you for your notes and help.

Sincerely, M. Sachs.

For the elderly Mrs Sachs childhood existed as a premonitory state of being, laden with foresight of horrors that could not be exactly known or named.

'Dusk' wasn't Mrs Sachs's only attempt at writing. Her personal papers also included four sprawling, handwritten pages headed 'Sketch – not used'. On the bottom of the first page was the note 'If I ever will emerge enough to write the book, which has to be written, it will be called "The Void". (An investigation of the mechanisms of certain types of depression.)' Poignantly dated Christmas Day 1954, 'Sketch' was clearly written fast. The handwriting is loose, the expression spontaneous and not reworked, and the pages are laced with crossings-out, unfinished sentences and thoughts enclosed in parentheses.

Conceived as a dialogue between 'M' (Margaret) and her friend 'L', 'Sketch' is based on a straightforward sequence of events, though no chronology is observed in the recounting of them. At its heart is the distress M experiences following L's rejection: after attending a lecture together L had gone off, in M's words, choosing to be 'alone, alone from me, but also alone so that you could just stroll around the shops, hands in pockets, carefree, nobody pulling at your skin or mind for attention'. From M's perspective L's actions are of great consequence. They illuminate not only their different expectations of the relationship but also her own profound loneliness. As M sees it, L conducts their relationship according to her convenience rather than in response to M's 'needs for intelligent company' and relief from her 'spiritual and intellectual loneliness'. M is alone and lonely in her 'self-made prison', all too aware of 'the struggle [crossed out], the frustration, the dangerous periods of darkness when I have lost myself, [and] live in the darkness of an emotional, intellectual void'.

Towards the end of 'Sketch' M abandons the dialogue structure, draws a horizontal line across the page and continues as Margaret. What follows, in rough, quickly formed handwriting, is as close as she comes to declaring her position on life:

But how, could I not be hurt [by L's rejection]? When everything is lonelyness [*sic*], when I hunger for exchange of ideas, of sharing life, which is denied to me to the point, that I can truly say – life is suspended, and to pretend to the outer world, it is going on – 'business as usual' while the very muscles of my jaws are cramped because I have not spoken for hours, for months, and in fact for years from the sources of my real being. Most of it make believe. Most of it substitute, at best, some glimpses of reality, of that reality, which is life to me. The rest is waiting. My strength of recovery comes from that waiting within me, which seems to know, it is for a purpose. <u>It must be that</u>. How else would I have survived the many deaths I have died. How else would I have come out of the black void of loneliness to a new start.

But there are only 2 ways out and up to that daylight ... To learn to understand, how much of it is of one's own making and to readjust one's own attitude. In the process of this readjustment ... one can't afford to give in to the feeling of being hurt. The only strength is to accept in order to learn ... Being hurt, but trying to absorb the lesson by finding out, why it is necessary to be rejected by people who obviously have quite a regard for ~~you~~ [crossed out] me – is the task – is my particular task: if I not only find out ... but am able to adjust myself to it I will have solved the problem of my loneliness. All I can say is: I want to have the strength and 'the infinite patience of the imagination to achieve the freedom of the spirit'.

3   VIENNA

Few traces remain from Margarethe Gross's early years – a birth certificate, a certificate of study, a number of employment references, and some postcards and letters. From these items, however, one can construct a story about Gross's involvement in photography. While the twists and turns the story takes are particular to Margarethe Gross's own life, its overall narrative is not unique. It applies to numerous women of her generation and class who chose photography as a career in the 1920s. They were the beneficiaries of the broad social changes that took place after World War I, especially the hard-won gains by European, English and American feminists, which saw increasing numbers of women entering education and employment. In Germany, by 1925 11.5 million women, or 35.8% of the active population, was in the workforce.[1] Photography, especially studio portraiture and commercial practice, was one of the fields regarded as ideal for women. In 1925, in an article titled 'Photography for girls', the English newspaper *The Times* reported that a special photography course was to begin at the LCC Trade School for Girls, in Bloomsbury, London. The course was

> designed to train girls as assistants to portrait photographers, whose demands the school has been unable to meet. The head mistress expects that girls will find employment with firms of repute, and that the most expert and enterprising of them will ultimately become studio managers or will start studios of their own.[2]

The Times's description of the career path for young, middle-class women desirous of social mobility and economic self-sufficiency could have been written for Gross.

From 1918 to 1921 Gross studied at the Institute of Graphic Arts and Research in Vienna, which since the late nineteenth century had been the principal institution for the education and training of photographers in

Austria. The course she undertook comprised a mix of art, science and business subjects, and she achieved excellent results in Commercial Accounting, Natural Science and Trade Hygiene, graduating with a certificate in photography and reproduction techniques.

According to Monika Faber, an expert on Austrian photography, the Institute of Graphic Arts and Research was conservative in its approach.[3] In her view, the Institute's virtual monopoly on photographic education prevented the generation active after World War I from finding its own voice and freeing itself from established conventions. Consequently, the influence of the three father figures of Austrian photography – Hugo Henneberg, Hans Watzek and especially Heinrich Kühn – remained dominant until the 1930s, perpetuated by the camera clubs that had proliferated since the turn of the century.

Gross's conservative training proved no impediment to employment. In November 1921 she began work with one of Vienna's most progressive studios, the famous Studio d'Ora, and a year later she took up a position with Grete Kolliner Atelier Für Porträt Photographie. Significantly, for the subsequent development of her career, both studios were run by women and specialised in portraiture, which at the time was the most extensive and important sector of professional photography in Austria. Both studios were also sympathetic to new trends in photography.

Studio d'Ora, which Dora Kallmus – Madame d'Ora – had opened in 1907, was known for its relatively unconventional approach to the practice of portraiture. Madame d'Ora and her assistant Arthur Benda both trained in Berlin under Nicola Perscheid, who introduced them to new photographic approaches.[4] Madame d'Ora pursued a more naturalistic style than was the norm in Viennese photography of the time; she favoured a mise en scène in which the subject's pose, attitude and clothing were the primary elements, and she abandoned the use of sets, props and retouching. Her style also owed much to her familiarity with contemporary painting, especially that of Gustav Klimt. She exhibited her photographs in private exhibitions and in salons or galleries – such as the Galerie Arnot, which exhibited Egon Schiele's work – where they were appreciated by an arts audience.[5]

As an assistant at Studio d'Ora, Gross's duties were wide ranging. When she left nine months later, the Studio's letter of reference stated that she carried out all duties, particularly negative retouching, to their 'fullest satisfaction'.

Gross then joined the well-regarded Grete Kolliner Atelier Für Porträt Photographie in Vienna, where she remained for five years. There she was trained in the various tasks associated with studio photography and proved her technical abilities as a laboratory worker as well as a camera operator. In her reference letter, dated September 1927, Grete Kolliner highly recommended Gross to all colleagues, praising her as a capable, independent, hard-working and intelligent co-worker.

Photography appears to have been at the centre of Margarethe Gross's life in the 1920s but very few of her professional photographs from that time exist. These were the years of her apprenticeship when her energies were directed towards the work undertaken for the studios – work that remained anonymous. Any photographs she did produce independently were also extremely vulnerable to her life circumstances and her frequent, and increasingly rapid, relocations during the 1930s. Those photographs that were left behind were far from safe, destroyed most likely or, at best, lost.

The small group of authored images that have survived were probably taken for personal rather than professional reasons. Of these, four are especially memorable: three studies of female subjects and a portrait of Gross, taken either by Gross herself or her friend and fellow photographer Edith Spitzer, in 1924. The portrait is typical for its day and displays the hallmarks of great deliberation. Gross wears a dress that was more likely to have been a costume than a contemporary outfit; she is positioned in front of a light-toned background, and adopts a beguiling pose with downcast eyes. The use of selective focus and directional lighting ensures that the centre of interest is her face, with its self-absorbed expression. Viewed on its own this portrait appears more backward- than forward-looking, its romantic aura seemingly out of keeping with the modernity associated with the 1920s; but seen alongside the other photographs from Gross's Viennese years it begins to look far more powerful. The companion photographs – two portraits of the same sitter and a nude study – are all of young women. With their bob haircuts and willingness to hold the stage, they personify the *neue Fräu* who made her debut in the years after World War I.

In July 1923 Gross and her friend Edith Spitzer took a bold initiative: they wrote to the directors of the Lloyd shipping line after meeting with the company's Representative-General in Vienna to make the following proposal:

> We envisage the establishment of a photographic studio on one of
> your large passenger or luxury steamers.

Self portrait 1924 Vienna 16.4 × 11.4 cm

Portrait of a woman in silk shawl, Vienna c. 1924 11.2 × 8.2 cm

Portrait of a woman with wavy hair, Vienna c. 1924 12.1 × 8.2 cm

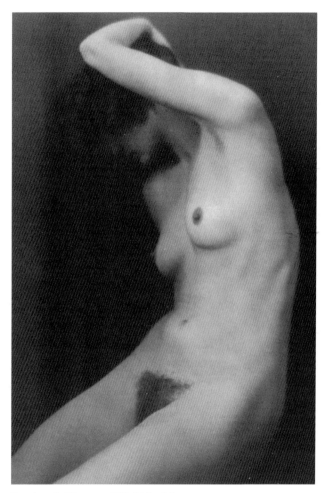

Female nude, Vienna c. 1924 12.4 × 8.2 cm

We are both qualified and have successfully completed a course at the Institute of Graphic Arts and Research. We have each worked for two years in various Viennese studios. To successfully bring our proposal to fruition and to achieve the most favourable results we would require two rooms, a brightly-lit room to be used as a photographic studio, and one small room as a darkroom.

It would surely be advantageous to have on board one of your passenger liners a world-class Viennese studio.

We humbly request that you consider our proposal and ask for your agreement in principle. Please advise us of your conditions to allow us to realise our plan.

Yours very faithfully.

The proposal was rejected but the letter is interesting because, as the only extant 'document' from this period, it conveys a sense of the young Margarethe Gross: her confidence, enthusiasm and adventurousness.

Gross's departure from the Grete Kolliner Atelier in 1927 inaugurated the peripatetic lifestyle – initially chosen then forced – that characterised the next decade of her life. Her employment references chart a path that led next to Berlin, where for two months she was employed as an assistant at Binder Photographie, located on the fashionable Kurfürstendamm. Other prominent studios sharing the same address included the Suse Byke Atelier Für Photographische Porträts, for whom Gross later worked, and the studio of Germany's leading fashion photographer, Else Neulander-Simon, known as Yva. At Binder Photographie Gross 'copied photographs, developed and retouched prints, and completed all other tasks which came before her, except retouching negatives'.

In November 1928 Gross took up a position in Prague at Fotostyle studio. For the next ten months she worked as an operator and technical adviser, expanding her repertoire to encompass industry, advertising and fashion photography. Her employer was sorry to see her go and gave her an excellent letter of reference, writing:

she contributed a great deal to the growth of the business, and was in every way a first-class employee. She was independently in charge of the photographs and she presented them to both our and our public's great approval. Apart from this she also took photographs for industry, advertisements and fashion with great success.

We are very sad that Miss Gross is leaving our gallery. We are losing an extremely hard-working and ambitious co-worker, who was not only conscientious and capable at photography, but who also showed an interest in the development of the studio.

A year later Gross made the life-shaping decision to return to Berlin, for reasons that are not known. Berlin itself may have been the attraction. Along with Paris, Berlin was regarded as the quintessential modern metropolis in the early twentieth century; in the heyday of the Weimar Republic its rich cultural and artistic life attracted an uninterrupted flow of visitors and new residents.

Berlin may also have offered the prospect of expanded professional opportunities, given that photography appeared to be flourishing and drawing high levels of support. By the late 1920s Germany was recognised as a world leader in different fields of photography – in commercial photography, including advertising and portraiture; in modernist experimentation, originally centred on the Bauhaus under László Moholy-Nagy; and in the Worker Photographer's movement. Germany also dominated the new area of photojournalism, pioneered by Erich Salomon and Felix Man; the illustrated magazines, which began publication in 1923, gave prominence to photo-essays of contemporary life and events. In addition, photography's high profile seemed assured through exhibitions such as Neue Wege der Fotografie (the first exhibition of modern photography in Germany), held in the provincial town of Jena in 1928; it had been preceded by an exhibition of advertising photography in 1927, also organised by the progressive Jena Künstverein. The landmark exhibition Film und Foto, which celebrated the New Photography movement, was presented in Stuttgart in May 1929, and in the same year the influential books *Foto-Auge* and *Es kommt der neue Fotograf!* were published.

Women, too, were prominent as independent practitioners of photography. Irene Bayer, Aenne Biermann, Florence Henri, Annelise Kretschmer, Germaine Krull, Alice Lex-Nerlinger, Lucia Moholy, Anne Mosbacher, Cami Stone and Yva were among those who exhibited and published their work in the proliferating magazines.[6] These high levels of participation and visibility – the subject of much recent scholarly attention – were conspicuous at the time. The conservative photographer Erna Lendvai-Dircksen remarked at the end of the 1920s, 'It is now recognised that women have become an important factor in the realm of intellectual and physical work'.[7]

The timing of Gross's return to Germany, however, was not auspicious. It is now generally recognised that photography was at a watershed in 1929, with the Film und Foto exhibition marking the end of a dynamic and fertile era rather than a beginning. And Gross was faced with far more important problems than the state of photography. The country that had endured the instability and hyper-inflation of the early 1920s was on the cusp of the Great Depression, signalled by the collapse of the New York stock exchange on 25 October 1929. By the following June, 2.7 million people were officially registered as unemployed; by June 1931 it was 4 million; and by June 1932 the figure had reached 5.6 million, one tenth of the population. In July 1931 the magazine *Die Tat* reported that Germany was undergoing a period of 'hidden famine of enormous proportions'.[8] Doctor and nutrition scientist Helmut Lehmann stated that this 'threatened to have serious consequences for physical and mental health. What we are seeing imminently endangers the next generation. People from all strata of society – all over Germany – are already eating less than half of the nutritional minimum!'[9]

Not surprisingly, work in Berlin proved difficult for Gross to obtain and her short-term positions alternated with periods of unemployment. From October to December 1929 she worked briefly as an assistant at Atelier K. Schenker, from March to April 1930 she was a copier at the Suse Byke Atelier Für Photographische Porträts, and from October 1931 to August 1932 she was a retoucher at Photos Winterfeld. The references from her employers continued to be extremely positive: Atelier K. Schenker 'fully recommended' her and Suse Byke 'came to know her as a diligent and conscientious assistant'. Photos Winterfeld wrote that she completed her designated tasks to their 'complete satisfaction' and concluded that she 'leaves her position of her own volition'. If her departure from paid employment was voluntary, it may have been to establish her own studio; two photographs in the archive dated 1932 are stamped on the reverse 'Fotogross' and carry a phone number, presumably for the nascent but apparently unsuccessful business.

Although the work Margarethe Gross performed in the Berlin studios did not appear to carry the same level of responsibility as her position in Prague, it remained consistent in other ways. As previously, her employers specialised in portraiture, often involving a relatively privileged clientele. The Suse Byke Atelier, for instance, had established its reputation for portraits of public personalities and artists, many of which were published in various illustrated magazines during the 1920s. Byke's subjects, who included the famous African-American dancer Josephine Baker, epitomised what conservative forces regarded as the decadent nature of Berlin as, in Stefan Zweig's words, the city 'transformed itself into the Babel of the world'.[10] Studios like Byke's were hit hard by the stock exchange crash and the resultant loss of clientele.

Gross's return to Berlin also coincided with the dying days of the Weimar Republic and the disintegration of Germany's first democracy. In the Reichstag elections held in September 1930 the National Socialists achieved a landslide victory, winning an unprecedented number of seats. The first session of the newly elected Reichstag a month later was accompanied by violence. In his diary German aristocrat and republican Harry Kessler, known as the Red Count, described events in Berlin where Nazis smashed the windows of Jewish-owned department stores in Leipzigerstrasse before assembling in the Potsdamer Platz to shouts of 'Germany awake!', 'Death to Judah' and 'Heil Hitler'. Kessler continued, writing 'If the government does not take matters firmly in hand, we shall slide into civil war ... The vomit rises at so much pig-headed stupidity and spite'.[11]

While Margarethe Gross's years in Berlin were interwoven with the development of her photographic career, another story also began there. It is not told through historical documents and publications of primary and secondary material, but through the small bundle of notes and letters that Mrs Sachs kept with her until her death. One of the earliest is a short note that reads:

> Darling, I woke up so late that I couldn't do the dishes. I hope I manage to make the dole queue on time.
>
> I intend to wear my red dress tomorrow, it seems appropriate. But if you think it's so important and want me to wear another one, then ring me up.
>
> Mój kochany [my love] thank you for the apple and your writing. I was pleased with it, with the content and the fact that you gave it to me. In everything that you write, in every sentence, your whole being is reflected. I embrace you.
>
> Yours, Grete.

4   DEAR GRETL

My dearest life, I am here in your room ... Owing to your absence I
only now become fully aware of how deeply you are imbued in all
things around me, how deeply you are involved in my life. I am gaining
a perspective of the beauty of our joint life, of our joint home. I am all
excited about how you squander love on even the smallest things and
I am asking myself humbly whether I am worthy of it, my love?

I would prefer to be here this evening ... it would be better if you
could come to my place. Will you come? Pack everything you need
and arrange it so that you can stay with me ...

I am longing for your lips as if I had been deprived of them forever.

Yours

I am just reading a report about a trip to Spain. Michele, darling,
couldn't we go with it? Can't such a dream be realised? We have to
talk about it.

Margarethe Gross and Rudolf Michaelis became lovers towards the end of
1930. She was twenty-eight years old and he, born in 1907, was five years
younger. When they met she was well established in her photographic career
and he, also a relative newcomer to Berlin, was a restorer in the Near Eastern
Department of the Berlin State Museums. As it happened, Grete and Michel
were lovers for only a brief period – four years at best – but their relationship was
enormously consequential for them both. It didn't end, as a lesser relationship
might have done, when they parted company in Spain in 1934 and divorced in
1937, but entered a new phase thirty years later after Mrs Sachs visited Michel
and his wife Marianne in East Berlin. Following the visit Grete and Michel
began to write to each other again, letters that Mrs Sachs tucked away with
those she had kept from the beginning of their relationship in the early 1930s.

For a long time I believed that Rudolf Michaelis was peripheral to what has become this story. I wrote to him only once, just a few months before his death, hoping to glean from him more information about his former wife's photography. That was in 1990 and I hadn't really expected a reply, as the address I used – taken from what appeared to be the last letter he'd written to Grete – was fifteen years old. My letter did reach him but unfortunately he was too ill to respond himself and so one of his colleagues in Berlin, Dieter Nelles, replied on his behalf. This inaugurated a rewarding trickle of information, mostly biographical, that still hasn't dried up. What has been interesting is the consistency of the various accounts of Michel's life that I have received over the years: all are framed in terms of his politics – first as a member of the anarcho-syndicalist movement in Germany in the 1920s and early 1930s and then as a participant in the pro-Republic campaign in the Spanish Civil War. Any personal details, including his relationship with Grete, are mentioned only in passing.

When Grete met Michel he was already a committed political activist. According to his obituary, written by Hans-Jürgen Degen and published in *Direkte Aktion* in March/April 1991, he was politicised by his early experiences of 'proletarian misery'. Degen explains that Michel's

Senya Flechine,
Foto-Semo
Rudolf Michaelis working
on an archaeological
fragment, Berlin
c. 1930–33 12.4 × 16.8 cm

mother died directly after his birth. From the age of six days the half-orphan was placed in a proletarian foster family. His foster mother was a washerwoman and his foster father was a bricklayer. His foster father was often violent, particularly towards Michel's mother. Even as a child Michel rebelled against the violence of his father. He would stand protectively in front of his mother without thought for himself. This was the root of two of his lifelong determining characteristics: extraordinary courage and unconditional solidarity with his fellow man.[1]

At the age of fifteen Michel joined the youth branch of the anarcho-syndicalist movement, Anarchistisch-Syndikalistischen Jugend Deutschlands, in his hometown of Leipzig. The initial reason for his involvement was pragmatic: he was in revolt against what he later described as 'the constant betrayal of workers' interests' in the printing trades in which he worked. However, through his friend Helmut Rüdiger, who was editor of the journal *Der Syndikalist*, he also acquired a theoretical understanding of anarcho-syndicalism.[2] In Berlin, where Michel moved in 1925, he continued to participate in the movement through his membership of the Freien Arbeiter-Union Deutschlands (Free Workers Union of Germany), or FAUD. He led children's groups in Berlin-Schöneweide and gave lessons in handwork, folk dancing and the appreciation of worker's poetry; he also contributed articles to *Der Syndikalist*.[3] In 1930, the year he met Grete, his political activities ceased; he later described himself as being 'politically inactive' until 1932.

In contrast to Michel there is very little information about the nature of Grete's political beliefs and activities. One of the only direct comments on the subject was made by Michel decades later in the first and only completed chapter of his memoirs, 'Encounter with Spain', where he wrote that

> My wife was a tabula rasa as far as politics was concerned. As a Jewess, the role of an anti-fascist came to her, so to speak, from nature. Her clear reasoning and her good talent of observation enabled her to correctly evaluate her surroundings and arrive at conclusions which came very close to my own convictions.

The fact that Grete does not appear to have been formally involved in politics at the time she met Michel is not surprising, given that she had arrived in Berlin only a few months earlier, was an Austrian citizen and a woman. The latter is of particular significance. During the Weimar Republic women were less likely than men to join political parties and often did so only in conjunction with their spouses. As a result, Marsha Meskimmon has argued, narrow definitions of politics have obscured the contributions made by women in the Weimar years. Women participated in politics in different ways: their 'very presence in the public sphere as workers, activists, and even professional artists were themselves political statements'.[4] In this sense Grete can be seen as a thoroughly modern woman with her own career and interests, including a love of dancing – of which Michel thoroughly disapproved – and the visual arts.

Grete's approach to her relationship with Michel also appears to have been self-consciously modern, for the couple did not marry until October 1933 – and then perhaps only as a means of securing her citizenship in Hitler's Germany (Michel was not Jewish). The years they spent living together suggest that Grete and Michel were liberal in their views and open to the possibilities of the social experimentation of the 1920s, which saw the emergence of companionate or egalitarian relationships and marriages known as *Kameradschaftsehe*.[5] Such relationships were based on the emotional compatibility of the partners and the mutual enjoyment of sex, independent of the need for having children.[6]

From the outset Grete and Michel frequently wrote notes and letters to each other. The notes were a means of keeping the absent partner up to date with the other's activities and of making arrangements for their next meeting.

Four such notes have survived: three of Grete's notes to Michel were amongst Mrs Sachs's belongings when she died and one of Michel's notes to Grete was recently retrieved from Michel's papers by his biographer. It intrigues me that Grete and Michel retained these ephemeral items whose main virtue, like a quick telephone conversation or an email message, was their immediacy. Even more curious is the fact that the notes they had kept were their own, possibly returned during the ritual exchange of objects that follows the break-up of a relationship.

At the end of Grete and Michel's first year together letters, by necessity, became their primary form of communication. From November 1931 until March the following year the couple lived apart while Michel worked on an archaeological dig in the Middle East, in Baghdad and Babylon. As a member of the Berlin State Museums' team he was involved in the excavation of the Tonstift-Mosaikfascade, an Assyrian mosaic facade, fragments of which were subsequently displayed in the Pergamon museum. The most informative description of Michel's work experiences comes in a letter he wrote to Grete's father, Henryk Gross, in February 1932; the letter also speaks of Michel's closeness to and genuine affection for Grete's parents:

> Dear Father
>
> It was really nice of you not to wait for my reply before writing your second letter. I have only today found the time to reply. The great quantity of work and of new impressions has not allowed me a moment to myself. Everything has to be thought about in peace and quiet and considered as a whole.
>
> You do not need to be concerned about cholera in this country any more. Not because Basrah is so far away, it is only half a degree of latitude to Basrah, but because this disease is considered to be extinct. About fourteen days ago two travelling salesmen stayed at our expedition camp, and confirmed this message. Your recommendation of Samaicarnm and wine is not valued by me as I do not value these things in general.
>
> ... I have been in Warka for about three weeks with three other Germans. Which is north west from the 31' of latitude and 46' of longitude.
>
> Warka, which was called Uruk in biblical times, is the birthplace of the Babylonian hero Gilgamesh. The ruins are characterised in the white desert by the chain of hills covered in innumerable clay splinters

on the top. Otherwise there is nothing else to see apart from the great desert. The course of the Euphrates, in the old days, apparently touched the city in the north-east and now flows 20 kilometres west of Warka. In clear weather reflections in the sky bring the flow of the Euphrates close to the ruins. You can see the white sails of the ships and it seems as if the dream of a past time is coming alive after sleeping deep in the earth.

My work in Warka consists of the reconstruction of a mosaic facade, which we have dated at 300 BC. An incredible atmosphere has been created by this. Never before have I been so close to the dawn of human culture as at this moment. During the day the sun shines on everything, or dust storms pass over everything, and it could be as it was on the first day.

It is a different world, and still it is the same eternal world, which could also touch you in Dzieditz, if you only tried, my dear father. Hold your head up high and don't become weary. Mother, and this is my rock-hard belief, will be better soon. It will be like Gretele recently wrote to me: that Mother's recovery, my homecoming, and our visit to my parents' home will be a double celebration for us.

Until then, my dear Father, hold your head up high, cheerfully look at the world, and see the beautiful things in it. Greetings to you and Mother.

All my love, Michel.

During their five-month separation Michel wrote constantly to Grete. In his neat, tight script on small sheets of airmail paper he described in detail his work and his impressions of the country, its people, their customs, the weather and the behaviour of fellow Germans on the expedition. However, his preoccupation in these letters of love was his relationship with Grete, his seesawing feelings about their separation and his hopes for their future life together.

It seems that Grete, too, was an ardent and conscientious correspondent but only one of her letters has survived. In his own letters Michel recorded the dates he had heard from Grete and sometimes wrote directly in response to whatever she had sent him. Because Michel's extensive correspondence remained in safekeeping in Grete's hands, reading the Warka letters is like listening to one party in a two-way conversation. And yet, while Grete is mostly silent, she is not absent. Every now and then fragments of her thoughts, feelings and desires flicker through Michel's prose.

Three years after returning from Warka, when their relationship was ending, Michel wrote one last letter to Grete in which he analysed the circumstances behind their break-up. As he saw it, the Warka period represented a moment when 'things that wanted to break apart' were 'bound firmly together', when in fact the couple had been at their best. He tells Grete that their letters from this time reveal 'the pure and truest bond, in which our love is demonstrated in its intensity and helplessness and with all the limitations that we had to face'.

Michel to Grete

Express Berlin–Istanbul, 16 November 1931

Moja kochanko [My love]

It was all too much for me to have been able to stay calm. You, my brave one, Helmut and Dora [Rüdiger], the moving train, the long corridor with all its brass, the passengers. It was all too much for me … the six months of separation push themselves between us …

It took time for me to calm down. Gradually I came to realise that we are only really separated by a stringing-together of the miles. Otherwise we are still with one another in our feelings, thoughts and wishes. In six months we will see each other again. You will have become calmer, more tender, I hope. Me and my ingrained pigheadedness will have been a little burnt from the Arabian sun – just the thing in order to live happily with, and for, one another.

I have calmed down now. And you? …

To finish up: be brave and good, and remember that really there isn't anything which can come between us. The railway tracks have their absurd side: they separate, but in the end they bring people back together again. I kiss you. I dream of you. I feel for you.

Love Michele

Michel to Grete

Baghdad, 27 November '31

My dear Gretele,

It will take some time for me to get my emotional stability back again. At least my work is over and done with for today. That's a small consolation.

When I sit in my dreadful hotel room after work is over, I always believe that at any moment the door will open and you will come in to me. But that is just daydreaming. What would be more likely, though, would be to receive word from you. I shall be very happy when a letter comes.

What keeps me together is the hope that these six months will pass by really quickly. Then Gretele, my love, you will be born for me once again, then we can have a second honeymoon, like that time a year ago, when we showed each other our best sides. And then we must be more persistent in our wishes and actions – to be good and serene. Do you believe that too, moja kochanko [my love]?

Do you know that with all my worries I completely forgot our wedding day. That is certainly material for psychoanalysis (I'm reading Freud at the moment). But you will already have gathered how near I was to you, how completely I was with you. [Here Michel had written in the margin, 'A slip of the pen! With a plus!' The translator noted that instead of writing 'war', meaning was, Michel wrote 'wahr', which means true.] Among the many thousand differently formed things and beings in this world, you are the only constant thing besides my mother and God.

I simply can't imagine how beautiful the world would be here by your side. I don't know. But I believe our four eyes would behold some miracle, in which the whole world would reveal itself. My dear Gretele, I kiss you, your breasts, your thighs. My dear Gretele, I hug you, I hold you. My dear, dear Gretele. What is the world to me without you. You know it: an hour at odds with you is more beautiful than the most beautiful world without you. What will the world be like for us if we live in harmony? You only need to be more tender, and I more understanding.

Grete to Michel

December 1931

My love, my love, my love, my solely loved person, tender, faithful and quiet Michele, I want to kiss you and hold you tight in my arms and not let you go except to grab you back and kiss you again.

How can I bear it that you are always so sad, my dear, you should not be sad. You should not spend so much time thinking about me. You should lift yourself up on the newness and uniqueness of this experience and have patience. Patience, a thousand times patience.

Why is it that you still don't have letters from me? Why didn't they deliver my telegram to you? I sent it on the 7th, it should have arrived on the 8th, therefore on the 9th or 10th in Hillah. In a letter from the Consulate it was stated that letters arrive at the Consulate, and until now at the Post Office, as poste-restante. But you should have been advised about it. This is just not on. You should make inquiries at the Consulate. It has to be established whether the telegram has arrived. I sent it for this purpose so that you would have instant news from me.

My dearest, I came home at 10 o'clock. It was after five days, which seemed endless to me, that a letter from you finally arrived. Just now I read it, breathed it, smelled it and searched for your hand on it, for your eyes which rested on it. I read it again and went for a walk with you to the Nile, to Hillah, on to the Euphrates and back to the house. It was so marvellous that you also drew a plan of Baghdad. I am much closer to you straight away and can now visualise how you walk, in which direction you are heading, as if I were there.

Darling, my bright eye, you dear soul. I wish to have a diary from you, containing each and every bit, everything you do, think, read, dream, talk, eat, how you sleep, everything: the way the plaster turns out, the distance to the scaffolding, how it is constructed. The time you get up, what you wear. How you wash yourself, what you drink. What is 'Good morning' in Arabic? How do you communicate with Salman Mohamed? How many Arabs are there? Is it cold, is it warm, when? What kind of person is Salman Mohamed? Is he nice to you, can you get to know him better without speaking his language? Does he learn English? Do you take photographs? Please, send the films back straight away and take many pictures and quickly. I am going to send you some more films again. I would like to have an exact description of a whole day, with all your thoughts and feelings. Tell me what thoughts you have while you are working, what do you have to consider when you start restoring the lion? How tall are the palms? Do they cast shadows? Are there wells and drinking water? Do you take care with the water and follow the strict warnings not to drink water? ... Darling, will you promise me this? Do not take things too hard, but also not too lightly. Don't forget that the Orient has strange laws and customs, which you, as a foreigner do not know, do not sense, cannot grasp instinctively as you do here.

Have the mice eaten your suitcase or have they got an upset stomach from it? Do you shave or let your beard grow? Who is cutting the nails on your right hand? I would like to have the menu for the whole week. Are clouds in the sky? Has it rained as yet? Is there some grass and are there flowers out in the open? Where do the roses and the yellow blooms grow, the scents of which were in your last letter? Do you love me and in which way do you love me and what do you love most about me and what the least? And what things are you missing, clothes, books? I could keep on asking questions endlessly and want all my questions to be answered, then to ask thousands more. One wish! Write to Fabers, say something about the Song of Solomon, and that you enjoyed it, do it soon please. They send their love and enquire often about you. And write to Milli, who is as sad as a mother that you haven't written.

My sweetheart, how are you going to spend Christmas Eve, will you sense that I am with you? I am going to light a red candle which is to shine for the two of us. And you didn't get a red candle from me for Christmas Eve. I looked everywhere and finally found one ... you will receive it tomorrow by mail. It should burn on 16 January. And I will light another candle and think of you and her [Michel's mother], whom I love, because she loved you. And the other candle, you should light on March 31 and April 6, our birthday candles. It is still a long time till then. Until then. But by then you should be back.

Oh, my sweetheart, how could it be possible for me to come? How could I realise it when I don't possess anything, besides my yearnings, my wishes and dreams, your longing and your desire to make it possible. It is only the damn money. But where can I get it from? Nobody lends you anything. Nobody has anything and how could he get it back? The other day Marianne W. told me she talked to Mrs Andrae, with whom she sings in the choir. Mrs Andrae told her, her husband has pangs of conscience because he had to deny me the chance of accompanying you. Isn't this decent?

Michele, do you write to Andrae? You have to and in detail about everything, especially the job. How did the lion in Baghdad turn out? You should tell me everything personally.

My treasure, Michele. My father writes such sad letters again. I decided to go to visit him, to cheer him up. Mum is still in Ernsdo and she is slowly getting better but he is so lonely and sad. I can't come to you, my dearest. So I will travel to him and show him much love which will give him a lift again. Winterfeld gave us 11 days off till the 4th of January. Had you been here, how exceedingly nice that would have been. I could have been with you. I could, but it will not happen because there is still no magic carpet by which one could fly to Baghdad. Not even in fairy stories. I still can't get 'Thousand and One Nights'. It is booked out …

The Grosses and the Steners send their love to you. They also intend to write to you. I planned to make Fabers a little happier and asked Helmut for his advice. He talked me out of it and said: Faber is a difficult person, you may spoil it for yourself if you give him a present. Therefore I did not dare. But later on he will get a rubber tree. As well as the Rüdigers when they shift house and I visit them in the new year. So far I haven't managed, despite all good intentions. Helmut is away very often and is, by the way, very busy. The piano will arrive between the 24th and the 1st. I won't be here. Lotte will receive it. I am looking forward to it.

24.12

I kept writing this letter till 1 o'clock and fell asleep. The reason for my handwriting becoming skewed is that I wrote it in bed and my supporting left elbow became tired. Tonight is Christmas Eve. I still have a lot of errands to do and to wrap things. I am invited with Lotte to Erich's. Later I will go home and be with you alone and have a silent chat over thousands of miles. My all and only, your love. Goodbye, I love you endlessly and ever more, your Gretele.

Michel to Grete

Hillah, 23.12.31

My dear Grete, my brave one, my heart of gold, my beloved, my one and only, my I-can't-find-the-words-to describe you, my darling Grete.

Just now I picked up three airmail letters and two parcels from the station master. I had to skim through everything in a rush. When I get back to Babylon tonight, I want to lovingly read through everything. I saw your photos, I'll have to think about them, they look so strange to me. But that too in a rush. I have lots to do in Hillah.

Kiss upon kiss, love Michele.

Without roses, due to being in Hillah.

Michel to Grete

Babylon, Christmas 1931 in the evening

My heart-love, my Gretele

I kiss you. Maybe this is my saddest Christmas, even though I am nearest to the land where 'the rose bloomed, of whom the ancients sang'. I have never felt so much abandoned by God and the world as in these last few days. This is how my mother must have felt six years ago, a few weeks before her third and last attempt when she committed suicide. On Christmas Eve I gave her two shirts and I received a pound of sugar. I was happy and mother not much less so, as it then seemed to me. One shirt, she told me, should be her funeral shirt. This was her last wish, which came to be fulfilled.

Perhaps you are asking yourself, why don't I think of anything more light-hearted? My Grete-heart, my sweetest, far, far from me, I had plenty of time last night and today for reflection. I thought only of you. Gretele, my Gretele, if only I could touch you, feel your breath, your eyes, your forehead, your skin, your hair, your breasts, your belly, all of you, and have you here with me in your entirety. It would be much nicer to start a letter to you, my Grete-heart, in another vein. Only a few more months, my Grete-heart, since you can't come to see me, a few more months … then my dearest one, I will have all of you. I am waiting for you, my sister, my bride, every day …

Last night I cleaned up my table. On it, alongside a glass with wilting roses, I put the two photographs of you and of my mother, as well as your farewell gift, the words from the Song of Solomon. Then I yearned for you for a long time. Outside the starry sky. I went to bed at eight. Maybe, I thought, she will feel that I went to bed early, maybe she is with Lotte or with friends. In Germany the air will be filled with the scent of Christmas-trees, candles will be burning; last year, my Gretele, my Grete-heart ... tears ... and sleep. What a child I am.

All day I was unable to form a clear thought. A few minutes ago I washed a couple of hankies, only to kill time. I gave Salman leave; he should go to his wife and his children at Hillah. I am alone, all alone.

There was a change of weather during the night. I have never experienced anything like it. A terrible storm, without rain, whirling up the dry clay soil; everything is covered by a grey dust cloud. The whole landscape is nothing but grey dust, it penetrates the window joints and gets into my room, settling as in Germany, the dust of centuries, on everything, it gets into your throat, gets into everything. Here it is cold, very cold. I am sitting at the table, well rugged up but shivering. And it all happened overnight. Yesterday the day was still nice with lots of sunshine.

It must be frightening at Warka, where there is only sand on the ground, a desert, nothing but sand; here in this country it is called 'raml' ...

My Grete-heart, I would like to continue writing tomorrow. My hands are getting stiff and it is getting unpleasant. For the time being feel kissed a thousand times. I love you my Grete-heart. I am embracing you. I press you to my chest, very lovingly, deeply and quickly. Do you feel it?

Good night. The clock shows that at your place at home it is 6.00 pm.

Michel to Grete

26 December 1931, in the evening

My Braveheart

There was no mail for me over the holidays. This does not disturb me much; I am still drawing support from your second letter. My experience with the second letter was the same as the first ... the date of the letter alone speaks of the distance of our separation. I am getting to see in it the face and the feelings of my Gretele as she looked twenty days ago. Ever and always it is this that forces its way between us, what you as well as I realise with sadness: the different lives we are both living.

I can well visualise your room; the fact that you like it pleases me. When I return we will acquire a flat of our own. I have never had such a yearning for a home to myself as just now in this foreign land.

If you don't come to me, Marianne's piano will have to come to you. In our own home there has to be music, for us and for my Christmas wish. Guess! My Greteheart, guess! Have you got it? For our child. Do you hear me, my darling, for our child. This is my Christmas wish. You know how much it would have to have from you and I know what it does not have to have from me (my pigheadedness it might have). Don't say there is still plenty of time, but familiarise yourself with this hope now; nothing requires more forethought, apart from our love, than our child. My Gretel-love, don't laugh at me, your silly Michele, let us lighten the time of our separation with this thought, next to God and the world, let this be our finest thought.

I have here so much time for introspection, that it seems like a voice from another world when you talk to me about lectures by Rocker and Haidn ... Haidn is a type of straightforward person in Germany – just think of Dehmel, Hilder ... and many more – who, for all his righteousness talks a lot of hot air and who knows his anarchism only from books and not from its organisational foundations; nor has he studied the syndicalism and activities of our Spanish comrades. While reading the story I could not help suppressing a wry smile. I wished more, much more of your reply to Haidn's words. Talk to Helmut [Rüdiger] about this matter. By the way, you should more often obtain advice from Helmut about such things; he is the right person to give advice on literature and many other things. While I am at it: my cordial greetings to Helmut and Dora.

And before you are told how much your letter pleased me, something about what you should not have written, or should have written differently:

'... the reverse side of the romantic Orient'. The Orient is not <u>romantic</u> and it never was, it had to have been a very long time ago.

'... That you can't be here, my dear, how much would we both enthuse over the fine lectures. The discussion was good and of a certain standard'. The last sentence, my Grete-love, should be in a provincial newspaper and not in a letter. The former is not enough, neither for you nor me.

'... Darling, you should not let your wellbeing be dependent on externalities' [which the translator noted referred to hygiene and accommodation]. Remember, my Grete-love, you pushed in all haste on the wrong button.

Enough, my Grete-heart, I want to tell you how much I enjoyed your lines. They are letting me have you in person, they are bringing a known world closer to me, and give me encouragement to shoulder our separation more easily. If only every week a few lines would come to me?

I still don't know how often my letters reach you; but I think more often than yours come to me. This is as it should be, because perhaps you are having it harder than me. Be patient if a letter gets held up and when, in the next few weeks, I will only be able to write a letter a week. There are good reasons for this.

During the eleven days of my work in Babylon I never had enough time for leisure. From 8 o'clock in the morning till sunset (5–5.30) I am at work, from which I don't look up very often and of which I have finished up till now about a third of my forming job. Dr Jordan was here today – he brought me a small basket of candies, nuts and fruit – and he asked that I complete the rest of the job, that is 2/3rds, in a fortnight, because I am required urgently at Warka. i.e. to work with utmost intensity and to be dead tired in the evening; whether I will manage it in fourteen days, I still don't know. I have to attend personally to just about the simplest of jobs here. These Arabs have not the slightest tradesmen talents to show. Therefore, my Grete-heart, don't expect anything superhuman from me and be patient; you will receive a letter from me every week.

Michel to Grete

Babylon, 28 Dec '31, evening

My dear Gretele,

I have just learned how Iraq is written in Arabic – from right to left. So, my darling, if you want to be absolutely sure with your letters, which are so few and far between, then apart from Iraq also write this in Arabic. It will be able to be read by every post-office official from Istanbul onwards ... In future, I will write the date only in Arabic, it's called good practice, my darling Grete ...

I will soon have to write 1.1.32 in Arabic, and in spite of our separation (you know an hour at odds with you is more beautiful than an hour without you), I will look back on the best year of my life with a cheerful heart. My sweetheart, my dearest, like this year, we want to live the rest of our lives with one another and for one another with just a little more love and understanding between us. This year was like our car trip to Beethoven's Ninth Symphony. Do you remember? We came to our senses after many detours, not too late, just a little late, like that New Year's Day when we missed the first chords of the first phrase. Moja kochanko [My love], can you sense how close I am to you with these words? I taste your first kiss, I hear your first laugh, and feel our souls and bodies trembling. When we see each other again I'll court you so much, like on the very first day of our love.

My brave Gretele,

If I look in the mirror now, I see a brown, sunburnt Michele who hasn't shaved for eight days, and has an awfully blocked nose. It's bitterly cold here. Salman has caught a cold, Muse is barking like a dog and I'm not faring much better. I had such a headache today at work that I would have ripped my head off if I had had the time ... In every respect I am a spoilt European, who thinks: Oh, but if only I had a warm bath right now, a heated room and a warm bed. In spite of all this I play the 'Titan' at work. I sing and keep in good spirits, in order to cheer up the Arabs a little, who complain and are frozen stiff. My hands are like sandpaper, the skin is all cracked. In the mornings the water and clay are still blocks of ice. It should get warmer soon.

... Tomorrow I want to go to Hillah and make a fuss about the plaster supply. I used up the last of the plaster today and unfortunately ... cannot work. Apart from that I want to look around for cheap crates to transport my work in. It sometimes seems like I'm the manager of a small business: I grumble, though somewhat nicely, but I grumble like nothing on earth when Salman and Muse do everything back to front; I have my problems 'with the people' in Hillah. My precious, there are so many things that one can become in this big wide world. And now to finish up: on the whole I've made a good impression on the Arabs. They like me a lot, they sense another type of person in me; there is much evidence of this. Only the women in this country, Allah's special creations, will probably always remain strangers. I only get to look at their sunburnt feet, sometimes with silver chains around their ankles, and a face, which immediately hides behind a veil and leaves all questions unanswered.

Many kisses, my love and good night,

love Michele

the clock says 12.30 am

Michel to Grete

30.12.31

My darling

I am so happy, so unspeakably happy. My whole body is shaking with happiness. I excitedly pace up and down the room, excited by love. Three letters and two parcels, two dear photographs, and so many dear, very dear words, and still more surprises from you. There are a few short passages which Helmut [Rüdiger] sent you and which bring my homeland back to me again; there is the 'world stage', which tells me how serious things are in Germany; ... there are the dear fairytales by Andersen, which I loved to read as a child; there are Walt Whitman's anthems; there are your dear written caresses jotted down on the side for your Michele ...

My darling Grete, you are everything.

Michel to Grete

31.12.31 Babylon

At the end of our first year together

My Grete-heart,

I have already sent all my New Year's thoughts in my last letter. This is good as the day-to-day activities and the large amount of work do not let these thoughts come out. I worked until dawn.

Even though I am tired I want to tell you, moja kochaneczko [my sweetheart], of my last words in the old year. Thank you for your letter from the 13–14th December. When we are back together we will have a lot of quiet Sundays, where we will have time to get to know more about our differently lived lives. The being with and for one another was put totally in our hands ...

The last thing in the old year has to be a wish, that you are coming to me soon. Do you hear this my Grete life? Very quickly, but with care. I have been thinking about it for a long time, and I think that for me – this means for us – this country has to be experienced by you even if it means a year of poverty for us. You get to Baghdad via Mosul. From Kirkuk you telegraph to the German Consulate so you can be picked up at the Baghdad train station. Before your journey you should inform Prof. Andrae, show him this letter if you have to. Your first steps in Baghdad should take you to Dr Jordan. Don't be intimidated by the severe or surprised look on his face. In the end he has to understand that two people who lead a life together, do not want to lead it in different places. Ask for his help for the ongoing journey.

Something is being decided here. Either you are coming to Warka, or if this is impossible due to various circumstances, you go to Babylon. In Babylon you would be well looked after. We would feel close as it is only a day's journey away. You would live and absorb my experiences; we would be able to see each other during this time. On my journey back I have to go to Baghdad to finish off some work there but I will come to Babylon to pick you up. The last days will be ours in Baghdad. My love, my sister, my bride.

You will live in the expedition house in Babylon, in the same room that I stayed in. I will ask Josef Effendi to give you the basic things, a bed, table, chair and lamp for your room, and to supply you with food during your stay. In Babylon the food is cheap, living is for free (you will probably have to eat meat). Josef Effendi is the most righteous man I have ever met and he will be happy to help you and me. We will pay him back when he comes to Germany in autumn. If you want, and if he agrees, you could continue my German lessons. He will really need it in Germany, and he will teach Arabic to you.

My Grete-heart, do not forget to dress warmly, lace-up boots are essential and please bring your photographic materials, your pictures will make our time in poverty easier. Find the money for the trip here. For the time in Babylon, give yourself up to my help.

These are my last thoughts of the old year. No word said is too much or too little. It is up to you – and here again it should be us – to consider the hindrances of your journey and to think about them. I am looking at your two photographs, smiling my last smile in the old year. I kiss you, and I will await you in the new year in this country.

Your Michel

It is an hour before midnight in Germany where you are.

Michel to Grete

Warka, Friday 5 February 1932

My Grete-heart

This week you are being showered with caresses a few days sooner. Dr Holdeke travels to Baghdad tomorrow morning to deal with expedition business and agreed to take our mail with him. These last few days I have been pondering what Warka would have been like for me without Dr Holdeke; I dare not say. I am sure this world would have been much duller for me if his calm voice and quiet understanding had not reached across to me.

Yesterday after lunch the two of us spent half an hour in the expedition yard. The sun shone warmly and the deep blue sky hung over our court. A wonderful mood for a yarn. The white plaster products in the yard shone in the sun and a cat played with its two kittens. To questions regarding expeditions and diggings Dr Holdeke talked about his last Egyptian diggings in the following terms:

'When I was in Egypt, I travelled with the Egyptologist Schott in a car, apparently displaying a very worried face about the forthcoming diggings. To which Schott inspired some confidence by saying, don't worry about it, we will just dig a hole in the ground, something will always turn up with that. We can't dig like this any more today. When the first diggings started one proceeded in this fashion: a well was dug in the ground and a search made for findings. It may still work this way in Egypt today because huge stones were used for building purposes there and sometimes also large bricks which immediately catch the eye of the archaeologist. But here in Mesopotamia and specially with us here at Warka it is sheer impossible to work that way. By these means we see nothing but grey clay when we work. And it took a long time before we managed to identify walls of bricks not kiln-burnt from this clay. With such work concepts for diggings we could not achieve much out here.

'First we look at the picture of the ruins properly and according to what we assume to be under the earth surface, or what is known to be, the first cut is made. From the gaping wound of the soil we can then read the layers of deposits and continue thereafter with work, either horizontally or vertically, whichever seems best.

'It is because of this that the architects took hold of the diggings in due course. One started to realise that the written word was inadequate in view of the complexity of the diggings. A different form of expression had to be adhered to: it was the drawing. In addition, as things are in this country, they required technical knowledge of construction. And who was here more qualified than architects? This is how it came about that in this country the architects take predominance among the German excavators. This is the more plausible as the brick material and the mode of construction are the only means by which the historical connections of the ruins can be reconstructed.'

To relate this in a letter, my Greteheart may appear idle; but one can't avoid it to make my present world comprehensible to you ... In fact you can see from my enclosed diary entries that well over 60% of my time here is taken up by work. The above is part of the most interesting aspect, of the problems of digging activities, which affect me without my being involved with them. My job consists simply of cutting-off the already dug-out facade sections, the throwing on of plaster, the tilting over and transport home of the pieces; nothing problematical, a craftsman-like contribution to the whole of the excavations from which I should only derive real pleasure later on in Berlin. Real pleasure from an artwork can only arrive with a certain distance from the completed work. At present there are the many little worries, which can turn out to be mighty: the plaster is badly mixed, the wire with which I am sawing through the facade pieces is bad while the proper one never turns up, the assistants are not up to scratch. But what does this all matter, weighed against the impression one gets from the picture of the ruins; here a wall structure appears, an ancient world and in the midst of it a hundred working people. The pickaxe surges carefully into the ground, the broad pick scrapes the soil into the small basket, it travels to the lorry, a rail track leads to the dumpsite. A hundred working people, with no worries in this wide world and sharing the same niggardly worries as me, a hundred working people for whom work still means play and for whom a monotone song arouses from their rough throats, a sarcastic song or one longing for knock-off time. These are men with large families, men who would like to woo a wife and who are earning the money to buy a wife, children who have a narrowly defined life ahead of them.

Goldheart, I am trying to convey my world to you as best as I can. I don't always succeed; sometimes my yearning makes me ill and other times, like now, the tiredness sits in my eyes. But I am trying.

Which I can't claim as far as you are concerned. Between the last three letters, of 10 January, 17 January, 20 January alone there is a span of 10 days, mention of which I am searching amongst your lines in vain. Two letters make excuses for the late hours and the last one seeks to 'chat' with me, to 'polemicise', to 'argue'. But telling stories, reporting to keep your world alive for me, hardly any of your letters achieve this. In each one you claim to be dead tired and the remainder you leave for me to guess. Your siblings hardly warrant a mention, friends and comrades always send only their regards, you do not ever labour in your letters, my own letters remain unanswered and with all that midnight stays away from the end of your letters.

Still, I am grateful for every word. Even if I had to come to terms with the fact that you could not manage to write more than your and my own name, and could connect the two only with a greeting, from the bottom of my heart, I would still be very obliged to you, and your world would come alive to my eyes through these few words. But I know that you can do better, if only you would apply yourself.

I kiss you, my Gretele, and I am thankful that time is bringing us nearer to each other day by day.

Farewell, I embrace you.

Your Michele

Michel to Grete

Warka, 23 February 1932

My heartlove,

At least last week I still received a letter from Lotte. However, this week the mail has deserted me completely. All the other gentlemen received their mail. I can only explain that it failed me through a delay in the airmail. Owing to the winter weather in the faraway northwest from here it seems that the railways are still the most reliable means of communication. Maybe it would be better if you sent all letters by surface mail. I am thinking in this way because the first airmail letter that was supposed to be in Baghdad before my arrival reached there only after I had left the town and had your first surface mail letter in my possession. On the other hand, if kept to time schedule the aircraft has the advantage that I know of your thoughts eight days or even earlier. The best example for this is your last letter and that of Lotte of 29.1.32. In short: one has to have patience.

Hopefully you received my letters in time. As much as I try to anticipate a 'mail-delay' and keep calm, in reality I always feel as if dunked into a deep hole.

Now I have arrived where we were, with many repetitions, several weeks ago when I already wrote at length about the 3 April, a time just before your and shortly after my birthday. This date is not fixed, it is just a benchmark and can either be too short or too wide of the mark. An alternative possibility could be envisaged, for which there is actually not much chance, namely the days after the 12th of March, if I manage to dissuade Dr Jordan from the job at Baghdad. Anyway, it's all up in the air and in an emergency a telegram could give you final notification, but of the dates mentioned the 3rd of April carries the best chance.

Measured against the time of our separation, our reunion does not seem to be too far away. For me it is self-evident that our meeting should have to be celebrated festively. Nothing seems better than a trip by the two of us to your parents' home. My feeling is that you do not have enough resolve for such a trip, because it would probably involve your dismissal from your job. For me this would constitute the pinnacle of cowardice. My dearest Greteheart, my adorable Gretelove, let me be quite frank: through your indecision in the last two months you have deprived us of the most beautiful experiences of our life.

Except for a bit of effort, nothing stood in the way of your trip here. Your pointing out the lack of money I dismiss, the trip to your parents' home would have cost about 150 marks, whatever was missing one could have made up with a loan. In this country daily living would not have cost you anything and any other expenses you would surely have defrayed with photographs. I took this dithering quietly and I would not like to touch upon it again. More indecisiveness would break my heart. I want to embrace you at last, I don't give a hoot for all the arguments, which can dish up nothing but the damned and again damned money. Listen, spare me the thousand arguments on that subject; take them into consideration but don't stumble over them.

The starting point of my return trip, my trip to you, will be Baghdad in any case. From there I will arrange my itinerary in line with your proposals. If you decide on Constantinople or Balkan cities like Bucharest, Sofia, Belgrade, Budapest as a meeting place, I will promptly follow the way familiar to me from my journey here: Mosul–Nissibin–Aleppo–Constantinople. Otherwise if your longings drive you to the Mediterranean Sea I will come via Damascus–Beirut and by sea to meet you. The Balkan cities lie closest to your parental home and may therefore be more appropriate. My Gretelove, I must place everything into your hands, even in this matter, owing to my seclusion from all the 'world'; and even in Baghdad … could find only scarce information. Don't hesitate and try, as far as possible, to avoid the percentage on costs imposed by the travel agencies.

Moja kochaneczko [My little sweetheart], I have such terribly strong cravings for you that I can hardly wait for the day of our reunion. I kiss you, I embrace you, I cuddle you like on the first day of our love.

Your Michele his Gretele

5 LOVERS

Between 1931 and 1932, while Michel was in Warka, he and Grete could only communicate through the exchange of letters, photographs and objects. The objects, limited to what could be sent through the mail, ranged from practical items Michel needed, like clothes, books and films for his camera, to the symbolic, such as the candles Grete sent him to burn on their respective birthdays. Michel also sent Grete something that was not visible: the scent of roses that apparently grew near where he was staying. These varied objects, photographs and letters had an individual and collective importance. They were all part of an address to the absent and loved other, which if it was to succeed needed to conjure in him or her the desire to reciprocate quickly, without delay.

Grete and Michel appreciated the complex, fraught nature of this exchange almost immediately, especially given its dependence on the vagaries of the mail system. For her the five days of waiting for his letter 'seemed endless', while even if Michel tried to anticipate a delay in the mail he felt desperate, 'as if dunked into a deep hole', when none was delivered. When a letter did arrive Michel was faced with the reality that he saw in it something already long past: Grete's face and feelings from twenty days earlier. Such lags in time and space are anathema to lovers whose moment is the present. So, like other lovers who have been parted, Michel and Grete (in her only surviving letter from this time) developed a new language, one that above all else was insistent in its immediacy. Its features include descriptions of the place or environment in which the letter was being written, the sensations being experienced, the time of day and the weather. Michel wrote at a table in his room in Baghdad, 'Here it is cold, very cold. I am sitting at the table, well rugged up but shivering'. Upon receiving one of his first letters Grete revelled in her sensory responses, writing 'Just now I read it, breathed it, smelled it and searched for your hand on it, for your eyes which rested on it'. Michel often noted the time he had started or finished a letter – six o'clock, eight o'clock, Christmas Eve – and sometimes projected himself into Grete's time.

These strategies had their successes, especially in the first days and weeks that the couple was apart. Michel could visualise Grete's room and, after receiving a letter and a plan of Baghdad from Michel, Grete could walk with him to the Nile, to Hillah, on to the Euphrates and back to the house. 'I am', she wrote, 'much closer to you straight away and can now visualise how you walk, in which direction you are heading, as if I were there'.

Another key part of their language is the emphatic use of the present tense. Ending letters can therefore be a highly charged moment, as it means stopping talking and turning away to continue life alone. For Michel this was often the point where he was most upbeat, having readied himself for the parting: 'These lines', he writes, 'are only a short note, for you, for us. I want to go to bed now. It is freezing in this room. Good night, moja kochaneczko [my sweetheart]'. On another occasion he writes in haste, dedicating the last minute before the mail is collected to Grete, 'to a kiss, my love ... my Gretel heart'. Only as the misunderstandings and distance between them increased over the months did the endings of letters become more perfunctory, sometimes verging on the formal. A few weeks before their reunion, after scolding Grete for not applying herself to bringing her world alive for him, Michel signs off, 'Farewell, I embrace you, Your Michel'.

To create a sense of being in each other's space, Grete and Michel also frequently used repetitions of endearment and imagined actions. Sometimes words become the aural equivalents of a caress: Grete begins her letter, 'My love, my love, my love, my solely loved person, tender, faithful and quiet Michele'. Michel tells her 'I am embracing you ... Do you feel it?' and concludes two other letters with the respective refrains, 'I kiss you, I embrace you, I cuddle you', and 'I kiss you, I hug you, I love you'.

Photographs offered another means of evoking the other's presence and are woven into the couple's language of separation. In Warka Michel placed two photographs of Grete on his bedside table alongside a glass with wilting roses. They were probably copies of two small self-portraits that I eventually came across in Mrs Sachs's own collection, with her inscription on the reverse: 'Weihnachten [Christmas] 1931'. The photographs appear to belong to a group of four self-portraits taken in the same session; in them Grete is wearing the same dress with its distinctive white scalloped collar. In the first image she is holding a white cat and smiling, in the second she is posed with hands clasping the back of a chair, and in the final two portraits – the ones she probably sent Michel – she appears in three-quarter profile. Of these, the portrait titled *Christmas*, in which her head is gently tilted downwards, is by far the most evocative.

What I find interesting about this self-portrait stems from the fact that it has been made for a lover in his absence. One can imagine that in the taking of it, as in the process of writing a love letter, Grete was conjuring up Michel, attempting to make him present. But the portrait goes further than this evocation of the absent other. It can also be seen as an attempt to deal with the projection of desire; that is, Grete was trying to see herself as Michel might, trying to imagine what it is about her that he responds to.

My partner keeps a portrait like this among his most private things. It was sent to him a long time ago by a lover then living interstate. Theirs was a relationship charged with erotic energy; years after it was over you could still sense its power if you saw them together or if either one talked about the other. Like Grete, my partner's lover wanted a photograph that could speak to her lover on her behalf. She wasn't a photographer herself and so commissioned a photographer to take a portrait of her nude from the waist up. As I remember the image, she is posed with her body in three-quarter profile and her head is turned back towards the camera; she is gazing into the lens to make eye contact with the imagined viewer of her portrait, her lover. But in this instance it is the photographer's presence, rather than the lover's absence, that is made most palpable and the self-consciousness of the portrait speaks of strain, of what I interpret as her strain to speak to her lover through the photographer.

This is where the 'success' of Grete's portrait for Michel becomes apparent, for she was able to determine the outcome herself. The result is affecting in its intimacy, both as an object and as an image. It is a small print, of a size that is given to mobility. You could hold it in your hand, insert it inside the pages of the book you're reading, or place it on your bedside table so that it stays beside you while you sleep. As for the image, its intimacy is suggested in a

Christmas 1931. Michel in Warka 11.4 × 8.9 cm

Christmas 1931 11.8 × 8.8 cm

number of different ways. These include the use of predominantly dark tones that hint at a known or private world where it is neither possible nor necessary to see everything. The choice of a background with no topographical or specific reference ensures that Grete's face, set off by the collar of her dress, is the centre of attention. But even here the specificity is muted. By this I mean that the portrait is not confined to an unremittingly detailed description of Grete's facial features; instead, what is sought is the evocation of a state of mind, or being, arising from her situation as one who is separated from her lover. She therefore shows herself to be serious-minded, verging on melancholic.

The soft, indirect nature of the portrait is enhanced by Grete's choice not to make eye contact with the camera. This was a significant decision, which parallels the much-published public images of desire from the 1930s onwards. Hollywood photographer George Hurrell, for example, used averted eyes to great effect in his consummate portraits of film stars Hedy Lamarr and Johnny Weissmuller, each of whom look downwards and out of frame. For Hurrell this was a means of enhancing the images' seductive appeal, enabling the viewer to scrutinise the glamorous subject at close range and, for a moment at least, to possess him or her. In Grete's self-portrait, however, the downcast eyes signify something different to the Hollywood glamour portraits' seductive but mechanical control of desire. The interior state suggested by her self-portrait is without conceit. It has a specific focus – she is thinking only of Michel – whereas we know full well that Lamarr and Weissmuller will never think of any one of us.

But if Grete's portrait succeeded by creating a space for Michel (who would surely have recognised that he was in the image), it is beset with difficulties when it comes to the projection of oneself as the object of another's desire. Could Grete know Michel's desire? Indeed, can the desire that is unique to each individual be known at all? And, if so, can such a thing be represented?

There is a companion piece to Grete's self-portrait that Mrs Sachs had shown me: a portrait of Michel, probably taken in 1932 after he returned from Warka and the couple was reunited. This, too, is an image about desire, not an imagining of the other's desire, but of one's own. Yet while the portrait deals with the 'specialty' of Grete's desire, it does more than this. As well as being part of her own collection of photographs of Michel, it belongs to the extensive family of photographs of lovers taken this century. I find such images captivating, when and wherever I come across them, because they speak with such immediacy, such insistence, demanding my complete attention.

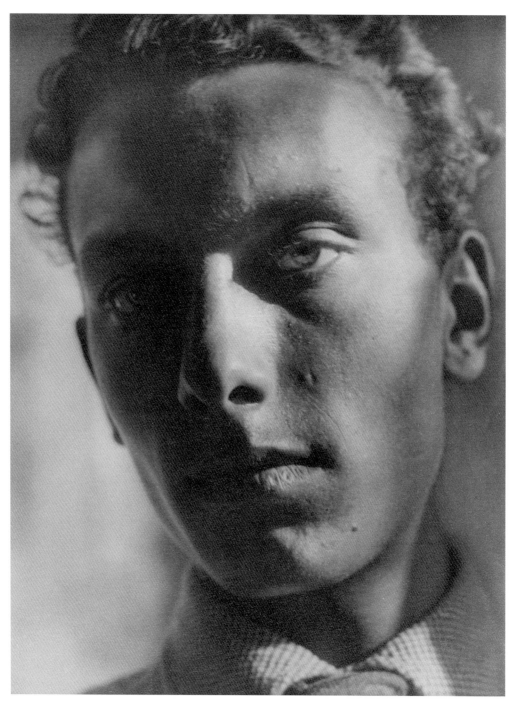

Michel, Berlin c. 1932 23.6 × 17.6 cm

What Grete's portrait of Michel shares with other photographs of lovers is a remarkably consistent code. Its features include the use of neutral backgrounds, eye contact between the photographer and subject, and sharp focus to give detailed renderings of the lover's face or body. But it is the close-up, with its multi-layered functions and meanings, that is at the heart of photographs of lovers and, one might add, of photographs of babies and infants, such as American photographer Nicholas Nixon's portraits of his daughter Clementine. In both categories a particular kind of photographic space is created. It is charged with sensory triggers so that you can almost feel the breath on the cheek, the brush of the eyelashes, the smell and warmth of the body. Photographs of lovers and babies also share a paradoxical relationship between what can be read as detachment and extreme connection, between the cool description of the beloved's features on one hand and on the other, the evocation of a state of rapture that is dependent on that description.

The close-up is a hallmark of the best known photographs of lovers, mostly men's portraits of women: Alfred Stieglitz's of Georgia O'Keeffe, Paul Strand's of Rebecca, and Man Ray's of Juliet are among the international examples that immediately come to mind. But it is also a feature of lesser-known Australian photographs, including Olive Cotton's of Max Dupain and Carol Jerrems' of Esben Storm. Grete's portrait of Michel is typical in this context. She photographed his face full frame, so that it literally filled her vision. The close vantage point enables verisimilitude, a linchpin of photographic representation, to come into its own by describing Michel's features in detail: his hair, eyes, lips, a tiny mole on his chin, a scar by his nose, another on his forehead. This photographic journey across a lover's face or body is akin to the 'scrutinising' that Roland Barthes considers in his *A lover's discourse* – 'To scrutinise means to search: I am searching the other's body, as if I wanted to see what was inside it'.[1]

At the same time as the close-up enables the photographer to scrutinise his or her lover it affirms the connection between the two of them. The photographer is there with permission, occupying a space that has nothing to do with the respectful 'personal space' observed by strangers. Within that space – almost too close for the viewer, an outsider, to feel comfortable – the photographic rendition of detail just holds. If Grete were to take another step towards Michel his features would have begun to dissolve into the blur of a kiss or an embrace. The close-up is an obvious means of signalling that the physical space, the actual distance between photographer and subject, is a corollary for the closeness of the relationship. Georgia O'Keeffe described this with a studied matter-of-factness when she recalled the circumstances behind the first portraits Stieglitz made of her around 1916. When they were first exhibited she recalled that:

Several men – after looking around a while – asked Stieglitz if he would photograph their wives or girlfriends the way he photographed me. He was very amused and laughed about it. If they had known what a close relationship he would have needed to have to photograph their wives or girlfriends the way he photographed me – I think they wouldn't have been interested.[2]

The close-up also permits the photographer lover to enter into the field of view and it is here that eye contact plays a crucial role. While Grete was photographing Michel he was looking at her, admitting her into his vision, his presence. Consequently the portrait, rather than simply being of Michel, is a representation of the relationship between the two of them. André Kertész tenderly plays with this idea in his famous photograph *Elizabeth* 1931, in which his hand – the hand of the photographer and the lover – curls around Elizabeth's shoulder. It is all that we see of Kertész but it is sufficient to signify that we are not looking at her alone; she is with him.

While the close-up may be pivotal to those photographs of lovers I have mentioned, it should be said that its use is now historicised. The close-up doesn't mean what it once did, having been altered by those who have appreciated its transgressive possibilities. We are now familiar with instances where use of the close-up has little or nothing to do with an agreement between photographer and subject – about either the nature of the photographic transaction or the outcome. Diane Arbus was a key figure in inaugurating this shift, given that much of the controversy around her practice was based on the issue of whether or not she had the license to photograph her subjects as she did. Photographing them in close-up, in sharp focus and with eye contact was acceptable if predicated on a relationship, or at least a friendship, but immoral if not. With the proliferation of images by paparazzi photographers, the close-up has become even more suspect with the likely fakery of a telephoto lens. After all, the close-ups of celebrities that are the standard fare of contemporary magazines are invariably achieved without the photographer having been bodily present. Now we can know 'intimacy' easily and also falsely. Yet some practitioners, like William Yang, continue to use the close-up in a redemptive manner, as a way of asserting a sense of connectedness with their subjects and of making an emotional investment in the act of photographing them.

For Grete, photographing Michel – like the act of writing to him during the months he was in Warka – was deeply embedded in the here and now, and the intimacy of their relationship. And yet, what is paradoxical is that the photographic devices she used, so tightly and inextricably bound up with verisimilitude, could not adequately describe what was wanted. Desire cannot be caught by the hard facts of the photographic image; it slips away into another space that has no ties to concrete reality, leaving its trace in a lack or an absence.

It is here that more details about Grete's portraits of Michel become illuminating. During their four years together she often photographed him – on his own, with people, and in studied and informal poses. Almost invariably, only one print remains of each image, suggesting that she was content to close the loop that had begun with the taking of the photograph and ended with the choice of the final print for safe-keeping. But her close-up portrait of Michel tells a different story. It exists in more than one format with a variation in size and cropping. Mrs Sachs kept these different prints with her until her death, giving no indication of whether she considered any to have been the final version. It is tempting to think that this was the portrait that she struggled with most, the one that could never be completed.

And yet, even if its possibilities couldn't be condensed into a single print, this portrait speaks more strongly than any others of her desire and love for Michel. This is not a simple matter, as two conversations occur simultaneously. While each single print speaks with gentle certainty about desire and love, the existence of multiples introduces a shadow of doubt, not about the experience of such states of being, but about being able to adequately speak of them.

Seventeen days after Michel returned from Warka, Grete wrote a note that was amongst the papers I retrieved after Mrs Sachs's death. It may have been a diary entry or a letter that for some reason she never gave Michel. Then again, perhaps he had received it and chose to return it some time later. It reads:

> For a whole evening and night I did not succeed in making you happy. But you managed to make me sad, the kind of sadness that has no tears. The seventeenth day after the day of joy is a day of mourning.
>
> I do not wish to make you sad. I would like it to be undone. But something else makes me dispirited. Your lack of understanding of my motives which I am encountering for the third time.
>
> I imagine you call it cowardice, bourgeois, lack of greatness, and even if you did not think these words it seems to me that this is what

you feel. For your agreement is always a painful renunciation ... an accusation directed at me. You are wrong, both as far as you and as far as we are concerned. This evaluation makes me suffer. I don't want to have what is beautiful between us disturbed and am thinking of tomorrow and the future. You don't want what is beautiful between us disturbed and think 'now'. Which of these is right?

I love you and long for you with all my soul.

6 A SORRY STATE

19 April 1932, Wilmersdorf

My sweetheart

The clock shows it's ten. I will go to bed, to read a bit and to wait for you. But should my tiredness get the better of me and lull me to sleep, please, wake me with a kiss after snuggling down next to me in bed.

My second day at work is already behind me. I went to the canteen to eat and you'll find the proof when you look carefully at your dinner. I came home at quarter to six, stretched out a bit and went to sleep in no time. At half past eight I cooked dinner and prepared lunch for work tomorrow, that's when I noticed that you hadn't even taken a morsel with you to work. I hope you bought yourself a bite.

Gretelheart, please read the pamphlet that Helmut sent to me. I find it sweet of him. In the canteen I read in the <u>Frankfurter</u> that Bulgaria never had a written history of art until recently. Now a professor at the University of Sofia, Bogdan D. Filow, has compiled a History of Ancient Bulgarian Art ... Such a news item sounds like a fairy story, when compared to the over-supply of German histories of art.

An ardent kiss, Your Michele.

In March 1932 Michel returned to Berlin and he and Grete set up home in an apartment in Breitenbachplatz in Wilmersdorf, a suburb of Berlin favoured by artists and leftists. Michel returned to his position as an archaeological restorer at the State Museum, while Grete continued to work as a retoucher at Photos Winterfeld in Bamberger Strasse. Her employment was relatively short-lived; she resigned from the studio in August 1932 and from this point on found no more work in Germany. The photographic profession was in decline and by the following year was judged to be very poor.[1] The Depression and runaway inflation dramatically impacted on the numbers of clients and numerous studios faced collapse; successful independent practitioners like Germaine Krull also earned only a scanty living at this time.

The backdrop for Grete and Michel's reunion encompassed more than the difficult economic conditions. Michel was home in time to witness the escalating political crisis that had gripped the country since 1929 and which in March 1932 began to move into its final stages. Exactly what he and Grete thought about the disintegration of the German Republican government is not known, as no relevant letters or diary entries from 1932 survive. However, other published first-hand accounts, such as those by Count Harry Kessler and Victor Klemperer, give compelling descriptions of events that Grete and Michel were party to. These included elections of the Reichstag held in March, April, July, September and November; political intrigues associated with jockeying for the position of Chancellor (Von Papen was appointed in June); and the breakdown of civil order and the eruption of violence throughout Germany. In his diaries from the period Kessler described the establishment of a Nazi reign of terror and the growing bloodshed as people were killed and injured in daily massacres.[2]

Despite opposition to the Nazis' ascendancy – including a huge demonstration of more than 100 000 people in the Lustgarten on 4 July 1932 – Adolf Hitler was appointed Chancellor on 30 January 1933. Kessler recorded his reactions to this unanticipated turn of events in his diary and elaborated on the celebrations taking place around him:

> Tonight Berlin is in a really festive mood. SA and SS troops as well as uniformed Stahlhelm units are marching through the streets while spectators crowd the pavements. In and around the Kaiserhof there was a proper to-do with SS drawn up in double line outside the main door and inside the hall. When we left after Coudenhove's address, some secondary celebrities (Hitler himself was in the Chancellery) were taking the salute, Fascist style, at an endless SA goose-stepping parade.[3]

Column with posters, Germany c. 1932 23.2 × 17.7 cm
[The lower notice on the column reads: CALL FOR HELP and was posted by a person who had been unemployed
for three years and was in need of work.]

A little over two weeks later the Reichstag was in flames. 'What follows from this,' Kessler wrote, 'remains to be seen'.[4]

For another diarist, Victor Klemperer (an academic and a Jew), the rapidity of change that followed the National Socialists' victory was staggering. On 10 March he wrote:

> Again it's astounding how easily everything collapses ... On Saturday, the 4th, I heard a part of Hitler's speech from Konigsberg. The front of a hotel at the railway station, illuminated, a torchlight procession in front of it, torch-bearers and swastika flag-bearers on the balconies and loudspeakers. I understood only occasional words. But the tone! The unctuous bawling, truly bawling, of a priest ... day after day commissioners appointed, provincial governments trampled underfoot, flags raised, buildings taken over, people shot, newspapers banned, etc. etc. ... Yesterday, the dramaturg Karl Wolff dismissed 'by order of the Nazi Party' – not even in the name of the government – today the whole Saxon cabinet etc. etc. A complete revolution and party dictatorship. And all opposing forces as if vanished from the face of the earth ... No one dares say anything any more, everyone is afraid.[5]

The mechanisms of state control and repression were rapidly instituted, with the first wave of persecution being directed at political activists, especially communists after an alleged communist was accused of burning the Reichstag. The ensuing anti-communist hunt resulted in the arrest of approximately 10 000 Party members and sympathisers, and their subsequent imprisonment in the newly created concentration camps[6]; mass arrests of Social Democratic Party members also took place. On 23 March the Enabling Act was passed, giving full legislative and executive powers to the Chancellor. In May trade unions were abolished, their assets were confiscated and their functionaries taken into 'protective custody', and the first book burnings took place in Berlin with more than 20 000 books being destroyed. In July all political parties, with the exception of the National Socialist German Workers Party, were banned.[7] By September state control of the press was confirmed with the dismissal of oppositional reporters and photojournalists from their positions; some were imprisoned, others were interned in concentration camps or forced into exile.[8]

Anti-Jewish measures were also introduced within the first few weeks of the National Socialists' assumption of power; these included the Law for the Restoration of the Professional Civil Service of 7 April, and the Law for the

Repeal of Previous Naturalization and Recognition of German Citizenship of 14 July. Violence against Jews that had flared up in the last years of the Weimar Republic became widespread after the Reichstag elections of 5 March 1933. Attacks against Jewish businesses and individuals occurred in the so-called *Boykott-Aufruf* (call to boycott), which was organised by the Nazis and commenced on 1 April. That day Kessler wrote in his diary that 'The abominable Jewish boycott has begun. This criminal piece of lunacy has destroyed everything that during the past fourteen years had been achieved to restore faith in, and respect for, Germany.'[9] Klemperer described the situation in more detail a few days later:

> Is it the influence of the tremendous propaganda – films, broadcasting, newspapers, flags, ever more celebrations (today is the Day of the Nation, Adolf the Leader's birthday)? Or is it the trembling, slavish fear all around? I almost believe now that I shall not see the end of this tyranny. And I am almost used to the condition of being without rights. I simply am not German and Aryan, but a Jew and must be grateful if I'm allowed to stay alive.[10]

While harassment against individual Jewish photographic studios and proprietors is known to have taken place in 1933[11], the economic sphere was not the primary target for Nazi persecution of the Jews in the regime's early days. Instead, the cultural domain was the first from which Jews and leftists were massively expelled. In September their participation in Germany's intellectual life was limited by the newly established Reich Chamber of Culture, which was under the control of the Propaganda Ministry. By the end of 1933, 1200 Jews had been dismissed from their academic positions.[12]

Like Kessler and Klemperer, Grete and Michel were immediately caught up in the maelstrom that accompanied the National Socialist regime's consolidation of power. Grete's arrest came first, less than two weeks after the burning of the Reichstag. On 9 March at 10.30 am the rooms of the ASY Publishing House, which served as the headquarters of the anarcho-syndicalist group the FAUD, were searched; books and stock belonging to the *Gilde freiheitlicher Bücherfreunde* (Club of Liberal Bookfriends), the cultural branch of the FAUD, as well as correspondence of the Internationale ArbeiterInnen Assoziation (International Workers Association, or IAA) were confiscated. Grete was among those arrested during the raid. Remarkably the statement she gave to the police has survived. In it, after being advised to tell the truth, she declared:

I deny any connection with the ASY Publishing House or to have carried out communist propaganda there. I have been living in Germany, or rather Berlin, since 1929 and with some interruptions have had positions as a photographer. At the moment I am receiving weekly unemployment benefits of 9.90 marks. About two years ago I attended a lecture at the Lessing Technical School and on this occasion talked to other members of the audience about the buying of books – the publisher ASY was mentioned as a firm that sells books cheaply. In order to buy books I went there on 9.3.33 and was arrested ... I had 46.80 marks in my possession and therefore could have easily paid for the book. I had not as yet decided on any particular book.[13]

This was a disingenuous but apparently effective defence, as Grete's presence in the ASY Publishing House was certainly not a matter of chance. At the time of her arrest Michel was the leader of the Berlin group of the Club of Liberal Bookfriends, which held discussion groups on literature and art. Grete may have belonged to the book club herself, or perhaps was on the premises to conduct FAUD business or to meet Michel. According to a statement she made in later life she was imprisoned in a single cell for five weeks[14]; the circumstances of her release are not known.

Michel was a far more conspicuous target for Nazi persecution because of the overt nature of his activities with the FAUD and his friendships with key members of the anarcho-syndicalist movement, including Gerhard Wartenberg (one of the FAUD's theorists and their 'expert' on fascism)[15], Helmut Rüdiger (a FAUD leader), Fermin Rudolf Rocker and Erich Mühsam. He also knew Dutch anarchist Arthur Lehning, who was active in the IAA, and in 1928 had met the Spanish anarchists Buenaventura Durruti and V Orobón Fernández during their illegal stay in Germany. In May 1933 Michel travelled illegally to Amsterdam to participate in a congress of the anarcho-syndicalists, which considered the future direction the FAUD should take in fascist Germany. Despite the advice of his employer Dr Andrae, the Director of the Museum, that he 'should be as shrewd as a snake and as sensitive as a dove', Michel openly opposed the National Socialist regime. He condemned Nazism in several public speeches and at a public meeting of the FAUD in the industrial area of Berlin-Schöneweide was involved in a fight with the SA.[16] In Michel's own words, Andrae's 'biblical pearl of wisdom' had little 'effect on a fireball' who had immersed himself in the writings of the Russian anarchists Bakunin and Kropotkin.[17]

By midyear Michel's position at the Museum had become untenable and an internal investigation into his 'anti-fascist agitations' was mounted. On 26 July 1933 he was brought before the Chief Administrator, Dr Gierlich, and the Investigating Commission where he stated that he did not consider promoting his ideas to his colleagues at the Museum – he felt that 'there was no future in this'.[18] However, he did elaborate on a speech he had given earlier in the year, prior to an election for a factory committee:

> The content of what I said was something like this: The National Socialist Party may have won, but it was only a quantitative not a qualitative victory. This victory was not evidence of the truth of their ideas: where it is a question of belief the number is not important.[19]

A day after Michel's initial appearance before the Investigating Commission he was called back to continue with the interrogation. That evening, after it was all over, he wrote to Grete, who at that time was probably staying with her parents in Bielsko. Somehow this letter remained in Michel's hands, passing to his biographer, Hans-Jürgen Degen, after his death and eventually on to me after I had visited Berlin. As the letter was not part of the correspondence Mrs Sachs had kept, it is not possible to establish whether Michel ever sent it, or indeed whether Grete ever read it.[20]

27 July, Berlin

Dear Gretele

I have to admit that I have been quite angry with you since Tuesday when I discovered in the ice chest, hidden behind a stack of plates, three pieces of mouldy quark cake. I declare that this is the pinnacle of your achievement. Three pieces of quark cake ... my mouth is still watering even now ... to hide something clandestinely, this I could never bring myself to do.

Today I will forget it all. It is for another reason that I am feeling happy and that a stone has fallen off my heart. After the daily humiliations of raising my arm and the hypocrisy, I was finally able to shed the whole burden ... this cheers me up. This is what happened.

Today I went through a thorough official interrogation. It was to be the last one but the thick end is still to come. Not long after you left, the works councillor came over to tell me that Mr Gierlich, the Chief Administrator, wanted me to come over for an interrogation.

I was therefore 'interrogated' yesterday and today I was questioned about my various jobs, since leaving school till my job in the museum. My political statements in the development of my convictions were chronologically recorded, beginning with my activities in the children's groups, right up to the talks to museum workers. Finally I was asked for my attitude to the new government.

This proceeded in more of a humane than an official way. I said what I had to say. As for the last question, I could not answer otherwise than to say that the last six months of the National Socialist government have not changed my outlook on life and my view of society, and that I could assure the state of my passivity, but no more than that.

Admittedly this is not saying very much and despite the frankness it is not what the law requires. On this we both agreed, Gierlich and me. For this I received a warm handshake and was complimented on my forthrightness when I left.

Today I was once again asked to appear before Chief Administrator Gierlich, for the purpose of signing the record of my statements of yesterday. I was allowed to add a summary to the record that further clarifies my position and formulates it unequivocally. In both documents the chief administration of the State Museum, and maybe also the new Kulturministerium [Ministry of Culture] will for the first time hear something about Bakunin, Kropotkin and Proudhon, about the split in the First Internationale, about the FAUD and much more.

And in the short and clear summary that I have added, and that ends with the words of Beethoven – 'Do good where you can, love freedom above all else, never deny the truth, not even before the throne' – can be found words which indicate that the ideal of the National Socialist government may concern the German citizen but never the free Germans whom I am seeking.

I will tell you more about the whole story in person. In a time when all peoples' good qualities are in hiding, where openness and straightforwardness can cost you your job or your life, where hypocrisy, lies and betrayal are at a premium, my kind of approach must have evoked the sympathies of a man like Gierlich. Sure, dearest Gretle, this is not enough to live on, and in the end the decision does not lie with the Chief Administrator, but in the hands of the Minister.

But you must never reproach me. I have given it a lot of thought. I have raised my arm in salutation, I have allowed myself to be humiliated; but now I can no longer take it. Now that it has all been said my heart feels lighter. Perhaps it is in this manner that the world is opened to us, even if not in its full joy, but at least in its beauty and some pain. If we stick together, we can overcome everything. But we must wait a little longer, things are still up in the air. The decision is now with the Minister.

A kiss, my dear Gretele!

Michel didn't have long to wait. The Minister's decision was conveyed a few days later, and on 4 August Michel's position at the Museum was terminated. In the decree from the Acting General Director of the Berlin State Museums, it was stated that Michaelis was dismissed in accordance with the Law for the Restoration of the Professional Civil Service of 7 April 1933, and the second Ordinance for the implementation of the law concerning the restoration of the civil service with tenure from 4 May 1933. The grounds for dismissal were given as follows:

> [Michaelis] stated clearly that he was familiar with the works of Karl Marx, Bakunin and Kropotkin, that he rejected the authoritarian state and only recognised the free federal societal order ... He offered no guarantee ... that he would at any time without reservation support the nation state, rather the opposite was shown ... that he rejected the state on all important points in question ... His disapproving stance with regard to the National State is completely clear.[21]

Grete and Michel were now both out of work. They were also becoming increasingly isolated, as many of their closest friends and colleagues in the anarcho-syndicalist movement had already left Germany; for example, Helmut and Dora Rüdiger and Etta Federn had settled in Barcelona some time in 1932.

On 2 October 1933 Grete and Michel married, possibly in an attempt to secure Grete's residency in Germany; each gave their address as Wilmersdorf. A few weeks later their situation became more perilous when the Gestapo raided their apartment and confiscated their books, an event Mrs Sachs spoke about during one of our early conversations. I remember her telling me that in the moments before the raid – somehow she had been warned it was about to occur – she had successfully hidden one of the most damning pieces of evidence of the couple's leftist political sympathies. This was a scroll by the German artist Will Faber; it commemorated the lives of the communists Saccho and Vanzetti and usually hung on the Michaelises' living-room wall.[22]

Not long after this incident Grete returned to Bielsko, hoping to earn enough money from her photographic work to fund her and Michel's emigration from Germany. In her absence Michel was arrested – allegedly because he had objected to the confiscation of their books, but surely also because of his political activism – and so she promptly returned to Berlin. For five weeks from the middle of November Michel was imprisoned in the cellars at the notorious Central Police Station at Alexanderplatz, where many political prisoners were held and tortured before being despatched to the newly established concentration camps outside Berlin.[23]

Forty years after the event Michel returned to the circumstances behind his imprisonment and release, attempting to piece together the fragments of his memories. But, as he explained in a letter to 'Dear Gretl' in 1973, his memory was poor and he needed her to help him retrieve what he had forgotten. The only information Michel had about his miraculous escape had come directly from Professor Andrae, whom he had visited at the end of the war. Professor Andrae had told him that he had attempted to secure Michel's freedom 'through a friend of Goerring's, which then caused him considerable trouble with the Gestapo'. What Michel now wanted was Grete's account:

> So, how was it then, at the end of 1933? ... During my imprisonment
> in the Alex you had prepared everything. You had disposed of our
> possessions. Some of them went to Jussuf, others to the Buttkes.
> Were they given, or were they sold? I know nothing of that.

Grete replied a few months later. She kept a rough copy of the letter she drafted in German, elaborating on her version of the sequence of events. Upon returning to Berlin a few days after Michel's arrest, she explained that

> I asked Marianne if anything had been done to organise your release.
> She said that she had spoken to Professor Andrae who, however,
> didn't know what to do. I went to Prof. A and the substance of our
> conversation was, 'Please Professor, what can one do, what can I
> do?' Prof: 'Michaelis appears to be in a period of his life in which
> he appears to need this kind of experience.' Me: 'Yes, but before he
> can learn anything from it he will be killed. Please, please Professor,
> what can one do?' Prof: 'Come to my place tomorrow. I will think
> about it'. On the next day he gave me a letter in a big locked box
> and said 'This will need to be put in Goerring's letterbox personally.
> Who can do that?' Me: 'That could be dangerous, I will have to do
> that myself.' I went on the same day to the address that I was given,

a place at the Brandenburg Gate. There was a hedge made up from tall trees on the left and the right. A small gate in the middle led to the garden. There was a letterbox in the gate. On the garden side a soldier with a drawn bayonet passed by this entrance, from one end to the other. I stood at a distance under a tree and counted the steps he took from the last tree at the entrance to the last tree on the left side. It took ten or twenty times until I could be sure that he was the furthest distance away, then I counted another ten times with my eyes closed and opened them at the instant at which he should appear at the entrance. Once I was sure of this procedure I went away and came back in the evening, another ten times to make sure, then quickly to the letterbox, and the letter in the box. Because it was a big box it rang out in the stillness of the night. I turned to go and expected a shot in my back. But I returned home. The soldier had obviously not heard it. At that second he was at the other end. Three days later and you were home.

At the end of this densely written paragraph Grete had crossed out a sentence that read 'I remember that I told you this briefly, but your reply was: "No, I was released because I was innocent!"'

Michel eventually wrote his own detailed account of his experiences at the Alex. They were published posthumously in 1994 in a booklet entitled 'Rudolf Michaelis in protective custody', a copy of which his biographer Hans-Jürgen Degen kindly sent me.

Rudolf Michaelis in protective custody

After Hitler ... grabbed power I became acquainted with the cellar rooms of the Alex ... I was taken into 'protective custody' by the Nazis and incarcerated in those cellars.

Each of these cellar rooms of some 20 square metre floor surface was covered with bundles of straw. The people in 'protective custody' stood shoulder to shoulder during the day and at night, even if they crouched down, could not find sufficient room in order to sleep. They sagged together into a uniform human heap as a result of how tired they were. When the door to such a cellar room was opened to me I found companions with their teeth knocked out and bodies beaten, who bore everywhere the blue and yellow-green marks of inhuman thrashings.

These cellar rooms were guarded in shifts by two uniformed policemen of very different types. The younger of the two, somewhere in his thirties, was clearly a Nazi, who did not flinch from beating the people in 'protective custody' at the slightest provocation ... This Nazi prison guard ... took an interest in me. He did not like it that I did not greet him with the Hitler salute. When this Nazi was on the job he ... removed me from the cellar room at night and ordered me to clean the windows and doors and to scrub the floor of the corridor. Sometimes I also had to do this work for him during the day, and my companions assisted me when my special employment extended to the inside of the cellar rooms. They helped me with the cleaning and we used a handy brick to scrub the doors until the paint came off the wood. It was for us a form of protest against 'protective custody'. It also gave me an opportunity to make contact with companions in the other cellar rooms and to bring information and secret messages from room to room.

... We must mention the second prison guard in the cellars of the Alex. This man, who was closer to fifty years of age, had no doubt been a social-democratic police official in the Weimar Republic. We had no proof of this but his humane manner during contact with those in 'protective custody' gave this impression. He was very sympathetic towards me. When he was on duty he called me out from the floor and secretly gave me a part of the bread from his breakfast ... We also received the newspaper from him that did the rounds in the cellar rooms. I even entrusted this prison guard with a secret message that he took in an envelope to my wife.

The cellar rooms began to empty towards Christmas 1933. Some of the people in 'protective custody' were sentenced, others had to tread the heavy path to the concentration camp and some received the 'freedom' to live in an unfree Germany. I was among the latter ones. After having signed a waiver for my library, which had been confiscated, an intervention by Professor Walter Andrae, who was at the time the Director of the Section for the Far East of the State Museum in Berlin, opened the prison door for me. He was an archaeologist with a worldwide reputation who had done excavations in Babylon and Assur ... his influence was sufficient in December 1933 to effect my being freed from 'protective custody' in the Alex. I still remember quite clearly the moment when I left the cellar rooms and the words of the Nazi prison guard, who shouted in my face, full of hate, 'You, pig, belong in the concentration camp!' I was immeasurably relieved at that moment. However ... I had had to leave behind many manuscripts to which I was very attached, among which were volumes in whose spines I had hidden illegal pamphlets. They included a photocopied text that read 'Nero burned Rome and blamed the Christians – Hitler burned the Reichstag and blamed the Communists!' My wife, a very good photographer had made hundreds of very small copies of this and we had already distributed a large number of these. If the prosecuting officials had made a thorough search of my confiscated books my fate would have been sealed. Being mindful of this danger, the Executive Committee of the FAUD had made all the necessary arrangements for me to leave Hitler's Germany immediately. In the morning hours of a December day, shortly before Christmas 1933 I regained my freedom from Alexanderplatz and a short time later, on the very same day, I crossed the border in an express train.[24]

While 'Rudolf Michaelis in protective custody' is fascinating as a first-hand account of the brutalism of the Nazi regime, it is equally revealing for reasons particular to this story. It conveys a strong sense of how Michel saw himself, especially in terms of his unwavering political beliefs and subversive attitude towards imprisonment. The bravado and daring he highlights through his oppositional activities are confirmed in the recollections of Bertold Cahn (later shot by the Nazis) and Fritz Scherer, members of the FAUD and fellow inmates at the Alex. Scherer described an incident during Michel's imprisonment in which the SA made the prisoners

sing the Nazi songs. One day we were told to sing the SA song 'Die Fahne Hoch' ['Up with the flag']. Michel stepped forward and sang with a thundering voice, the worker's song 'Brüder zur Sonne, zur Freiheit' ['Brother to the sun, and freedom']. The SA were so confused that they hastily left the cell corridor. Nothing happened to Michel.[25]

Also of significance is the fact that Michel's account gives credit to Grete's photographic work on behalf of the resistance movement – the only firm proof of her participation in it. And yet he chooses to make no mention of her role in securing his release from prison or in arranging their departure from Berlin for Barcelona, both of which she had explained in her letter to him. Michel writes as if he arrived in Spain on his own, whereas Grete gives a very different version of their flight from Germany. In the mid-1980s she recalled:

My husband was in a dangerous position because he objected to the loss of our books and was imprisoned. As he had earlier lost his work in the State Museum and we intended to emigrate [*sic*] to Spain, I prepared everything for a quick departure. My husband was freed with the help of his museum director who was not a Nazi ... Two days after my husband's release from prison, we arrived in Barcelona. We didn't know a word of Spanish, had little money but could live with our friends.[26]

The circumstances of the Michaelises' departure meant that they could take with them only what was essential. This included Grete's photographic equipment – a crucial fact, for it was photography, not her relationship with Michel, that was the thread connecting her lives in Vienna and Berlin, and now Barcelona.

7 BERLIN

I came to Berlin with a small bundle of things from Grete Gross's time here, between 1929 and 1933, that I felt might be useful for my research. It wasn't difficult choosing what to bring, as not much remains. A few photographs, some of the letters she and Michel wrote each other in the 1930s and 1970s, and a list of addresses of places where she lived and worked more than seventy years ago. The addresses that I had meticulously collected over the years never meant much to me in Canberra. They were like strangers' names that I would have to say over and over, sometimes out loud, to keep them in my mind: Martin Luther Strasse 6, Kurfürstendamm 225 and 230, Breitenbachplatz, Budapester Strasse 6, Bamberger Strasse 4. Now as I follow them around my map they are taking shape and are becoming easy to remember. Just to be sure I can hold them there I take a photograph of each site, always including the street sign in the foreground for future reference. Of course there is little left of the buildings that Grete inhabited; I didn't expect otherwise in this war-scarred city.

At night, in my hotel room just off the Kurfürstendamm, I re-read the letters and look again at the photographs that I have come to know almost by heart. One photograph is an interior view of Grete and Michel's apartment, perhaps at Breitenbachplatz in Wilmersdorf. I took the S-bahn there yesterday and in the gentle rain walked around the area that is now a mix of residential and office buildings. Grete's photograph of their home is a houseproud image in which everything has its place; it is a light-filled inventory of the couple's brief domestic life together. Michel is at the heart of another photograph taken in the same room – book in hand, he stares into the camera Grete is holding to her eye. The third photograph is the one I like most. It is about desire. Grete has moved in close to Michel, as close as possible before the features of her lover's face began dissolving into a blur. The space she has created is eroticised, a shared space where, with the license granted by intimacy, she can gaze on Michel's features. Who hasn't wanted to fix in one's mind every detail of a lover's face?

Michel with open book, Berlin c. 1932 17.1 × 21.4 cm

I have decided to put aside the portraits of Michel for the time being. It is two interior shots that seem most resonant on my journeying around Berlin. For a long time I have responded to them as images of 'home', as the centre of a world, but now I see that they speak simultaneously of home and its loss. The rugs, table, chairs, pot plants, bookcases and books that appear in the photographs don't look as solid and as resolute as they did in Canberra. Here their future is almost upon them. Take the books as an example: they are signs of civilisation and domestic order, yet are harbingers of chaos, fuel to the Nazi fires that would force the Michaelises from this quiet, neat room. Books, after all, were behind each of their arrests in separate incidents in 1933.

What we see so clearly delineated in Grete's photographs is precisely what was lost when the Michaelises fled to Barcelona. The books, furniture and room were all left behind, leaving their traces only in gelatin silver and memory. But the loss of the objects so present in the photographs is only part of it. Much harder to talk about, but more affecting, is the loss of other things that have no physicality and can't be properly named – a time, a relationship, a state of being. They are inside the photographs, in the light, in the space and in the aura woven around the objects. Although Grete and Michel might not have been sure of it at the time, the small, peaceful world of the photographs vanished as it materialised. A few months after arriving in Barcelona they would separate and go their different ways, and across Europe fascism would thrive.

However, Grete did not abandon everything in their hasty departure from Berlin. Somewhere out of view, maybe inside a chest of drawers in the bedroom or in a cupboard beside the bed, are some of the things she took with her to Barcelona, Bielsko, London, and then on to Sydney and Melbourne: notes and letters, mostly from Michel during his time in Warka, photographs and personal papers. No more than would fit in a shoebox, easy to stow inside the suitcase that went with her from one country to the next.

Somewhere in the Michaelises' apartment there was also a bundle of photographs, forty-eight to be exact, that Grete could not take with her. For forty years she didn't know their whereabouts, telling Michel in a letter written in 1974 that 'When I moved I often wondered what happened to the photographs, but I couldn't remember'. This morning I found myself thinking about them when I visited an open-air museum in the ruined foundations of the former SS internment cells, in what was once the administrative centre of the Nazi state. It was only in the 1980s – in the desire to restore 'to public consciousness' the Prinz-Albrecht area – that the remains of the buildings were unearthed from the great piles of dirt and rubble that had rendered them invisible after the war.

Grete's photographs were on my mind, too, as I walked through the
Potsdamer Platz and other areas where the Wall had stood in the decades after
the war. In an orgy of construction the earth is being opened up for the laying
of cables, pipes and the pouring of foundations. From footpaths and temporary
viewing platforms you can peer into clay pits, some small and shallow, others
larger than any I have ever seen. And everywhere you can smell the earth; it is
a smell I knew immediately from childhood play in freshly excavated housing
estates on the other side of the world. I imagine that all sorts of things are being
unearthed in these frenzied excavations, maybe even domestic treasures, such
as letters, photographs or a piece of crockery.

Half a lifetime after leaving them behind in Berlin, Grete's lost photographs
were returned to her by Michel. They were accompanied by a long, tender
letter explaining that they had been buried in the Nazi era by their friend Carl
Buttke, one of the fortunate who had been able to return to the burial site and
retrieve what he had hidden. In Buttke's case, writes Michel,

> they buried everything that was suspicious, in crate loads buried under
> the earth. After the annihilation of the Nazis they dug everything up
> again. This is how Carl is in possession of an enviable book collection,
> which contains books by Thomas Mann, Sigmund Freud and classic
> editions ... Sometimes I borrow a book from this collection. On such a
> visit Carl's daughter Gabriele spoke of your photographs, which were
> still in her father's possession. Of course I insisted that they be given
> back so that I could send them to you.

Left Berlin, November 1933 Grete and Michel's living room in Wilmersdorf
16.6 × 22.6 cm

For Michel the recovery of the photographs is a potent event. 'As it sometimes is,' he told her, 'a word, a song, a letter, a photograph, they wake memories. In my very concrete case, it was forty-eight photographs.' It's not the subject matter of the images that unsettles him – the photographs were taken before he had met Grete – but rather the fact that Grete is their creator. As Michel and Buttke admire each photograph Grete becomes the centre of their conversation, which extends for a long time. But there's more to Grete's re-emergence than that. Aged in his late sixties, a reflective stage of life when the remembrance of things past becomes a preoccupation, Michel is faced with what he has lost: 'You have to begin to lose your memory,' writes Spanish filmmaker Luis Buñuel in his autobiography *My last breath*, 'if only in bits and pieces, to realize that memory is what makes our lives. Life without memory is no life at all ... Our memory is our coherence'.[1]

In response Michel asks Grete for help to retrieve his memories. He explains that his memory is full of holes, not because of increasing age, but because of the appalling treatment he suffered during five years' imprisonment in Barcelona at the end of the Spanish Civil War. Grete, he hopes, will enable him to recover those fragments of his life that were entwined with hers. Their possessions in their Berlin apartment, for example, what happened to them? Were they 'given or sold?' he asks her. 'I know nothing of that. Books, photographs, the silver eggcups that I brought for you from Baghdad. And what else was there?'

There is also a pragmatic dimension to Michel's desire for memories. They may help him identify in some of their former belongings he cannot recognise on his own.

> Perhaps you could remember other things that Carl might have in his protection? He doesn't like to get things out. I already know that! Over his seventy years he has developed a certain stinginess, something that one would really not expect from him. But with Gabriele's help I was able to tear your photographs away from him. This work will surely mean more to you than to the amateur archivist Carl Buttke, even though I can understand that one would not willingly let such good photographs go.

Unlike Buttke, the amateur archivist who hoarded his own and others' possessions, Michel apparently has nothing at all from his past. 'But which things,' he asks Grete rhetorically, 'have we not had to part from over the course of our lives? I was able to rescue nothing.'

It doesn't surprise me that five months lapsed before Grete was able to respond to the return of her past and the once buried photographs that included portraits taken during her years in Vienna and Berlin. She kept drafts of three letters she wrote to Michel; written in English they may have been her means of working out what to say in German, their shared language in correspondence. The first letter, a series of stops and starts and crossings-out, is unfinished and was probably never sent:

Dear Michel

I have had your letter for nearly five months. To leave a letter unanswered for such a long time deserves an explanation.

First of all I would like to heartily thank you for the 48 dug-up photographs that arrived safely in one piece. And certainly you will soon have copies of your letters from Babylon ~~and everything else that was there, birds~~ [crossed out], trees and your poems …

I have often 'written' my answer in my thoughts, but to write it down is a little harder. I really regret ~~that such a long time~~ [crossed out] that I didn't at least acknowledge receipt of the letter and the photographs. ~~Will you hold it against me?~~ [crossed out]. In some ways I am experiencing the same as you with your memory. There are holes that I also cannot fill up … When I moved I often wondered what could have happened to the photographs, but I couldn't remember. I can also hardly remember Carl Buttke, I don't know what he looked like, and now he is 71 years old. I can't remember his poor wife Edith.

I read with shock that you were in prison in Barcelona for 5 years and of the atrocious treatment that you had to put up with. Even though Marianne sent me a long letter shortly after the end of the war, she didn't tell me anything about it, she wrote about you and that you were with your family in Berlin.

The letter ends here. She goes on to compose another, shorter letter:

… that will at least say thank you for your (as always) interesting letter and for the 48 photographs, which arrived safely. You brought me a lot of you with them … I hope that the letter, which should clearly answer everything for you, will soon be sent off. But this short one should be sent early tomorrow, so that you know that everything arrived, for which I want to thank you again.

The third letter is the most sustained and fluent and, as far as I know, is the last she ever wrote Michel. She explained that she could not remember what had happened to their things: 'I thought that we left the apartment as it was and locked the door as if we were going on holiday. I know that you gave Carl the violin'. One of the photographs she enclosed is of their Berlin apartment – perhaps it was the same book-filled image that I have in front of me now. My copy, however, doesn't carry the inscription Grete wrote on the back of Michel's: 'On this wall hung the poem by Saccho and Vanzetti written by Will Faber. Do you remember?'

These copies of letters and photographs do their work: the photograph of their Berlin apartment, for example, Michel remembers well. As he looks at other photographs from their shared life he reminisces that

> A time gone by seemed as present as our current existence. This
> all makes me feel that you remained truer to yourself than I, who
> abandoned this and that or had to cast it off like a worn coat.

Early this evening I found my last address, Martin Luther Strasse 6, where Grete once lived. Now the site of a car yard, there was no building to photograph, just rows of brightly coloured pennant flags and new cars lined up behind them. From there it was a short walk to the woods at the Tiergarten, where Grete may have relaxed on her days off from the studios in nearby Budapester Strasse or on the Kurfürstendamm. I found the Tiergarten a cheerless place, even in early autumn it was dark, quiet and dank, and the water in the ponds inky black. The trees Grete saw were not those around me; they had been cut down for fuel during the war and were not replanted until the war ended. In the woods I was filled with a desire to leave my copies of Grete's photographs in Berlin, but I couldn't decide what to do with them. Burn them up in the firestorm that had been raging through my mind since seeing photographs of bombed-out Berlin in a display at the Kaiser Wilhelm church? Or scratch a hole in the earth and bury them?

When I arrived back at my hotel a package was waiting for me at the reception desk. It was from Michel's biographer, Hans-Jürgen Degen, whom I had been corresponding with for a few years and who I had hoped to meet. His cover note explained that a meeting wouldn't be possible, as he was about to go on holidays. Inside his package was a bundle of papers I had never seen before, including a copy of the first and only chapter of Michel's memoirs, 'Encounter with Spain', and a copy of Degen's obituary for Michel, which was published in *Direkte Aktion*. Most surprising – because I had assumed from Michel's own comments to Grete that he had lost everything – there are also copies of two letters he had written to her in 1932 and 1933. According to Degen,

> When Michel left Germany in 1933 he left some written things (books, pictures etc) with a friend. A few of these things were burnt during the war. The letters above-mentioned were saved.

How these letters came to be saved I don't know; buried perhaps by Carl Buttke along with Grete's photographs 'in crate loads under the earth'.

Degen's package also included photocopies of two portraits of Michel, taken in 1949 and 1980. The earlier portrait is of a handsome, earnest, though world-weary man, and the later is of a man in his seventies, elderly but very alert. The sight of these completely unfamiliar faces momentarily filled me with panic because I was afraid that they might not be the Michel I had come to know through Grete's images and her images alone, but proof of a mistaken or constructed identity. To reassure myself that I was looking at one and the same man I lay down Degen's photocopies next to Grete's early portrait of Michel. The physiognomic markers seem to be there, making it possible to link the three faces together, but as the young man grows into the old I am left with a sliver of doubt – not about Michel, as such, but about Mrs Sachs's represenation of him to those she had shown the portrait, myself included. However, it is the differences in the photographic codes, rather than the way Michel looks over time, that preoccupy me. All three portraits have different public and private roles, signalled by each photographer's choice of vantage point and use of space.

Seeing them together made me realise something new about Grete's portrait of Michel. It concerns the relationship between stasis and flux that is a problem peculiar to portraiture: how to create a living image of a still subject. Photographers have developed different ways to deal with this conundrum. Max Dupain, for instance, often introduced casual poses and gestures as a means of animating his portraits: one expects the conversation occurring between Walter Gropius and Harry Seidler to continue beyond the photographic frame. Grete, too, in one of her most outstanding portraits – that of the Australian writer Cynthia Nolan – used an unusual pose to create a sense of flux. The portraits of Michel that Degen has given me are frozen and self-enclosed but

Grete's portrait of him is alive – in it one can anticipate some kind of extended movement, a hand passing through his hair, perhaps a tongue sliding across his almost-parted lips, a word, a gesture, a move towards an embrace.

I made the trip to Berlin because of Margaret Michaelis, though I greatly enjoyed visiting a city that I had last seen still divided by the Wall. As I left I was preoccupied with thoughts about Michaelis's own relationship with Berlin, a city she had lived in only briefly, fled and not returned to for thirty-four years. Another émigré photographer, German-born Wolfgang Sievers who settled in Australia in 1938, once told me that he felt unable to revisit his hometown of Berlin for many years. When he finally did so in the late 1950s he hated hearing the sound of the German language. For the first few days, or maybe even the first week or two of his visit, he couldn't bring himself to speak German; English was all he could use. I feel sure that Mrs Sachs, like Wolfgang Sievers, would have had her own form of resistance to being in Berlin – though what it was, of course, I don't know.

8 CRACOW

Some time, probably in the early 1930s, maybe even in the tumultuous years of 1932 or 1933, Grete Gross visited Cracow. It wasn't far from her hometown of Dzieditz, less than 100 kilometres, and even closer to her parents' home in Bielsko where she stayed intermittently during these years. While in Cracow Gross took a number of photographs in the Jewish quarter and also photographed some of the buildings of Cracow University. The fourteen prints she kept have the coherence of a series and could easily have been part of a self-imposed assignment to document particular aspects of the city.

It's not simply the shared subject matter that binds the photographs together but also their loveliness as objects. Each image has been carefully and lovingly printed in a small, rectangular format (only one is vertical in orientation). Gross must have been happy with the results, signalling their state of completion by inscribing titles on the backs of some of them one or two years later. The longest inscription, referring to the image of a smiling peddler, is written in Spanish and reads: 'Cracow, Poland, secondhand clothes market in the Jewish quarter. Lleba has his whole shop on his head. Offered for sale, seven hats, all ready to own. In spite of everything he is content.'

In these Cracow images Grete Gross explores different photographic approaches. Her photographs of the university are artful architectural studies in which shadows play a major compositional role, whereas those taken in the marketplace are more documentary. The latter exploit the mobility and spontaneity made possible with a lightweight, easy-to-use camera – probably the Leica she had purchased in Berlin. One senses Gross moving around the market with ease, photographing whatever and whoever catches her eye. Most of her subjects seem unaware of the camera; only Lleba and the child Gross describes as a gypsy look directly into the lens.

Facade of building, Cracow c. 1930–33 12.2 × 14.4 cm

The Jagiellon University, Cracow, one of the oldest in Europe c. 1930–33 12.1 × 16.8 cm

Hat seller in the market in the Jewish quarter, Cracow c. 1930–33 12.1 × 16.9 cm

Like fellow photographer Roman Vishniac, Grete Gross could have been working with a hidden camera. For Vishniac, a Russian-born Jew, this was the only viable means of securing photographs of the Jews of Eastern Europe in the 1930s; he noted in his book *A vanished world* that 'Jews did not want to be photographed, due to a misunderstanding of the prohibition against making graven images'.[1] However, in Gross's case it seems more likely that she was working quickly rather than surreptitiously. This was the approach she took in Barcelona in 1932 and again in 1934 when she photographed the inhabitants of the Barrio Chino – the infamous old Chinatown. In a document held in the Arxiu Històric del Col.legi d'Arquitectes de Catalunya (ARXIU) Archives in Barcelona she describes in some detail the circumstances behind her photograph of cardsharps:

> I took my small Leica and went for a wander through the Barrio Chino. My friends were there, the cardsharps. Around them a crowd of gypsies and accomplices. I could really take a photograph there! I took one, and set myself up to take a second when they noticed me. Everyone looked at me with hostility, they thought that I was a spy for the police, and would use the pictures against them. They all took a threatening stance. The cardsharp who had played Kummelblattchen got up instantly and started to complain 'Have you already taken photographs of us?' I had just started, but they had noticed me too early. Three of his accomplices moved towards me, 'What are you doing here? Go away! We don't want to see you here again!' I laughed at them ... and continued on my way.[2]

That Gross had an eye for the picaresque is borne out in her photographs of the hat salesman, Lleba, and the gypsy child. Like the cardsharps of the Barrio Chino, such subjects are ubiquitous in the history of photography. They are exotic, outside the photographer's own realm of experience. Gross visited the market as an independent and socially mobile woman whose material circumstances were far superior to most of those she photographed. She was not their social equal. And yet, as a Jew herself, she was an insider. This may explain the respectful, almost reverential nature of two of her photographs of Jewish stallholders, which seem more concerned with the dignity of the subjects than with detailed documentary information; the compositions are tight, with an emphasis on gesture and expression, and the prints are sonorous in their range of dark tones.

Having just bought a pair of shoes, Cracow c. 1938 12.0 × 15.6 cm

It would be a relatively simple matter to end the discussion of Grete Gross's Cracow photographs at this point – having located them in her oeuvre, considered some of their most significant formal and stylistic qualities, and briefly contextualised them in relation to Roman Vishniac's work. But this sidesteps what is most compelling about them: their retrospective 'value', or their burden. For it is not possible to look at these photographs of the Jewish quarter without seeing the Holocaust in them. The individuals inhabiting the marketplace represent communities that will soon disappear, either through forced dispersal or extermination, and the site of the marketplace is one that will soon be irrevocably altered. For any Jewish survivors who returned to the quarter after the war, all would be gone – in place of their homes fragments of building materials, with only the sky remaining unchanged.

And so I find that the less formally resolved of Gross's Cracow images also have much to say. Take as an example the photograph of an old man, walking stick in one hand and a pair of leather boots over his other arm. This is not as visually satisfying as other images; the background is distracting and competes for attention with the centrally placed figure and the print is flat in tone. And yet my eye is drawn back to this photograph because of an apparently incidental detail: the boots the old man carries. These ordinary objects – a little worn through but in reasonable condition – are laden with signification. For civilians and soldiers, children and adults, boots could literally mark the line between life and death in a harsh European climate. When Vishniac photographed a shoemaker in 1937, it was to acknowledge and celebrate the shoemaker's critical role in the community, a sentiment reinforced by the shoemaker himself in the statement he made to Vishniac that is published alongside the image: 'Without soles, nobody can exist,' he wrote, 'neither porters nor peddlers. Even to go to synagogue, you need soles on your shoes. And to feed your family you must walk on the cobblestones ... Leather soles last six weeks on stones.'[3] As I look again at Gross's photograph, dozens of other images of obscene mountains of leather shoes, and piles and piles of bare-footed corpses crowd into my mind.

Of all photographs related to the Holocaust, whether taken by Jewish people themselves, by German soldiers or by allied photographers[4], it is Vishniac's that are most relevant to Gross's images of Cracow. Both photographers were working in the 1930s before the enactment of the Final Solution and they shared common subject matter. Roman Vishniac is especially known for his depictions of 'the rabbis ... peddlers and their customers, the beggars and the cantors, the

Second-hand clothes market, Cracow c. 1930–33 12.1 × 16.9 cm

sad old men and the smiling young ones'.[5] However, it is the differences between Gross's and Vishniac's work, both contemporaneously and retrospectively, that are most illuminating. Vishniac's vast project was underpinned by personal and social imperatives that he reiterated in print at different times. In 1974, for instance, he wrote:

> My friends assured me that Hitler's talk was sheer bombast. But I replied that he would not hesitate to exterminate those people when he got around to it. And who was there to defend them? I knew I could be of little help, but I decided that, as a Jew, it was my duty to my ancestors, who grew up among the very people who were being threatened, to preserve – in pictures at least – a world that might soon cease to exist.[6]

His documentation of the life of Jews in Eastern Europe grew to more than 16 000 photographs, of which only 2000 survived, although Vishniac's hope was that the remainder would eventually reappear. As he saw it, he was 'unable to save my people, only their memory'.[7]

The rediscovery of Vishniac's work in the 1970s coincided with the boom in the photography market led by the United States. Modern reprints of his photographs were widely circulated through various publications, especially the portfolio *A vanished world* (published in 1977) and the book of the same name that followed. As a book and a portfolio *A vanished world* makes a solemn public declaration about the enormity of what happened in the Holocaust, not only to the Jews whom Vishniac had photographed, most of whom were subsequently killed, but to all Jews. Large in format and heavy to hold, the book demands to be read at a table or a desk. Similarly, the portfolio commands serious attention, the large museum-scale of the prints maximises their physical impact while the sharp, modern style of printing emphasises their graphic qualities.

Why Gross photographed the Jewish quarter of Cracow isn't known. The primary motivation was probably personal, as there is nothing to suggest that the series was exhibited or published, either at the time it was made or subsequently. In contrast to Vishniac's work, Gross's small, modest prints remained invisible throughout her life. Friends and fellow photographers in Australia were unaware of them, as they were of most of her European oeuvre. Thus, when the Cracow photographs quietly slipped back into view after Mrs Sachs's death, some things about them – their tiny size, for instance – were as they had always been. For Gross, who either abandoned or lost her European negatives, re-printing and enlarging earlier work in response to its historical importance and contemporary interests and tastes was never an option. The captions for the Cracow images had also stayed as they were, unlike the Spanish photographs that she had added inscriptions to or reinscribed later on. In the case of her photograph of Lleba, the impoverished hat salesman, the frozen caption has a discomforting effect. Gross wrote of her subject that 'In spite of everything he is content'. In light of our historical knowledge such a statement, once merely patronising, slips into another register to become ironic, portentous and awful.

For me, the power of Gross's small, gentle Cracow images derives from this slippage between two worlds: the world she photographed in a relatively untroubled present (her subjects' poverty does not appear to have been a major issue for her) and the post-Holocaust world that she, and we, came to know. This represents not only the photographs' burden, but also the photographer's. Somehow Grete Gross had to live with this knowledge, with both the presence of the photographs and the absence they signified. Her response, not surprisingly, was to keep them invisible.

Bearded man in the Jewish quarter, Cracow c. 1930–33 14.3 × 9.2 cm

9 ENCOUNTER WITH SPAIN

The first and only chapter of Michel's memoir 'Encounter with Spain', given to me by Hans-Jürgen Degen, isn't dated but was probably written in the mid-1970s. Michel had told Grete in his letter of Christmas Eve 1975 that he was busily recording his adventures in Spain. In the process, he noticed the shortcomings of his memory – 'not surprising,' he wrote, 'after what I have been through' – and he once again asked her to help fill in 'some of the gaps'. He continues,

> You have done this once before when dealing with my liberation from the Alex. In fact, your impressions of your stay in Barcelona are important to me.

> ... Tell me some names and then I will remember everything again. Key events and words will do. And why you left Spain. And at what time things happened. That will help me with one chapter of my writing. Perhaps you have a few photographs.

And, he adds, 'If this is asking too much, forgive me and don't do anything. I won't be cross'.

There is nothing in the archive to suggest that Grete responded to Michel's request or, indeed, that she ever wrote to him again. No further drafts or copies of her letters to Michel exist. Nor, it seems, did Michel continue his correspondence. His Christmas Eve letter appears to have been his last, the unceremonious end to their irregular but intense eight-year exchange.

Nevertheless, Michel went on to finish his first chapter. Most of it deals with political matters, outlining the formation of his political beliefs and his views on the Spanish political situation, in particular the role of the anarchists during the Spanish Civil War. Curiously, in contrast to his essay 'Rudolf Michaelis in protective custody', which describes his experiences in Germany, Grete assumes a greater presence in 'Encounter with Spain'. The chapter opens with Michel's very specific recollections of their shared experiences and describes the couple's arrival in Barcelona in December 1933 the following way:

Now we were standing at the railway station in Barcelona where heavily armed Guardia Civil checked our entry permits. Instinctively we compared the affected manners of this Spanish police corps with that of the Nazi SA and SS. Had we fallen out of the frying pan and into the fire?

Our friends, Helmut Rüdiger and his wife Dora, were expecting us at the station. Both of them must have seen the surprise and dismay on our faces. 'State of siege', was their brief and serious greeting. They took us to the tram, which slowly made its way upwards to the city under escort by two civil guards. Strong characters, who threw dark looks, without letting the silent passengers out of their sight ... In their green uniforms with black leather and with the strange three-cornered helmets rounded off at the forehead, they looked like theatre extras. However, the strap across the chin, the carbine over the shoulders and the ammunition pouches at each side left no room for doubt, that their deployment was not at all staged. The Guardia Civil dominated the face of Barcelona like an occupying power.

Rüdiger quoted and translated into German several verses from the 'Ballad of the Spanish Civil Guard' by Federico García Lorca for us:

Their skulls are leaden,
which is why they don't weep.
With their patent leather souls
they come down the street.
Hunchbacked and nocturnal,
where they go, they command
silence of dark rubber
and fears like fine sand.

So even before we had reached our place of refuge at Rüdiger's, we had been confronted with the current political situation in Spain. The poetic image from the 'Romancero Gitano' ['Gypsy Ballad Book'] of García Lorca affected us strongly. We thought back to the Germany whose prisons and concentration camps we had escaped.

At the south-west of the Carrer Rossello, we found accommodation on the top floor of a modern apartment building, very close to the model prison, Carcel Modelo. From the terrace we could see into the prison courtyard. This hexagonal prison building was swarming with political prisoners. During the day they clustered around the barred windows. At certain times they carried on excited discussions between the high walls of the prison yards, as if they wanted to give voice to their protest against their arrests. When they caught sight of us they waved up in our direction. From time to time their cry rang out in unison: "Viva la CNT–FAI' – Long live the Anarcho-Syndicalist Union and the Anarchist Association of Iberia'.

In 'Encounter with Spain' Michel explained what drew him to Spain, relating his attraction to his experiences in Warka and the Near East. He wrote of 'the expectation of encountering a kind of people ... who, like those of the Near East, hadn't degenerated under the pressure of the capitalistic way of life' and remarked that he was especially interested in 'the interplay between Occidental and Oriental influences'. However, in reality, the reasons for settling in Spain appear to have been much more pragmatic and urgent given the nature of the Michaelises' departure from Berlin.

Barcelona was an obvious choice as a safe haven for a number of reasons. Fellow members in the anarcho-syndicalist movement the FAUD, including the Michaelises' long-term friends Helmut and Dora Rüdiger, had already settled there and were able to provide valuable material and moral support. These expatriate Germans were vitally interested in the Spanish political situation, which the Michaelises had also been following for some years – through the German anarchists Rudolf Rocker and Erich Mühsam Michel had met the Spanish revolutionaries Buenaventura Durruti and V Orobón Fernández in 1928, in Berlin.

In Barcelona the political situation had improved considerably with the declaration of the Second Republic in April 1931. The new coalition of Socialists and Left Republicans, with Manuel Azaña as Prime Minister, had begun the complex and fraught process of re-shaping a traditional and deeply conservative society; they attacked the privileges of the church, introduced reforms of the education system and of the military, granted autonomy to Catalonia, and made the first attempts at agrarian reform. For those in the Michaelises' circle who, as anarchists, were opposed to any form of parliamentary democracy, it was not the modest gains being made by the Azaña government that were the source of great hope, but rather the growing strength of the anarcho-syndicalist movement, especially in Catalonia.

Membership of anarcho-syndicalist organisations – the Confederación Nacional de Trabajo (Federation of Anarcho-Syndicalist Trades Union, or CNT), formed in 1911, and the more militant Federación Anarquista Ibérica (Federation of Anarchist Groups, or FAI), formed in 1927 – rose dramatically in this period. With more than 700 000 members by 1931, the CNT claimed to be larger than the Socialist Trades Union: the Union General de Trabajadores (UGT).[1] Trade unions, or syndicates, were regarded as a crucial tool in the revolutionary struggle – as the means by which labour was organised, they would provide the basis for the establishment of libertarian communism in post-revolutionary society.[2] In the early 1930s anarchist activity escalated across Spain, with general strikes, riots, uprisings in the south, peasant revolts in Andalusia, and in the creation of revolutionary communes in rural areas throughout the Levant.[3] A spontaneous revolution, it seemed, was imminent.

However, Barcelona also offered professional possibilities to both Michel and Grete Michaelis. She had visited there in 1932 (perhaps to meet Michel on his return from Warka), and had apparently already established contact with the group of Catalan architects, the Grup d'Arquitectes i Tècnics Catalans per al Progrés de l'Arquitectura Contemporània (Group of Catalan Architects and Technicians for the Progress of Contemporary Architecture, or the GATCPAC), who were to become her major clients from 1934 to 1935. Supported by a reference from Dr Walter Andrae, his former Director in Berlin, Michel was able to obtain part-time work as a restorer at Barcelona's Archaeological Museum.[4]

Grete Michaelis did not write directly about her experiences in Spain; her short story 'Dusk' is confined to her childhood and early adult years in Vienna. However, she made it clear that her time in Spain was of great significance. A magazine article published in Australia in 1951 stated that she regarded her Spanish years 'as the most interesting period of her life. She found plenty of character in Spain's landscapes, its people, its slums, its architecture'.[5] A newspaper article from the same period declared that Spain was her 'greatest love ... with its uninhibited peasantry, colourful festivals and half-pagan rituals'.[6]

In Barcelona Grete was finally able to establish her own photographic studio and achieve professional autonomy. In one way it seemed her timing could not have been better. It is now recognised that the interwar years in Spain, 'though plagued by conflict and intolerance', were notable for 'an extraordinary cultural and artistic vitality which was particularly intense in the field of photography'.[7] Catalonia was at the centre of this burgeoning activity. In a little under four years, against the turbulent backdrop of Spanish and, more specifically, Catalonian politics, Grete produced her most coherent and finest body of work, examples of which she kept until the end of her life.

It was also in Spain that Grete's personal circumstances were irrevocably altered. Within a month or two of their arrival in Barcelona she and Michel separated, divorcing three years later.

A few years ago, as part of that half-blind, intuitive search biographers make, I went to Barcelona with the limited information on Grete's life in Spain that I had gathered to that point. As in Berlin, I had the addresses of a few places where she had lived and worked and it was these that gave shape to my experiences of the city. The first task was to find the apartment on Carrer Rossello 36, which the Michaelises shared with the Rüdigers after arriving in Barcelona and whose address Grete stamped on the back of her earliest Spanish photographs.

It was easy to find – a six storey apartment block just a few numbers up from the huge prison Michel described, so noisy in his day, quite silent now. A modern building, more interesting than its neighbours with its pleasing proportions and sympathetic disposition of street-facing balconies, it is somewhat tired in appearance. For a while I stood on the footpath opposite, looking closely at the building, photographing it from different angles and watching the comings and goings of people in the area. A man came out of number 36; after he disappeared into a café I crossed the street, walked over to the entrance of the apartment and peered through the glass door into the vestibule. I felt vaguely disappointed. Nothing seemed out of the ordinary. Returning to the other side of Carrer Rossello I took a seat in the pocket-handkerchief-sized park almost diagonally opposite the Michaelises' apartment. There I felt a surge of excitement and relief; I had found what I was looking for. Along one border of the park was a row of olive trees, old olive trees with trunks far thicker than any I have seen in Australia. As soon as I saw them I felt sure that Grete Michaelis had seen them too; maybe she had rubbed her hand along their trunks just as I had done.

Later, reading through the *Barcelona architecture guide* I had purchased on arriving in the city, I came across a reference to the apartment block at Carrer Rossello 36. According to the Guide it was architecturally significant, having been designed in 1930 by Josep Lluis Sert, leading Catalan architect and co-founder of the GATCPAC. Together with another apartment block on Carrer Muntaner, it is seen to represent the first phase of Sert's mature work. In these apartments, the Guide continues, Sert 'utilises the repertoire of concepts and forms habitually associated with the Modern Movement: duplex apartments with double-height interior spaces, studio flats on the attic level with terrace gardens, a metal structure with plaster-rendered brickwork facades ... and so on'.[8]

I still don't know how the Rüdigers and Michaelises came to be living in what was then one of Barcelona's most modern apartments, but the connection with Sert was perfectly appropriate. For Grete Michaelis the association with Catalan architects, and above all with Sert and the GATCPAC, was crucial, resulting in the production of some of her most outstanding photographs that would eventually come to be identified as exemplars of Barcelona's modernity.

10   PARTING

When Grete Michaelis arrived in Barcelona the modern movement in photography was finally gaining a foothold. The deeply conservative views that had prevailed among photography circles during the 1920s had finally dissipated and the innovation and experimentation associated with modernism had begun to yield impressive results. Josep Sala, Pere Català Pic and Emil Godes were among those Catalan photographers whose prominence was assured, with an expanding commercial sector and burgeoning opportunities in advertising, publicity and magazine illustration.

For a little over two years – until the outbreak of the Spanish Civil War – Michaelis's German background may have given her a competitive advantage over some local photographers. Germany loomed large in the consciousness of the Spanish avant-garde because of the cultural activity that had occurred during the Weimar Republic. Of direct relevance to Michaelis was Germany's pre-eminence in the fields of architecture and photography, and the GATCPAC's appreciation of the interconnections between the two disciplines.[1] Modern architecture needed modern photography and Michaelis was thoroughly familiar with its aesthetics, techniques and applications. She quickly demonstrated her command of the modern style in the architectural work she undertook for the GATCPAC, individual clients and *D'Ací i d'Allà* (*From Here and From There*) magazine. Her cool, clean photographs are analogous to the architecture itself.

Grete Michaelis contributed to the imaging of Barcelona's robust modernity through the publication of her photographs in the flagship modernist publications of the day, but her position in Catalonian society was tenuous. She was an outsider – a contributor to, rather than an active participant in, local life. There is no evidence to suggest that she was intimate with the architects, photographers and editors for whom she worked; she is absent from memoirs and historical studies (whereas references to Michel do occur). The tenuousness of Grete's position related in part to gender – an independent, free-thinking professional woman, she was an exception in a conservative, deeply religious society in which the majority of women continued to face very limited educational and employment opportunities. In marked contrast to Austria and Germany, where Michaelis had trained, Spanish women photographers were virtually non-existent during this period; those who were active hailed from other countries.[2]

Paradoxically, while Michaelis's German training may have given her a slight edge in terms of employability, it also kept her apart socially. As a foreigner, she had arrived in Barcelona without being able to speak a word of Catalan or Spanish. The friends around whom her social life revolved were fellow émigrés she and Michel had known in Berlin and who, like them, had been forced into exile after Hitler's rise to power. Most were anarcho-syndicalists, former members of the FAUD. Helmut Rüdiger noted that by May 1934, sixteen members of the FAUD were in Barcelona, and by early 1935 nearly the whole group had emigrated, with twenty members in residence there.

Exile presented the émigrés with numerous difficulties. The first and most pressing problem was earning a living during the so-called *bienio negro*, Two Black Years, of right-wing governments that followed the defeat of the Azaña coalition in November 1933. Spain was economically stagnant with high rates of unemployment, especially in the rural sector, and no new investment in industry; exports plummeted during these years. In economic terms, both Grete and Michel fared relatively well, securing work in their chosen fields of photography and archaeology. Others in their circle were less fortunate and were unable to find work that related to their former occupations, a situation exacerbated by language barriers. All of the émigrés lived frugally, relying on life skills they had developed during periods of intermittent employment in their final years in Berlin.

Émigrés were also affected by the social unrest that was widespread during the Black Years, as Spanish society polarised into what Hugh Thomas has described as two antagonistic blocs.[3] Earlier political reforms were either halted or reversed and the government's actions were increasingly challenged by those on the left. General strikes, often initiated by the CNT and FAI, became commonplace. In 1934, during what is now known as the October Revolution, uprisings occurred in Barcelona, Madrid and in the mining area of Asturias.[4] The rebellion in Asturias was brutally suppressed; the battle against the workers was directed by General Franco, assisted by the Foreign Legion and Moroccan troops. More than 10000 people were killed in Asturias alone.[5] Predictably, mass imprisonments of socialists and anarchists followed, with estimates of up to 30000 political prisoners being taken during October and November 1934.

In the face of growing political repression, German émigrés had to tread carefully with the local authorities, ensuring that their registration papers and work visas were in order. This sense of vulnerability was heightened by the presence of powerful Nazis in the German Consulate to whom passports were presented if an extension were required. Etta Federn, also an anarcho-syndicalist, described this pervasive sense of insecurity in a letter to her friend Milly Witkop-Rocker, then an exile in the United States. In 1935 she wrote:

> They call me in the german [*sic*] colony the general consul of the émigrés, but this is done much too much honour to me. I keep apart from most of them just as I have to keep apart from the really revolutionary circles in Spain, they denounce here and expulse here very easily now.[6]

For their part, those in Grete and Michel's circle were wary of meeting with Federn; they believed that she was being observed by the Spanish police and at risk of being expelled because of her support for newly arrived political refugees from Germany.[7]

Another area of difficulty for émigrés centred on their relations with local Spanish people. Like their exiled comrades elsewhere in Europe – notably in Stockholm, Amsterdam and Paris – the FAUD members formed a group with political intent some time in 1933. The Deutsche Anarcho-Syndikalisten (Group of German Anarcho-Syndicalists, or DAS) aimed to forge links with like-minded individuals and organisations in Spain – above all with the Spanish anarcho-syndicalist group, the CNT – and to work with them on political programs. However, little useful contact occurred between the German émigrés and the Spanish anarcho-syndicalists until the outbreak of the Civil War. Proposals by the IAA and DAS to organise a boycott against Germany failed, as did requests to provide financial support to German refugees. Helmut Rüdiger later summed up the situation:

> The tragedy is that, as a refugee yourself, you cannot get the smallest amount of material help or even assistance with the creation of employment opportunities, from the Spanish movement as an organisation. On this point there was 100% disinterest.[8]

Rüdiger was also fully aware of the failings of DAS members in their dealings with local people, elaborating on their circumstances in a letter written in 1935:

> The German comrades who are here have been eaten by pessimism. This is terrible. They don't see the big picture in things, they know only their closest circle, they complain about the mistakes that naturally

occur on a big scale. And then the comrades are surprised when no one listens to them. You can only take part when you confess to these people, and when every trace of the damn arrogance, of vain middle European civilisation is laid aside. But they don't want to do this.[9]

Grete's friend Karl Brauner was one of the few German émigrés who, prior to the Civil War, was successfully integrated into the local community. A member of the CNT, though not of the DAS, he 'was seen as the comrade, not the German, not the foreigner'. For a brief time, he later wrote, 'I was one of them'.[10]

As would be expected in such circumstances, the DAS members formed a tight-knit community. They regularly met at the home of Helmut and Dora Rüdiger – which Dutch anarcho-syndicalist Arthur Lehning regarded as exceptionally beautiful – to exchange information and discuss political events in Germany and Spain.[11] The community was mutually supportive; although everyone was poor, Helmut Rüdiger noted in 1935 that the 'comrades always helped ... and supported each other'.[12]

However, relationships were not always harmonious. Arthur Lehning described the German group as 'hopeless' and avoided them as much as possible during his visit to Barcelona in the early days of the Civil War. Etta Federn, who did not join the DAS, remarked on those fellow émigrés who lived 'as if we were in a very small German province town with all its slandering and all its meanness'.[13] It was within this environment, under the watchful eyes of their comrades, that Grete and Michel began to negotiate their separation.

―――――

Soon after arriving in Barcelona Grete and Michel's relationship began to unravel. No, perhaps that's not true. It is certainly not as Michel saw it. For him, the process of 'breaking apart' had begun years earlier. In December 1931, a year or so after the beginning of their relationship and a few weeks after leaving for Warka, he wrote to Grete asking 'What will the world be like for us if we live in harmony?' Obviously mindful of the tensions and arguments they had already lived through, and hopeful of a successful reunion, he told Grete that she needed 'to be more tender, and I more understanding'. He also spoke of his desire that they show each other their 'best sides' and that they be more persistent in their efforts for 'goodness and happiness'. If Grete did discuss their difficulties at the time, she is now silent; none of her letters from this period have survived.

In the summer of 1934 Michel embarked on an extensive bike trip around Spain. Although I now understand that this was a common anarchist activity, a form of reconnoitring, it is also tempting to ascribe personal reasons to Michel's trip. Perhaps it gave the couple a cooling-off period to allow them to compose themselves before finalising their impending separation. Whatever the case, Grete and Michel corresponded while he was away. He wrote at least two letters (on 22 June and again on 22 August) that have unfortunately faded and are now almost impossible to read. My translator has remarked, however, on the coolness of their tone and the formal nature of their signing off. Each letter ends 'With regards, Michel'. Grete was also in no mood for endearments. Her only surviving letter from this period is equally reserved and reads:

Barcelona 19.8.1934

Dear Michel

I am answering today, Sunday, because I won't have much time to write in the next few days.

It is a pity that you misunderstood my letter, it is really quite clear.

I am of your opinion. It is the most natural thing in the world that two people part again. (What may be less natural is the way in which it is done.)

I had second thoughts about your possible return to this flat. I did not want it, but I did not know what you intended to do. I also knew that M.L. as yet has no flat and lives with Schonfelders. As his wife is away at the moment you may be able to stay there too. Address: Avenida Gaudi 56.

The way I anticipate events is this: that you will notify me of your arrival in Barcelona by letter, and that you won't come up here for the time being. We meet somewhere and talk it over.

You tell me the day of your arrival and we could meet at about half past seven on the Plaza Espana in front of the main entrance to the exhibition.

It is clear that there is no point in delaying the news. But I would like us to agree on it and talk it over before you visit any of our acquaintances.

It should be done in a very dignified and formal way. How ridiculous! I want to protect myself from ill-mannered people – I want to have my peace. In order to achieve this it is best not to worry about anything, to give them nothing to talk about and to make everything look as natural as possible. That is what I wanted to talk over with you.

You can't imagine all this on your secluded journey but I have had experience with it and unfortunately my work forces me to talk to such people and to meet them frequently even though I would much rather have nothing to do with them.

Well, I think we will settle everything, but not in the way we did before our departure.

(It is silly that you did not get the money. Now it is in La Linea near Gibraltar.)

By chance I received an invitation to view the collection of the German who was mentioned by Paul Eichelmann some time ago. The things are wonderful. The whole flat is really a museum – 14th century capitals, the remnants of an altar picture, primitive early Christian paintings, 16th century carpets, Chinese sculptures, pictures belonging to well-known schools. I could not see everything in the two hours I was there.

Goodbye, I send you my greetings,

Grete

By September Grete and Michel were living apart. The following month, in a letter to their friend Milly Witkop-Rocker, Etta Federn wrote that she now saw little of Michel, of whom she was 'very fond', because he was living in an outer suburb and always had to leave very early in the evening because there was no train later on. She didn't know why the Michaelises separated but imagined it was because their characters were 'very different'.[14]

Michel wrote one last letter to Grete – to 'Poor Grete' as he calls her – on Christmas Day 1934. It is a long, detailed and merciless account of the history of their relationship and what he sees as the reasons for its disintegration. As part of his summing-up of their past Michel includes a diary entry written a year earlier when, imprisoned in the Alexanderplatz, he had had time to reflect on their relationship. Though the letter does not appear to have been finished – it is not signed off – it clearly reached its target. Grete kept it with her throughout her life. I find this surprising as I imagine that when reading it she would have been breathless with pain, with the kind of pain you wouldn't want to revisit or remember.

Michel to Grete

Barcelona 31.12.34

Poor Grete,

Perhaps these lines are the last ones that I have to write to you, certainly the last ones this year in which I still wish to tell you something.

Our relationship, which for your sake and for the sake of our friends, I am still describing as mateship makes a mockery of the most basic attitudes towards our fellow men. That we were not spared, this is hard to take ... Our last meeting was dominated by the wish to demonstrate to you at all cost in my non-bellicose, silent way how much the feeling of shame regarding the two of us had entered my heart.

At the moment I do not know how each of us will find himself and in that process the other person. On Saturday when I revealed myself to you I had the sad and glad feeling that what had joined us until then was over for ever – everything that had been edifying and shameful. I only did what had become obvious for some time – I made the break between the two of us final.

This break-up has a long history that becomes more and more concentrated, recently becomes more confused, is not clear to both of us as we both see and understand the world in different ways – in fact it will remain unclear for ever. If I try to remember I see the process of our break-up as follows.

First there is the studio time in Kreuzhacherstrasse, which was after our marriage in the studio in Steglitz. This is dominated by what we have in common. This is our music period – not only making music but also the music inside us. Here begins, God knows why, our first argument. I only know that as our fights increased I started to attack things – smashed bottles – until I attacked the person most dear to me – as you had done from the very beginning.

I know that this does not explain the reason for our first fight. I do not wish to interpret things in my favour. We fought for ridiculous reasons, finding a different way of expressing our feelings. You tended to be more brutal than I, who was more reserved. This does not explain the origins of our fights but it does explain their extent. If I want to interpret things in your favour it would be that I was the cause of all of it. In that case you are without blame, even if you had killed me. But as things were not as clear as that, it is futile to seek the cause of our first fight. It was always you who made peace, regardless of whether you had caused the fight or had been innocent. And something else, the extent of our fights made me sad and helpless. Today, living at a healthy distance from you, I try to understand and excuse everything. I know that I lacked strength where it would have been necessary, just as you were lacking the power to make peace in the middle of the fight.

After that came the Warka period, the pause in which as I told you things that wanted to break apart were bound together firmly for a time. For almost half a year we wrote letters to each other that reveal to me the pure and truest bond, in which our love is demonstrated in its intensity and helplessness and with all the limits that we had to face at the time.

Even if the following seems incredible to you, the day of our reunion and the whole time afterwards, the days around Breitenbachplatz were mainly estrangement and alienation. I am telling you this for the first time – even our reunion I see it so clearly – everything had become remote – the flat, the things around us, you, the tone of your voice, the loveplay, your non-ecstatic being and in the way we lived our daily lives. I have often wondered what you experienced in our half year of separation that I had not gleaned from your letters, but which was now obvious. I found no answer. Or whether I had walked too quickly in my loneliness in Iraq forwards, or backwards, who knows? The fact is, that I became ill, mentally ill as a reaction to this undeniable reality. This was the first time that I experienced fear. If I remember that at that time I was afraid of the leopard head at Naidu I am looking back at a solitary and sick existence for neither before nor afterwards would I have been afraid to look into the eyes of the wildest cat. I am endowed with fearlessness that no one can comprehend ... But at that stage I had lost this for quite a while because after our Warka period I found myself to be a different person from the one I had been at the end of our music period.

In the many arguments that we had so frequently in the days round the Breitenbachplatz, I lost myself, I tried to fight back against your accusations and allowed the things that you wished to rescue to bleed to death. It was obvious that we each went our separate ways. Hence, is it surprising that I sought refuge with a person who for many years had been a friend and more than a friend, and came to love Marianne? Neither in our music period nor in our Warka time would this desire have become overpowering in me. I know it was made easy for me. I should not have jumped at it then, only when I had fallen lower. But I had the feeling that I could sink too low, and allowed myself to be lifted up by Marianne's love – perhaps too soon. That was selfish, but also true and pure, like everything experienced on emotional highs. Perhaps you could not have acted differently, I felt free of all guilt and believe that I was meant to go that way.

The five weeks imprisonment on the Alexanderplatz that I experienced without fear left me time to think about our relationship. I kept a diary that I could take with me from the prison without any difficulties.

Diary entry

I feel restless. I can't experience or feel anything without Marianne and Grete, the two dearest people in my life. I don't know where this will lead, but it troubles me.

I feel and experience more with Marianne, which is understandable as everything between us is pure, unmuddied and thriving. Marianne's whole thinking and feeling is closer to mine. Everything is rounded and formed like her body, and her being is childlike. I still clearly remember the night when we stood embracing each other in the light of a lantern and she revealed to me that she wanted to bear my child, not today, but later on. That was uttering my own wish since our first kiss, which burns forever in my heart and unites us forever.

After such feelings and emotions it is difficult to remain fair to Grete. There are three years of a life together, which may both unite and divide, there are countless hours of great joy that I like to remember and hours that burn my soul like a nightmare because they made the differences between us more powerful than everything that united us. This is shared guilt and shared misery from which arises the duty to do good, nothing but good. But I don't know. I have discussed it with Grete but I am not strong enough for that, both of us are not strong enough for that, we are too different, the difference is stronger than what unites us. This conviction, I am conscious of that, has undermined our wish to let what unites us prevail. It's no use, to say anything else would be cowardice. Two people who want to live as one must admit all existing obstacles in order to remain faithful to each other and if they can't do that they should have the courage to be friends or to split up. I believe being good makes it better than a bad marriage.

Having reached that conclusion my honesty becomes exhausted, I close my eyes in order not to have to face the final truth. For a short time I believed in the possibility of a marriage of three, even though it was a remote idea. But both Grete and Marianne were against that. This was perhaps my first act of dishonesty, me closing my eyes. But I understand that this does not help. My whole being longs for a clear resolution.

This diary entry was followed by a year in Spain, a time of alienation and estrangement, our darkest hour. But because Spain showed me its wonders and light I sometimes experienced it like one of Beethoven's sonatas. Hiwu in Spain turned out to be the equivalent of Marianne in Germany. She is the youngest in the league, freer and perhaps more confused than you two. If Marianne gives peace to my soul, I find that you get over all contradictions with cool cordiality and spiritual abandonment. Hiwu, however, is unique dark passion. In you three I find everything that is held in common and that is different as I experienced it in the Romanesque abbey church of Maria Laach, the cathedral of Bordeaux and the Spanish cathedrals … My year in Spain can be summarised by part of my diary entry of 30.4.1934 – this one day stands for a large part of the year.

'Why did it have to end like this? Life had posed a task for me that I could not master. That is a proof of weakness. It burdens me, but only because of this, to have been too weak.'

11   A NEW SPIRIT

In 1993 I received a letter containing the only known account of Grete Michaelis's working life in Spain. It came from Karl Brauner, an old man by then, soon to be ill with cancer. Dieter Nelles, an expert on the German anarcho-syndicalists, had told me to contact Brauner because he had known the Michaelises in Barcelona in the early 1930s and, like them, had been active in the anarcho-syndicalist movement. Nelles also told me that Brauner had been Grete's lover for a short time; or rather, Grete had been his 'mistress ... after she had parted from Rudolf Michaelis. They [Grete and Brauner] did a lot of work together. Brauner was a lithographer and also had some knowledge of photographic work'.[1]

I liked the way Karl Brauner wrote. His letter was carefully considered and informative but it was the gentleness of tone that most appealed to me.

> Dear Ms Ennis
>
> ... In September 1934 I went to Barcelona. There I met Rudolf Michaelis who worked as a restorer in the archaeological museum in Barcelona. We decided to share a flat. This is how I heard about Margarete. She did not live far from us, they had agreed to part for good. As I knew something about photography and retouching he suggested that I should work with her in order to support her if necessary. This is what happened. [The translator noted here: 'It is not clear to me whether this means that they worked together only or that he supported her as well'.]
>
> At the time she was working in the business area. She produced photomontages as advertisements and I helped with their completion by retouching them. This sort of work was popular in Barcelona and elsewhere. It was easy to sell them and they were of a very high standard ... She intended her work to be original and good advertising. She combined the ... many separate shots ... enlarged

them to various sizes and completed them as pages of a prospectus that could be printed. She was very conscientious when doing that and she offered a choice of 2 and sometimes 3 versions. As far as I can remember her clients were owners of businesses, shops and car sales yards etc. who could afford advertising at that time. I do not remember her circle of friends that undoubtedly existed, for she did not like to be sad. We had friendly relations with the Konigs (owners of a bookshop in Barcelona in which German was spoken). We often went on outings with them – into the country and to the sea. Photographs of the landscape and of us were taken there and Margarete searched indefatigably for typical Spanish themes. Traces of these should be found in the archive.

I know that Margarete liked to do portraits but do not know anything about her commissions. From time to time I saw some that she had taken with the fixed camera. They were portraits of friends.

Margarete lived in a modern skyscraper in the Avenida Republica Argentina, which at that stage was already in the outer suburbs of Barcelona. Her flat was furnished in a very tasteful way. Her laboratory was small but practical. There she did her daily work and she had very, very little time to rest. Life was expensive and there was little time for artistic activity. Only once did we use a fortnight to have a winter holiday in the Pyrénées. There I experienced a relaxed Margarete full of enthusiasm for nature, free from the constraints of the struggle for a living, working in a region which at the time was little known, using her camera, a Leica. We had a great time and the friendship that originated there could have lasted if adverse circumstances had not destroyed everything.

Until 1990 I did not know anything about Margarete's life. It was Mr Nelles who cleared up the mystery. I am glad and grateful for this.

Dear Ms Ennis, there is not much I can tell you. If it is only a stone in the big mosaic that you are trying to create, I still hope that it will be of some assistance. I wish you strength and success and remain with friendly greetings,

Karl Brauner

The Montjoy's pen: La Estilografica de Calidad c. 1934–37 gelatin silver photograph, colour pigment 24.6 × 21.8 cm

By the time Brauner became involved with Grete Michaelis, she was already well established in her photographic business; she had relocated from the Rüdiger's apartment at Carrer Rossello to Avenida Republica Argentina and changed her business name from fotostudio to foto-elis. Unfortunately, very few examples remain of the advertising work Brauner remembers. Michaelis herself kept only one photomontage – presumably the rest went to the clients who had commissioned them – a striking advertisement for a Montjoy's fountain pen, which for some reason may never have been used.

However, she did keep many other photographs she took in Spain. These can be usefully divided into two main groups. The first photographs were produced between 1934 and the outbreak of the Spanish Civil War in July 1936. The second date from July 1936 until some time towards the end of 1937, when Grete left Spain. The photographs from these two short periods are quite different – in subject matter, emphasis, print quality and so on. The earlier photographs are far more diverse than the second group, encompassing snapshots of friends, photographs of Spanish traditions, rituals and festivals (such as the Blessing of the Animals), and a large body of work produced in association with the GATCPAC. The latter is particularly impressive, both in terms of the individual photographs and the group. From the works held in the collections of the National Gallery of Australia and the ARXIU in Barcelona, and from extant documents, it is now possible to obtain a clear picture of this vital area of Michaelis's practice. Despite its importance, Michaelis's GATCPAC-related work alone would not have secured an adequate income; other architectural photographs by her, including interior shots, were regularly published in magazines such as *D'Ací i d'Allà* and *Cronica*.

The GATCPAC photographs can be looked at in many different ways: within Michaelis's own oeuvre, in relation to the work of women photographers in the interwar years, or within the context of other documentary and architectural photographic projects of the 1930s. But it is the photographs' position within Spanish and, more particularly, Catalonian cultural life in the years immediately before the Spanish Civil War that is crucial.

Affiliated with the broader Spanish group Grupo de Arquitectos y Técnicos Españoles para el Progreso de la Arquitectura Contemporánea (Group of Spanish Architects and Technicians for the Progress of Contemporary Architecture), or GATEPAC, the GATCPAC was the focus of avant-garde architectural activity in Barcelona, and indeed in Spain, during the 1930s. Established in 1930, the GATCPAC's members included Josep Lluis Sert, Josep Torres Clavé, Rodríguez Arias and JB Subirana.[2] The GATCPAC – especially through

Two men in traditional costumes, Barcelona c. 1934–36 16.9 × 11.0 cm

June in a baker's shop, Barcelona c. 1934–36 16.0 × 23.1 cm

Stairwell, Barcelona c. 1934 23.9 × 16.8 cm

Josep Lluis Sert and Torres Clavé, who are generally regarded as its driving forces – is credited for introducing into Catalonia the innovative architectural and cultural movements that swept through Europe in the late 1920s and early 1930s.[3] Sert had studied with leading French architect Le Corbusier in Paris in 1929 and was familiar with contemporary architectural developments in Germany, including the work of Walter Gropius.

As well as practising as individual architects and participating in the collective, members of the GATCPAC were involved in the publication of the GATEPAC's influential magazine *A.C. Documentos de Actividad Contemporánea* (*A.C. Documents of Contemporary Activity*) twenty-five issues of which were issued between 1931 and June 1937. Edited by Torres Clavé, *A.C.* positioned itself as an avant-gardist publication, experimenting with layout and typography, and making adventurous use of photography and photomontage. Now recognised as one of the most important Spanish magazines of the period, *A.C.* presented the GATCPAC's rationalist doctrines with 'passion and intelligence'.[4] It stands out for its openness 'to theory, to artistic debate, to culture, to technological advances, and to international congresses'.[5] While the core interest of the magazine was contemporary architecture and related issues, like the German architectural magazine *Das Neue Frankfurt*, on which it was based, it was cross-disciplinary in approach and also ran articles on film, popular art, gardens and interior design.

The GATCPAC gave Michaelis's photographs a public profile through their presentation in exhibitions and various issues of *A.C.*, but there was also a happy convergence of interest. The first and arguably most important of these was the Group's left-wing orientation; their social focus was evident in their preoccupations with projects centring on housing, leisure, health and education. They also put forward a radical new view of the city in the Macià Plan of 1932–33, developed in collaboration with Le Corbusier and Pierre Jeanneret, which proposed to transform Barcelona into a city that would serve the Catalan working classes.[6] A second point of connection was the enthusiasm for the vernacular that in the GATCPAC's case arose from their commitment to what is now known as Mediterraneanism, and in Michaelis's case from a delight in the unfamiliar elements of another culture. The GATCPAC aimed to produce architecture that was at once internationalist or modernist in spirit, and also decidedly Mediterranean and local.

Narrow street, Barcelona c. 1934 22.9 × 14.1 cm

Slum children, Barcelona c. 1934 17.0 × 23.0 cm

Exactly how Michaelis came to be associated with the GATCPAC is not known. The earliest evidence of their connection actually preceded her move to Barcelona: in 1932 the magazine *A.C.* (number 6) reproduced some of her photographs of Barcelona's notorious Barrio Chino, a harbour-side district situated between the Ramblas and Avinguda del Paral-lel. While the photographs in *A.C.* are unsigned – for ideological reasons the magazine preferred to stress collectives rather than individuals – the Arxiu Històric del Col.legi d'Arquitectes de Catalunya (ARXIU) holds a set of small, commercially processed prints that were probably the originals for the *A.C.* issue. These have now been attributed to Michaelis, along with an unsigned text in German, also in the ARXIU Archives, which perfectly describes the taking of the photographs during what is referred to as a 'brief raid' into the Barrio Chino.[7] This pairing of image and text suggests that Michaelis may have had a photo-essay in mind; the GATCPAC, however, was evidently interested only in the photographs.

Michaelis pictured an exotic and colourful cast of characters – cardsharps and tricksters, gypsies, pimps and thieves – underscoring her position of privilege in both the visual and textual representations of her subjects. While the inhabitants of the Barrio Chino slept in the numerous low-priced taverns along Calle Mediodia, Michaelis had accommodation in what she described as 'the best tavern in the neighbourhood, where almost only Germans stayed'. There she felt safe, and remarked that her 'pursuers' – the people she photographed – would not have dared to enter. Michaelis's anecdotes are charged with the thrill of taking photographs in difficult, even dangerous circumstances: in what she described as 'an exciting afternoon' she was shouted at by a group of gypsies who thought she was a police informer, and chased by a cardsharp 'waving a stick and shouting "Don't you dare photograph me!"'

This is not to say that her approach precluded having a social conscience – the two are not necessarily incompatible. Michaelis was appalled by the state of the children in Calle Mediodia who present 'a sad and terrible image'. She wrote:

> The statistics say that between 90 and 95 per cent of the children in the Barrio Chino suffer from syphilis ... crippled children ... bald, blind, walking on crutches. This is the dark side of Barcelona. The Barrio Chino is a disgrace to the whole of Catalonia. There they were, a silent accusation.[8]

Houses in the Barrio Chino, Barcelona c. 1934 24.0 × 18.0 cm

Though significant, the initial publication of Grete Michaelis's photographs in *A.C.* appears to have been more the result of chance than design. This situation changed after she had moved to Barcelona and began her association with the GATCPAC in earnest in 1934. Two main areas of activity were involved: taking photographs for individual GATCPAC architects and producing the photographic documentation of the Barrio Chino for the GATCPAC's Macià Plan. In addition, Michaelis took photographs for an important issue of *A.C.* (number 18), dealing with vernacular architecture, and contributed prints to the exhibitions La Nova Barcelona and Barcelona Futura, organised by the GATCPAC.

In the first few months of 1934 Michaelis revisited the Barrio Chino, this time on behalf of the GATCPAC. Her brief, one can assume, was to document the unsanitary and squalid conditions that prevailed in the district and which the Macià Plan aimed to eradicate. Two of the Plan's tenets, which pertain directly to the Barrio Chino, were stated as follows:

> Provision of proper sanitation in the historic city centre
> The revision of zoning and regulations with a view to adapting them to improve sanitary conditions. The fixing of the measurements of interior courtyards and light wells so as to allow better ventilation and more sunlight to enter. The promotion of the use of modern materials.[9]

For the GATCPAC, the Barrio Chino was 'sick' and the architects made frequent use of medical-related metaphors in their writings on the area.[10] Describing it as a 'clinical case' they, the 'technicians', proposed treatment involving the 'closure of these centres of infection and destruction of unsanitary housing ... planning and gradual construction of the new urban development'.[11]

There can be no doubt that Michaelis admirably fulfilled her GATCPAC brief, bringing back from the Barrio Chino the visual evidence required to 'illustrate the graphs, statistics and plans' for the Macià Plan.[12] Her photographs were used in a number of issues of *A.C.* and were prominently displayed in La Nova Barcelona, a major GATCPAC exhibition held in the basement of the Plaça de Catalunya in June 1934. The large display panels juxtaposed her photographs with captions giving details on locations, critical commentaries or descriptions of the district's overall condition.[13]

While Michaelis's photographs could be readily harnessed to the GATCPAC's vision of 'a technocratic, classless society'[14], they also had another kind of life relating specifically to Michaelis's own experience of the Barrio Chino.

In the kitchen, Barcelona c. 1934–36 22.5 × 15.5 cm

La Nova Barcelona
exhibition. View of city
planning exhibition gallery
space, Plaça de Catalunya
1934 11.4 × 17.0 cm

The Barrio Chino was a highly contested site that meant different things to different people. Pictorial and literary representations of it are profuse – as a slum, as a hotbed of illicit activity and anarchism, and as a great genre setting for stories about sex, espionage and assassination.[15] For Michaelis it was an active, mobile site that elicited different and increasingly complex responses from her on successive visits.

Indeed, Grete Michaelis's extended encounter with the Barrio Chino represents her photographic coming of age. The photographs taken during 1934 are far more impressive than the results of the first quick raid made nearly two years earlier. Energetic, formally inventive and considered images, they demonstrate Michaelis's mastery of the stylistic features of the New Photography, including the use of sharp focus, unusual vantage points and bold, graphic compositions. In photographic terms, however, there is more to them than that. In them one sees the clear articulation of her position in relation to the highly influential New Photography movement. Michaelis did not pursue either the radical formal experimentation advocated by László Moholy-Nagy and others associated with the Bauhaus in Germany, or with the pure applications of the *Neue Sachlichkeit* (New Objectivity) advocated by German photographers Albert Renger-Patzsch and August Sander, and Catalan photographer Emil Godes. Instead she developed an approach that can best be described as social documentary, marrying the stylistic innovations of the New Photography to a social reformist and activist agenda. It is in the Barrio Chino that people and their environments – rather than the machine age and its materials – emerge as her principal subjects.

Olm Street, Barcelona c. 1934 24.0 × 17.9 cm

Michaelis's use of the now overly familiar devices of the New Photography was strategic. Sharp focus renders the disintegrating surfaces of buildings and streets in inglorious detail. Up and down shots (the so-called worm's eye and bird's eye views) offer a means of obtaining more information about the cramped living conditions in which the inhabitants of the Barrio Chino lived, worked and played. Look, for example, at the photograph of the street market in Olm Street, probably taken by leaning out of the first-storey window of a neighbouring building. Here the high vantage point enabled Michaelis to represent the mix of activities that were taking place amidst the piles of rubbish in the street below. She clicked the shutter at the critical moment when a horse and cart moved into view, and three incompatible activities are suddenly jostled together: those associated with the market (selling and buying), with pedestrian movement (a girl squeezes between a stall and the horse) and with the transportation of goods (the horse and cart).

Although Michaelis's photography for the GATCPAC was ideologically driven, the resultant images do not read as being pinched or programmatic. On the basis of the photographs themselves it is tempting to speculate that there was actually a disjunction between what the GATCPAC wanted from Barcelona's most notorious district and what Michaelis found there – a site not only of great interest but even of pleasure. I use the word pleasure deliberately, to encompass the guilty pleasures associated with making the most of photographic opportunities and the aestheticising of poverty (Michaelis did both of these things), as well as to invoke something more generous in spirit. In the Barrio Chino Michaelis found more activity, more flux, more life than a photograph can possibly accommodate. This is alluded to in different ways: in the blurring of figures who move too quickly to be frozen by her film's exposure – as in the street market in Olm Street – and more frequently in the suggestion of narratives that extend beyond the photographic frame. A woman leans out of an upper-storey window, watching something that we cannot see. A prostitute named Rosita stands in the doorway of a hotel in Carrer Cadena hovering in an in-between zone, neither outside where she will solicit her clients, nor inside where she will take them.

In another photograph, one of my favourites from this time, an apron-clad woman and a man are talking in the street, seemingly oblivious to Michaelis's presence. One suspects that their conversation began before the moment of the photograph and will continue well beyond it. While they are talking another kind of dialogue opens up on the left-hand side of the composition. This is a strictly photographic conversation, involving the photographer and two children who

Barcelona slum c. 1934 23.9 × 17.8 cm

Rosita, 1 Cadena Street, Barcelona c. 1934 17.9 × 11.3 cm

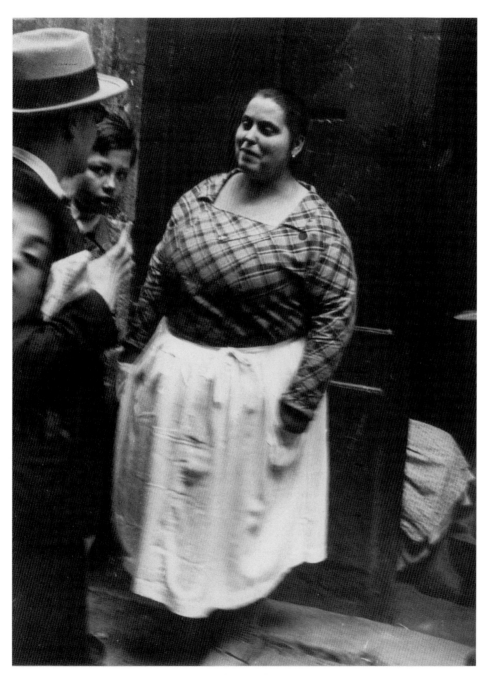

Woman in apron, Barrio Chino, Barcelona c. 1934 23.0 × 17.0 cm

look directly at Michaelis as she makes the exposure. Such exchanges are quite common in Michaelis's practice, especially when she is physically close to her subjects. Nowhere is this more apparent than the group of photographs taken inside the Taverna dels Tenors, a famous bar in the Barrio Chino known for its singing and culinary specialties. Here, within the tight interior spaces, Michaelis worked in medium to close range with her presence, both as a photographer and a participant, being tacitly acknowledged by her subjects.

There is one other aspect to the Barrio Chino photographs that charges them with energy and gives them their contemporary relevance. It is something less tangible than how they look or what they describe, it's more how they feel. This comes, I think, from the quality of Grete Michaelis's engagement with her subject matter, a kind of connectedness to what could be described as the body politic. Unfortunately, political circumstances render this experience short-lived.

———————————

When I was in Barcelona in 1997 I visited the Museu d'Art Contemporani; I wanted to see the new building designed by American architect Richard Meier and partners, as well as an installation by French artist Christian Boltanski that I had seen advertised in the local press. The museum was not far from Hotel Continental on Las Ramblas where I was staying and so I walked to it through a maze of narrow, winding streets. It was thrilling entering the wide, open Plaça dels Angels where the museum seems improbably berthed; I was unprepared either for the size of the building or its appearance. But, even on an early autumn day in September, I had to shut my eyes as I approached the museum, so bright was the glare from its surfaces and from the paving in the square. I could imagine that walking across the square in high summer would be almost unbearable. Later in the day I visited another architectural landmark, Gaudí's Casa Milà, which has been recently restored and opened to the public. Standing on its rooftop terrace I was surprised to see the Mediterranean – a blue strip, so close and unexpected – and to feel a gentle, late afternoon breeze.

Though I didn't realise it at the time, these experiences of the Casa Milà and the Museu d'Art Contemporani have made me reconsider Michaelis's architectural photography, principally because of her sympathy with particular qualities of the environment, especially the heat, the bright sun and the need for shelter. I have in mind two of the most resolved of the architectural studies she undertook for individual GATCPAC architects. The first is a particularly sumptuous, large exhibition print of Torre Eugenia, a house designed by

Four men in a bar, Barcelona c. 1934 22.9 × 16.0 cm

Man having his shoes shined in a bar, Barcelona c. 1934 16.8 × 11.0 cm

R Ribas Seva in 1936. Michaelis photographed the house in tandem with its in-ground swimming pool. She used the reflections of the building in the water to maximise the visual interest, achieving a satisfying interplay between different shapes and forms, straight lines and curves. The clarity of this image is informed by the New Objectivity wing of the New Photography movement, but its hardness is modified by a Mediterranean emphasis. The latter arises from the prominent role given to shadows and shade across the house and the pool; the shady nook in the right-hand side of the composition provides a place for the viewer's eye to wander and to rest.

Design for living, another very satisfying architectural photograph, has as its subject one of the weekend houses designed by Sert and Torres Clavé at El Garraf, on the coast seventeen kilometres from Barcelona. Michaelis did not picture a cool, neutral environment but a comfortable, casually furnished and inhabited space. She chose a vantage point inside the house looking out to the balcony where a woman – the architect's wife, Moncha – was seated; beyond her lies the broad horizontal band of the Mediterranean. This conjunction emphasises the tripartite relationship between house, inhabitant and its environmental setting.

In 1935 *Design for living* was published along with other photographs of the El Garraf houses in *A.C.* (number 19), alongside an article dealing with the evolution of interiors. For the astute reader Michaelis's photographs represented a significant contribution to the debate about Mediterraneanism. All its virtues were given visual representation – the finish of the room (white-washed walls and tiled floors), and the style and materials of the furniture and furnishings.

Michaelis's photographs were prominent in an earlier issue of *A.C.* (number 18), which was devoted to Mediterranean vernacular architecture. The cover image – a close-up of a ceramic jug and a wickerwork basket – was hers, depicting objects that were unequivocally associated with Mediterranean culture.[16] Inside the magazine were photographs taken during a trip to Andalusia with Josep Lluis Sert and Spanish artist Joan Miró in the spring or summer of 1935, a tantalising association but about which very little is known. Michaelis was presumably invited by Sert to produce the visual documentation: she photographed individual buildings in Cadis and Cordova, focusing on external views (facades, courtyards, and the relationships between the buildings and their immediate environments), and in Vinaros and on the hillside in Malaga she photographed clusters of houses. As in the Barrio Chino, Michaelis's studies of vernacular architecture were entwined with GATCPAC concerns.

Torre Eugenia Architect: Ribas Seva Barcelona 1936 22.0 × 28.2 cm

Design for living Weekend houses Architects: JLl Sert and J Torres Clavé 1935 16.9 × 23.0 cm

Elements of popular industry from a trip to Andalusia with JLl Sert and Joan Miró 1935
15.9 × 17.1 cm

The trip to Andalusia came towards the end of Michaelis's association with the GATCPAC. In September her name appeared in the group's ledgers for the last time, noting payment for photographs that were to be included in the exhibition Urbanismo y Habitacion, also known as Barcelona Futura, held in Buenos Aires in 1936.

Grete Michaelis's work for the GATCPAC occurred at a key historical juncture: that of the Second Republic, with which the group's fortunes were interwoven. As architectural historian Jaume Freixa has pointed out, GATCPAC opened its building on Barcelona's fashionable Passeig de Gràcia on 14 April 1931 – the day of the proclamation of the Second Spanish Republic and the autonomy for Catalonia that came with it[17] – and in the next few years received substantial support from the Republican government for the development of its projects. And yet, very few buildings by either individual GATCPAC architects or the collective were actually constructed. Work on the Ciutat de Repòs i de Vacances (the Leisure and Vacation City at Castelldefels), part of the Macià Plan, was abandoned in 1937 due to lack of finances and the fraught political situation.

The outbreak of the Civil War brought an end to GATCPAC activities: Torres Clavé died at the front in 1939, fighting in defence of the Spanish Republic, and other members went into exile, including Sert who migrated to the United States. In the final issue of A.C. (number 25), published in June 1937, Michaelis's Barrio Chino photographs – all of which had been produced before the Civil War – made their final appearance.

12 THE STAGE OF HISTORY

During my first forays into the Spanish material in the National Gallery of Australia's archive I paid little attention to a large number of small, quickly made prints. They bore no apparent relation to Grete Michaelis's work for the GATCPAC or various commercial clients during 1934 and 1935. Such work signals its serious intent in all sorts of ways: the prints are relatively large in size, the print quality is excellent, and the use of signatures and stamps ensures that Michaelis's authorship is recognised. In contrast, the photographs that I originally overlooked are more like work prints than finished objects. Now I realise that is precisely the point – in the very manner of their making they are a direct reflection of their time and their context. They are photographs of revolution and war.

During 1936, though documentary evidence is scant, Grete Michaelis's life circumstances were being dramatically changed by political events beyond her control: the military coup d'état on 18 July, led by Generals Franco, Mola and Queipo de Liano, and the spontaneous revolution that followed its suppression.

The elections of February 1936 brought victory to the Popular Front, in part because of the anarchists' decision to vote – they had abstained in earlier elections. The new coalition of Republicans, socialists and communists, led by a succession of Left Republican Presidents, re-committed to the reforms of the First Republic of 1931, with 'all the hopes, expectations and optimism of those days'.[1] For the anarcho-syndicalists, the political climate improved significantly with the easing of restrictions and harassment of the CNT and FAI. However, it was the events of 18 and 19 July that turned the tide, bringing the workers into triumphant control in Catalonia and effectively sidelining the government of President Luis Companys.

Rudolf Michaelis was on the streets of Barcelona on 19 July as a participant in the armed resistance to the coup. Years later, on the thirtieth anniversary of the outbreak of the Civil War, he recalled the day's events and his role in them in a report published in the East Berlin newspaper *Berliner Zeitung*:

> The rebels had pushed into the center of Barcelona. Around midday the fight for the Spanish Republic was decided in this city. The shots disappeared into the side streets. One of the streets … was the Calle de Lauria, where the German Club, a camouflaged Nazi institution, was domiciled … The German Club was occupied by us … I still remember the only destructive action taken. In the meeting room of the German Club there was a picture of Hitler on the wall. I grabbed it and threw it out of the window; it broke on the street to the applause of the crowd. The contents of the desk and the filing cabinets were put into a truck which had brought us there … On 19 July 1936 we brought a powerful branch of the Nazis to a standstill.[2]

In the thirty-six-hour struggle for Barcelona, the workers associated with the CNT and FAI played a decisive role in defeating the rebels despite the fascists' superiority in weapons. At that point it became clear, as Michel's colleague Rudolf Rocker stated, that the workers 'could not stop half way'.[3] What followed was anarcho-syndicalism's greatest, though short-lived, victory – a spontaneous revolution in which the principles and beliefs of libertarian communism were immediately put into practice. In Barcelona, where events proved most spectacular, committees of workers took over the functions previously performed by the state and by capitalist entrepreneurs.[4] All areas of life began to be transformed according to libertarian ideas about freedom and equality, and collectivisation of land, industry and small businesses was begun in earnest. (These revolutionary initiatives were often accompanied by violence; the murder of priests, burning of churches and political assassinations were widespread.) According to CNT member and writer Abel Paz, the situation during the first few days of the revolution was 'extremely chaotic but the chaos worked'.[5]

For those on the left, including international visitors to Spain – among them English writers WH Auden and George Orwell, Austrian political journalist Franz Borkenau, and Swiss journalist Hans-Erich Kaminski – the atmosphere was highly charged. Orwell, who arrived in Barcelona in December 1936 (when much of the revolutionary fervour had actually ebbed away), found the situation 'startling and overwhelming', especially compared to England. In one of the most famous passages in his book *Homage to Catalonia*, Orwell described what he saw:

> Practically every building of any size had been seized by the workers and was draped with red flags or with the red and black flag of the Anarchists; every wall was scrawled with the hammer and sickle and with the initials of the revolutionary parties; almost every church had been gutted and its images burnt. Churches here and there were being systematically demolished by gangs of workmen. Every shop and cafe had an inscription saying that it had been collectivised; even the bootblacks had been collectivised and their boxes painted red and black. Waiters and shop-walkers looked you in the face and treated you as an equal. Servile and even ceremonial forms of speech had temporarily disappeared ... There were no private motor cars, they had all been commandeered, and all the trams and taxis and much of the other transport were painted red and black. The revolutionary posters were everywhere, flaming from the walls in clean reds and blues that made the few remaining advertisements look like daubs of mud. Down the Ramblas, the wide central artery of the town where crowds of people streamed constantly to and fro, the loud speakers were bellowing revolutionary songs all day and far into the night. And it was the aspect of the crowds that was the queerest thing of all. In

outward appearance it was a town in which the wealthy classes had
practically ceased to exist ... Practically everyone wore rough working-
class clothes, or blue overalls or some variant of the militia uniform.[6]

Although Orwell appreciated that there was much about the situation he did
not understand, or even like, he recognised it 'immediately as a state of affairs
worth fighting for'.[7]

These were also heady days for those in Grete and Michel's circle, with much
improved prospects of working with the Spanish anarcho-syndicalists – the
DAS joined the Federación Local de Grupos Anarquistas in April 1936 – and
of direct political action. However, the events of July presented the anarchists
with a huge dilemma, the consequences of which are still being passionately
debated: whether to collaborate with the government, which was a violation of
anarchist principles, and whether to prioritise the social revolution or the fight
against fascism (Durruti argued that war and revolution could be waged at the
same time). As many saw it, the situation for the CNT was vexed:

> the only alternative of those who consistently opposed collaboration
> with the government was a heroic defeat ... there was no solution that
> would simultaneously preserve victory in the war against fascism;
> progress in the revolution; complete loyalty to their ideas and the
> preservation of their own lives ... they lacked the power to perform
> miracles.[8]

In September the CNT resolved to join the government, and from November
1936 to May 1937 was represented with four ministers.

Rudolf Michaelis was among the thousands of international volunteers who became directly involved in the fight against fascism. In the chaotic weeks following the failed coup he joined one of the militia columns, the Republic's main arm of defence. As English writer Raymond Carr has noted, militias formed haphazardly, almost spontaneously and varied bewilderingly in size[9]; each had its own flag and nomenclature, its own equipment, and its own command that, in accordance with libertarian principles, reflected a classless society. Michel joined the Columna Ascaso – named after Durruti's right-hand man, the FAI leader Francisco Ascaso, who had been killed in the fighting in Barcelona on 19 July – and formed a sub-group, the Erich Mühsam Gruppe – named after the German revolutionary poet and anarchist murdered by the Nazis in Berlin in 1934. The Erich Mühsam Gruppe comprised around thirty volunteers, including other German anarcho-syndicalists; Michel was their political delegate and, according to Swiss journalist Paul Thalmann, was an impressive leader. In his memoirs, published in 1974, Thalmann wrote that Michel

> was by far the most enlightened of them all and he made the effort to make convinced anarchists out of his men. This was made possible through his essential moral authority, which of itself could create respect and credibility. Michaelis lived like any other militiaman, without any privileges.[10]

The Erich Mühsam Gruppe was involved in the fighting for Huesca at the Aragon front in August, during which Michel was slightly injured.

For Grete Michaelis the outbreak of war and revolution also brought about a dramatic reorientation in her life and work. In November 1936 the secretary of the GATCPAC attempted to locate her on behalf of Josep Lluis Sert, who had been appointed architect of the Spanish Pavilion for the International Exhibition in Paris in 1937. The purpose was to obtain some of her photographs for possible inclusion in the related exhibition of ancient Catalan arts and crafts to be held at the Jeu de Paume.[11] Despite the secretary's best intentions – 'I won't sleep until I know where she is'[12] – surprisingly, Grete could not be found. She was, nevertheless, very active during this period, contributing to the revolutionary struggle through three principal and inter-related areas of practice: press photography, photography directly in support of the anarchist cause and 'official' propaganda photography.

This latter category, for which the most photographs have survived, appears to have been her main preoccupation, consistent with the broader situation

in which the production of anti-fascist propaganda, a governmental priority, dominated cultural activity. Leading Catalan photographers were employed by the central government authority, the Generalitat Propaganda Commissariat, which was responsible for the publication of magazines, pamphlets and postcards. Pere Català Pic, also known for his iconic anti-fascist poster *Aixafem el feixisme*, produced in 1936, was appointed Publications Manager, and Josep Sala and Gabriel Casas joined his team of photographers. Grete worked for the Commissariat during 1936 and 1937, undertaking assignments on child care, health care and industry issues. In 1937 her photographs appeared in the Commissariat's publication *Nova Iberia* and in the *Butlletí de la Conselleria de Sanitat I Assistència Social*.[13]

In response to the drastically altered circumstances, documentary photography became central to Grete Michaelis's practice. Links with her earlier documentary work remained – especially the engagement with people and aspects of their daily lives – but fundamental differences exist between the photographs produced before and after July 1936. In the months immediately following the coup, Michaelis developed a highly responsive, less formal way of working, taking her images quickly and achieving a far more urgent effect. Compositions are invariably haphazard and crammed with activity. The activity depicted is itself significant; it centres on work and physical labour, and ranges across such tasks as baking bread, washing clothes, shopping and tending animals. What one gains from the images overall is a sense of great industriousness and, equally significantly, communal activity. From Michaelis's perspective there was an important political point to be made about the value of people working together and so she rarely isolated individual workers for the sake of pictorial drama.

Schoolroom, Barcelona
c. 1936 7.8 × 11.0 cm

Men baking bread,
Barcelona c. 1936–37
5.5 × 7.8 cm

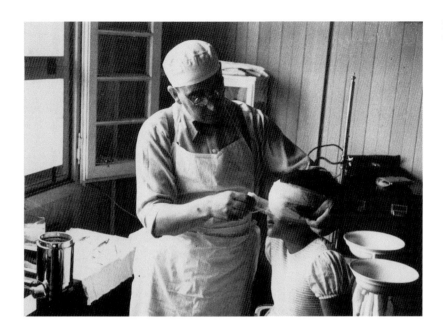

Doctor and child
c. 1936 7.8 × 10.8 cm

Women and fruit
crates, Barcelona
c. 1936–37
5.4 × 7.8 cm

Boys in the shower,
Barcelona c. 1936
7.8 × 11.0 cm

She was also especially attentive to the situation of women and children. In a particularly memorable set of images, probably taken outside Barcelona, Michaelis dealt with the effects of the war on young children, photographing a girl whose head wound was being bandaged, a group of boys showering together and a young boy studying at school. The point of view adopted here is deliberately matter-of-fact; eschewing heroicism and sentimentality Michaelis emphasised the ordered aspects of the children's lives and, by implication, the care they were receiving regardless of the mayhem brought by the war.

Another unique feature of these documentary photographs is their spatial compression: it is as though the space between Michaelis's subjects and her camera has been eliminated. As a consequence the viewer, presumably like Michaelis herself, experiences the sensation of being immersed in the action. Eye contact occurs less frequently than before and is no longer relied on as a compositional pivot; subjects are instead pictured giving their full concentration to the task at hand.

Although not so tangible, visually these photographs also represent a finely nuanced shift in political thinking. Whereas Grete Michaelis's work for the GATCPAC embodied a syncretic humanism (well suited to the architects' rationalist ideology and belief that society could be reorganised according to rationalist and planning principles), her photography from the Civil War and revolutionary period is less universalised, less generalised. In line with the Commissariat's propagandist brief, she dealt with more specific issues, highlighting current socio-economic realities.

In late October 1936 Grete Michaelis took an historic car trip from Barcelona through the anarchist-controlled region of Aragon to Valencia with Emma Goldman, one of the most famous anarchists of the twentieth century. Her other companions in the 'big, ancient Studebaker that swallows petrol like a drunk'[14] were also prominent in their fields: the journalists Hans-Erich Kaminski and his wife Anita Garfunkel, and Dutch anarchist and historian Arthur Lehning. The tantalising news of this five-day trip came to me in the early 1990s in a letter from Lehning, a friend of the Michaelises who they knew in Berlin through his work as secretary of the IAA.[15] Here, at last, was proof of the significance of Grete's links, not just with the German anarcho-syndicalists living in Spain but with the broader anarchist movement.

Significantly, Lehning's letter also mentioned that Grete took photographs during their trip, a fact that was reinforced when his Spanish diaries were finally published in 1996. In Barcelona, on 20 October 1936, Lehning had written: 'After an enormous amount of difficulty it has now been decided that we will go to Valencia with Emma and two others (journalists). Grete (of Michel) also, for photographs'.[16] The aim of the trip was to visit the agrarian collectives in anarchist-controlled areas and to enable Emma Goldman, in particular, the opportunity to witness the revolution first-hand. Goldman was still grieving from the death of her co-worker and former companion, Alexander (Sasha) Berkman, and her friends and colleagues hoped that exposure to the Spanish situation would boost her morale. This proved to be the case, as Goldman was greatly inspired by her experiences and wrote of being 'drunk with the sights, the impressions and the spirit of our comrades'.[17] She became passionately involved in the Republican cause, as a public speaker and broadcaster, writer, and enormously hard-working fund-raiser.

The group's choice of Aragon as their destination was entirely deliberate. The area was the jewel in the anarcho-syndicalist crown, because of the successful collectivisation of great estates and small peasant holdings into large agribusinesses controlled by the CNT Catalan militia.[18] Lehning estimated that in the area around Valencia, 615 collectives had formed during the first few months of the revolution; by mid-1937 in Aragon nearly all of the towns and villages had been collectivised.[19] The following year the scheme's achievements, in terms of scale and productivity, were cited with pride by Rudolf Rocker in his book *Anarcho-syndicalism*.

The mix of journalists and a photographer in the group was obviously strategic, providing a means of gathering information on revolutionary developments and of potentially publicising and promoting the gains being made. Kaminski's account, published in his *Ceux de Barcelone*, combined colourful descriptions of their adventures with observations about the revolutionary activity they saw occurring throughout the region. With a journalist's deft touch he began his account with an unexpected event: a car accident. Their chauffeur, Kaminski explains,

> is a nice chap, but unfortunately not a chauffeur in the better sense
> of the word. He drives on the left when he should be on the right, he
> always tries to overtake at exactly the moment that a car is coming
> in the other direction, and then fearlessly squeezes through between
> the two cars. On every bend ... we break out in a sweat. Suddenly
> a tremendous crash: our car breaks through the barriers on a train
> crossing. Shockingly a train rushes past right before our eyes. We got
> off lightly, others are less lucky. Gutted and overturned car wrecks
> lie all over the place on the side of the road, and in Barcelona itself,
> nearly all of the cars are battered to some extent.[20]

More importantly Kaminski, like Lehning in his diaries, detailed the efforts being made by the peasants in running their own communities – guarding the entrances to their villages, establishing hospitals and children's homes, introducing literacy programs, abolishing money, and so on. The only visible sign of destruction they witnessed was of churches, which had either been burnt, reduced to rubble or were in the process of being dismantled. As an historian, Arthur Lehning took issue with this wholesale destruction, believing that these 'historical monuments' should be kept.

On 25 October, in the final stage of their trip, the group visited the village of Alcora, which was, in effect, a model of libertarian communism. Here, as Kaminski put it, they found that the

> peasants want to 'share everything' ... And for them, the surest way of
> achieving a collective equality is in the abolition of money ... everyone
> still gets what he needs. Who from? From the Central Committee
> of course ... there are stores in Alcora that cater for people's needs

Grape pickers c. 1935–36 11.9 × 17.2 cm

as before. But these shops are also just distribution points. They belong to the whole village and their old owners don't make any profits any more.[21]

In Kaminski's view there was a naive quality to the different regulations the villagers had introduced and, as a social democrat, he expressed reservations about what he regarded as the limited freedoms permitted under libertarian communism.

For Lehning, what was most impressive was the extent to which the past had been done away with in the attempt to create a new world. In his diary on 23 October he wrote: 'Only if you have seen all this do you understand what this revolution means. An entire people here have really made a *tabula rasa* of the past'.[22] However, as the writings of both men demonstrate, they were aware not only of the immensity of the changes being made but also of their precariousness.

Lehning was certain that Grete Michaelis had taken photographs while they were travelling, but circumstances prevented him from ever seeing any – soon after they returned to Barcelona he left for Amsterdam and in the ensuing chaos of World War II lost contact with her. As it happens, however, Lehning's diaries and Kaminski's account of their historic trip throw light on a small group of unidentified photographs of rural subjects in the National Gallery of Australia's archive, making it possible to contextualise them. One series depicts the different stages of the grape harvest, probably near Alicante, which the group visited on 23 October, while another series of photographs (some of which were published in *Nova Iberia* in 1937) deals with hay-making, including threshing and transporting the loaded carts of hay. Both series present a very positive viewpoint of collectivisation – absorbed, busy workers are shown with their abundant crops, the fruits of their own labour.

For the most part Michaelis's approach was straightforward, more documentary than overtly revolutionary. An exception is her image of a farm worker, which appears to have been set up: he is posed holding his scythe, an immediately recognisable symbol of labour and struggle. Michaelis adopted a low vantage point that enabled her to bypass the distracting details of the worker's environment and to concentrate on essentials. The single figure, outlined against the sky, is monumentalised, an anonymous individual whose role is to represent a mass movement.

Michaelis's support of the anarchist cause through her photographic work also encompassed portraiture of key figures. None were more prominent than

Man with scythe c. 1935–36 12.0 × 16.9 cm

Emma Goldman, Spain 1936 29.3 × 24.0 cm

the Russian-born Emma Goldman, who she probably photographed on the Aragon trip (the portrait was taken outside, rather than in the controlled studio conditions Barcelona would have offered). A lifelong champion of anarcho-syndicalism and a passionate advocate of women's rights, Goldman was sixty-seven years old at the time of her visit to Spain; she had endured imprisonment, notoriety and long periods of exile. Michaelis adopted an heroic mode for her portrait, representing Goldman as a *grande dame*, dignified, composed and with an air of gravitas. Unusually for Goldman, she is pictured without her trademark round-rimmed glasses; photographed in three-quarter view, her unwavering gaze is directed slightly upwards and out of the frame, looking off into the middle distance.

The companion piece to the Goldman portrait in the National Gallery of Australia's Archive is a photograph of another independent woman and revolutionary, Etta Federn, one of Goldman's friends. Like Goldman, the Jewish-born Federn had rebelled against orthodoxy and conventional expectations, and devoted her life to revolutionary ideals. She was recognised as 'an outstanding personality with a formidable combination of intellect and political radicalism'.[23] Federn was associated with the German anarcho-syndicalist movement and in Barcelona, where she settled with her two children in 1932, she became involved in the anarcho-syndicalist women's movement Mujeres Libres and contributed to their publication.

Grete Michaelis knew Federn reasonably well; the warmth of the portrait is evidence of the relationship between photographer and subject, and by comparison Goldman's portrait is somewhat distant. In the Federn portrait Michaelis employed a strategy from her earlier work: a close vantage point that conveys a sense of intimacy. Federn's face fills the frame, her eyes looking into the camera lens with an expression suggestive of a lively intelligence.

In these portraits of remarkable women Michaelis is at her best, responsive to her subjects and determined to create photographs of them that exert a lasting impression.

Etta Federn, Barcelona c. 1934–37 17.7 × 13.8 cm

> We are not in the least afraid of ruins. We are going to inherit the earth.
> There is not the slightest doubt about that. The bourgeoisie might blast
> and ruin its own world before it leaves the stage of history. We carry a
> new world here, in our hearts. (Buenaventura Durruti, c. 1936)[24]

A few weeks after the Aragon trip the anarchist movement and the Republican cause suffered a major blow. The charismatic and powerful anarchist leader, Buenaventura Durruti, whom Goldman had visited only a short time before, was shot in Madrid (whether by 'a stray bullet', by the fascists or by a political assassin has never been established). He died at dawn on 20 November 1936 and his body was transported to Barcelona for burial at Montjuic Cemetery. His funeral, which Abel Paz ranks with the burial of Vladimir Lenin as the 'most important worker demonstration in the history of the proletariat'[25], was attended by more than 200 000 people with some estimates reaching half a million. Hans-Erich Kaminski, who wrote at some length about the occasion in his *Ceux de Barcelone*, reported that 'one inhabitant out of every four or five walked behind the coffin, without counting the masses who lined the streets, were at the windows, on the roofs and even in the trees of the Ramblas'.[26]

Both Michel and Grete attended the funeral, he as a soldier and she as a photographer. Michel was in Barcelona by chance, as his group were en route to Madrid to join the Columna Durruti for an assault on Saragossa. When news of Durruti's death came through it was, Michel later wrote, 'a massive loss for all of us'. As Durruti's coffin was carried out from the CNT–FAI headquarters, Michel was among the thousands of mourners who raised their fists for a last salute and sang the rousing anarchist song, 'Son of the people'. Greatly moved by the whole event, Kaminski also elaborated on the chaos that made it impossible for the funeral to proceed smoothly:

> by mistake two orchestras had been asked to come; one played mutedly,
> the other very loud and they didn't manage to maintain the same
> rhythm. Motorcycles were noisy, cars blew their horns, militia leaders
> gave signals with their whistles and the men who were carrying the
> coffin couldn't move.[27]

The funeral of Durutti, Barcelona 1936   11.9 × 16.9 cm

Kaminski came to the enthusiastic conclusion that, although it took hours to progress a few hundred metres, it was 'not a royal funeral, it was a popular one. Nothing was orderly, everything was done spontaneously, on the spot. It was an anarchist burial, that was its majesty!'[28]

Grete Michaelis took a number of photographs of the procession, using high vantage points – probably the roof of a parked vehicle and a room or balcony in one of the city's taller buildings – to enable her to obtain the most expansive view possible. The enormous crowds she depicted thronging the street and footpaths are the visual representations of what Kaminiski described as 'a human sea ... grandiose, sublime and strange'.[29] Michaelis's photographs simultaneously map the crowd as a whole and provide details of the individuals who have formed it: the faces, features and clothes of those in the foreground can be easily seen. A number of months later, in June 1937, one of her images of the funeral, taken at the moment when the crowd saluted Durruti, was published on the cover of *A.C.* (number 25). It appeared with the headline 'Problems of the Revolution' and proved to be the last issue of the magazine. With the anarchist flags as an integral but highly visible part of the crowd, this was a readily recognisable image of mass solidarity.

Michaelis's coverage of Durruti's funeral, possibly undertaken for the press, is a testament to the expansion of her repertoire from mid-1936 onwards. *The arrival of the international Red Cross at Portbou* is similarly concerned with the depiction of current events (presumably it was taken in the early days of the Civil War, though Mrs Sachs wrote 6 June on the back of the photograph). The action is largely self-explanatory due to the profusion of recognisable signs: text identifies the station as Portbou, a town on the French–Spanish border; the train is French, originating in Paris; and the five members of the international team, shown disembarking, are identified by the Red Cross insignia on their hats and armbands. It is an impromptu image dealing with events that were in the process of unfolding. Like all arrivals, this arrival marks a moment of transition. The Red Cross team is on its way to somewhere else – presumably the site of battle, of crisis. The image's narrative potential and power is drawn from an unexpected convergence, a purely photographic event in that it is solely dependent on chance. What is captured is simple enough: the similar facial expressions of two members of the Red Cross team, a young man and woman who are fortuitously positioned at either side of the foreground. Their expressions are full of significance; with what can be read as apprehension they look out of the camera frame towards their, and by implication Spain's, unknown future.

During the civil war, Barcelona. Durruti 1936 16.4 × 23.1 cm

The arrival of the international Red Cross at Portbou 1936 12.0 × 17.0 cm

For the elderly Mrs Sachs this photograph did not represent the beginning of something as 'the arrival' declared in the title would normally suggest. What she saw in it was the end, the end of the social revolution and the Spanish Republic. On the back of the print, in her elderly, shaky script, she wrote a long caption outlining the sequence of events in the Civil War that still, decades after the original events, impresses me with its tone of outrage and distress:

> I took this photo for the Barcelona press. When we arrived there was on the Road Border also a car with a Japanese Ambassador and his wife, who wanted to enter Spain from France. He was not let in – Japan supported Hitler – Franco's betrayal of his own country. Franco received 40,000 soldiers from Mussolini marching with them from Morocco, crossing Gibraltar and attacking from the South eventually braking [sic] all resistance and conquering Madrid. Hitler sent 200 Aeroplanes to Franco. – The legitimate very moderate social-democrat government (U.G.T.: Union general de trabajadores) – which had founded the republic in 1929 after sending the Monarchy and all their representatives peacefully to Marseille, where they wished to go. The monarchist flag was lowered only after the Royalists had landed and only on the return voyage of the ship – to Spain was the Spanish national flag elevated. As far as I know this was the only bloodless revolution in history. – The American and English governments looked on, did not help, preferred a fascist government, because amongst other reasons they had coalmines and industry in Spain, they didn't want socialised [sic] which would hardly have happened. Franco's prisoners are still in prison.

Like so many of her comrades in the anarcho-syndicalist movement in Spain, Grete Michaelis was devastated by General Franco's victory. For her colleague Arthur Lehning it was, in the words of his biographer, '**the** big tragedy of his political life'.[30] For years Lehning did not speak or write about what had taken place; only in the 1970s, in a more responsive and radicalised political climate, did he finally comment publicly on the events of the Civil War. Due to the particularities of Grete's own circumstances – her exile in Australia, her retirement from professional and public life, and the lack of knowledge about her earlier activities – she never came to break her silence.

Grete Michaelis's years in Spain were characterised by her most hopeful and committed period of political activism, as well as by a growing disillusionment with the state of humanity. In Spain her marriage to Michel ended and she kept a handwritten translation of the essential sentences of the divorce decree of February 1937, announcing that

> Mr Rodolfo Michaelis and Mrs Margarete Michaelis appeared today before the special department for divorces of the Ministry of Justice at the Generalidad de Cataluna at Barcelona and stated that they wished to apply for their divorce in mutual agreement and with firm determination.

Stapled to it was another paper handwritten in German and signed by both Grete and Michel. It confirmed that they had been separated for more than two years and that no 'marital relations' had taken place between them during this time.

Thirty-six years later, in a letter to Grete, Michel recalled the day their divorce was formalised. He wrote:

> I can still see us as we left the Barcelona Palace of Justice, and gave our goodbye kiss in the middle of the Paseo de San Juan. You left Spain and I hurried back to the Aragon front. We parted forever as married people. I don't know what you felt then. I ran to the end of the wide street and strode from one side to the other of the brick Arche de Triumph and thought to myself that this was the same number of metres as I was old: 30. T h i r t y! Turning point in human existence. Death, I said to myself, hits you in the back, if you run from it. Forward! To your place in the fight against fascism and for freedom. Then everything seemed so simple to me.

This final parting as a married couple may well have been the last time they saw each other in Spain. As the tide began to turn against the revolution and the Republicans' fight for freedom, it appears that they had no further direct contact and received only very scant information about their respective movements. It was not until 1967 when they resumed their relationship in letters that, for each other's benefit, they retraced their steps from 1937 onwards.

Michel's story was an especially brutal one. It has, however, been relatively well accounted for – through a booklet, *Rudolf 'Michel' Michaelis. Mit der Centuria 'Erich Mühsam' vor Huesca* (which, my translator tells me, is somewhat 'puffed-up in tone'); his unpublished memoirs, 'Encounter with Spain'; and in his letters to Grete.[31] In October 1937, in the continuing putsch against the anarchists, Michel was arrested in Barcelona by the Stalinist secret police and for several months was interned in the notorious Stalinist prison, the Puerta del Angel. Here Paul Thalmann, a fellow prisoner, observed Michel's behaviour first-hand; he later recalled an incident in which Michel broke out of prison on behalf of the imprisoned anarchists, brought their plight to the attention of the national committee of the FAI and then voluntarily returned to the prison, where he was promptly re-arrested. That, as Thalmann saw it, 'was Michel all over, unqualified solidarity and borderless trust in his anarchist [comrades] combined with unbelievable naivety and total misjudgement of a situation'.[32] Following this incident, Michel was relocated to a prison in Segorbe, near Valencia.

After being released from prison in 1938 Michel re-committed to the fight against fascism, although the majority of DAS members left Spain around this time. He became a Spanish citizen and joined a unit of the Spanish Republican Army that comprised former members of the anarchist militia. After the fall of Catalonia in January the following year, he fled to Paris where he lived illegally with anarchists Mollie Steimer and Senya Flechine, members of the close-knit anarcho-syndicalist group and close friends of Emma Goldman's. That autumn he was arrested on the French–Spanish border attempting to re-enter Spain. Caught with two false passports in his possession, he was tortured and sentenced by the fascist military court to twenty years imprisonment, of which – using Michel's own figures – he served 1595 days. In 1944 he was exiled to the village of Carabanche near Madrid where, with the granting of limited freedom, he was able to re-establish connections with anarchists, socialists and Trotskyists involved in anti-Franco activities. Through the actions of the allies and the German repatriation scheme Michel eventually returned to Germany, arriving in Berlin in June 1946 with nothing. Years later he told Grete that because he had been unable to find accommodation in the ruined city he lived 'in the bombed out museum where the rain came in and the walls were covered in mildew. If things were really bad I opened my umbrella. In those days I only owned the clothes I wore and there was little to eat'.

In 1973, in his key letter that accompanied the return of Grete's long-lost photographs, Michel elaborated on his experiences in Spain and their impact on him. He described his long and cruel term of imprisonment, which he felt was responsible for his memory loss:

> For a long time there were whole sections of my life that were
> totally erased, and it was necessary to have a direct prompt in order
> to retrieve what was lost. I am not referring to the type of memory
> weakness that is associated with increasing age. No. In my case it

is almost certainly related to the five years that I was in prison in Barcelona, during which the first three years were spent being turned into a skeleton. Additional to the hunger were the continual beatings that were carried out until consciousness was lost, interrogations with the Falangist police and the Gestapo, in which one would always answer with 'I know nothing' and 'no, no, and once more no'. Over time you really didn't know any more, even the names of your best comrades and fighting companions would be lost. And this has continued up until today. This should explain the situation to you.

On hearing these revelations more than thirty years after the event, Grete's distress was almost palpable. Her response made it clear that she had had no knowledge of what had transpired; she was shocked to learn of his long-term imprisonment and the atrocious treatment he had endured. Marianne had written her a long letter shortly after the end of the war telling Grete that Michel was with his family in Berlin. That is all she knew.

In contrast to Michel, there is little information about Grete's movements during her final months in Spain. Her only discussion of this fateful time occurred in an interview in 1985 where she outlined the convergence of political and personal events, and the circumstances behind her own departure from Spain:

Catalonia and its capital, Barcelona, did not fall into the hands of Franco's army. He marched west, up north to conquer Madrid, the capital ... My husband volunteered to fight in defence of the free country. Many men from Europe and England came to join the defence. An English convoy with doctors and nurses arrived, which I had to photograph. At the end of 1937, it became quite clear that Franco would win the war. I decided to leave and I managed to get a permit to take all my photographic work and equipment with me to go first to France then to my parents.[33]

Interestingly, however, Grete did not finish her account there. She went on to tell her interviewer that 'My husband agreed that I should go out and he was to join me when he could leave'. This despite the fact that by the time Grete left Spain she and Michel had been separated for nearly three years, and their divorce had been finalised several months earlier. Given that Michel was also in prison, her decision to leave could only have been made independently of him.

What lay ahead for Grete Michaelis was increased movement – from Spain to Marseilles, where she stored most of her photographic equipment and archive, to Paris and then on to Bielsko – and ever greater disruption.

These unpredictable, difficult months were the precursor to exile and the state of being that so many anarcho-syndicalists experienced during the ascendancy of fascism. In 1935, in a letter to Milly and Rudolf Rocker, who were themselves exiled in the United States, Etta Federn eloquently described her situation, presaging Grete's own:

> my life is so strange ... and I feel so absolutely disrooted [*sic*] ... I feel as if everything was lost ... [including] what I strived [for] and what I tried to do. It seems to me that I am too weak for life in exile. It is hard work and I feel tired and forlorn. I feel so absolutely lonely.[34]

A few years after her death, Margaret Michaelis's Spanish photographs began to have a new kind of life. The context for their re-emergence was the intense scholarly and popular interest in modern Spanish history, particularly the revolutionary period of the 1930s. The visual arts, including photography, were the direct beneficiaries of the now well-established processes of reclamation, analysis and interpretation. Michaelis's work was represented in some of the first survey publications and exhibitions focusing on avant-garde practices of the period, notably A.C.: Les Vanguardias en Cataluna 1906–1939, held at the Fundació Caixa de Catalunya, Barcelona, in 1992; and les avantguardes fotogràfiques a espanya 1925–1945, shown at the same venue in 1997. The latter exhibition included the work of photographers, as well as painters and architects, to emphasise the wealth of interdisciplinary connections during the period.

Margaret Michaelis was also one of the photographers whose work was examined in depth in the flurry of photographic scholarship that occurred in Spain in the late 1990s. In 1999 the solo exhibition Margaret Michaelis: Fotografía, Vanguardia y Política en la Barcelona de la República, curated by Catalan art historian Juan José Lahuerta and American art historian Jordana Mendelson, was held at the Institut Valencià d'Art Modern Centre, Julio González in Valencia and later at the Centre de Cultura Contemporània de Barcelona. This was only Michaelis's second solo show. It built on the National Gallery of Australia's exhibition Margaret Michaelis, mounted over a decade earlier (shown at the Jewish Museum of Australia in Melbourne in 1987 and the National Gallery of Australia the following year), which represented the initial phase of my research into the Margaret Michaelis-Sachs Archive.

The exhibition brochure, which Jordana Mendelson eventually came across in the files of the ARXIU in Barcelona, alerted her to the existence of a substantial body of Michaelis's photographs on the other side of the world. Whereas the National Gallery of Australia's exhibition surveyed Michaelis's career, presenting both her European and Australian photographs, the focus of the IVAM exhibition was her Spanish work produced between 1934 and 1937. It achieved a practical form of reunification by bringing together photographs from public and private collections that had been separated for decades.

Margaret Michaelis: Fotografía, Vanguardia y Política en la Barcelona de la República united major contemporary theoretical and thematic concerns. It dealt with the political and cultural life of the Second Republic, avant-gardism and photography, and took an interdisciplinary approach. In the words of the directors of the two institutions, it was conceived as an important reclamation project, marking a 'further dive into the origins of modernity and another advance in the salvage of names which are landmarks but which, for circumstantial reasons, have not been appreciated as they deserve'.[35]

The circumstances that had affected the appreciation of Michaelis's particular contribution did not relate simply to the disruptive effects of war and its aftermath, in which knowledge of Catalan avant-gardism in the 1930s was actively suppressed. Also crucial was the GATCPAC's own ideology and the group's commitment to collective authorship. As a result, Grete Michaelis's photographs that were published in A.C. were not credited to her as an individual. Thus, as Jordana Mendelson has persuasively argued, while Michaelis's images assumed prominence as emblems of Catalan modernity, their actual creator remained invisible.[36]

Through the exhibition and the fully illustrated catalogue, Michaelis's photographs returned to their Spanish viewers double images of their past, as they concerned Catalonian modernism but also to the Civil War. In the IVAM gallery, shortly after the exhibition opened, I watched people cluster around the photographs, including an image that showed two young men scrutinising the latest reports on the Civil War displayed on hoardings in the street. I stood close by, overhearing animated conversations that I could not understand, but which I interpreted as part of the process viewers go through to claim photographs as their own. I felt certain that this involved a range of responses; for example, curator Juan José Lahuerta had told me how 'emotionally attached' he was to the photographs and how moved he was by the experience of seeing them. Other viewers, I imagined, may have been excitedly – but as is common in the viewing of historical photographs, mistakenly – seeing themselves or people they knew in different images. For me, of course, no such self-identification or self-projection was possible. My experiences were naturally of a different order. What now began to make sense, however, were the photographs' rough, haphazard qualities, their uneasy urgency as well as the feelings of hope that I hadn't been able to see properly before.

At the close of the twentieth century Margaret Michaelis's photographs offered their audience images of a fraught, highly charged period in Spanish history that culminated in the defeat of the Republic and the entrenchment of General Franco's dictatorship. These events terminated the creative ferment that energised cultural activity of the 1930s, ushering in what is generally described as a dismal period, which saw the fracturing and dispersal of the avant-garde.[37]

13 EXILE

The year 1938 has become almost silent in Grete Michaelis's life. Only a few items remain to speak of it – an engaging informal portrait of her, inscribed 'Vienna, January 1938'; some snapshots taken at a market in Poland; and a German passport issued on 16 September. The snapshots are likely to have been among the last photographs Michaelis took in Europe. Embedded in the world of work and human activity, they are social photographs that reveal the constancy and continuity of Michaelis's interests. As in Barcelona and Berlin previously, Michaelis's identification with her female subjects is obvious: it is the women – selling fruit and vegetables, minding children, keeping each other company – who take her eye. In one strange image that comes out of nowhere, a young woman's dress is caught momentarily by the wind and balloons darkly in front of her.

Inside Michaelis's passport her place of residence is given as Bielsko (Poland) and her profession as photographer, suggesting that, as in the fateful year of 1933, she had returned to her parents' home in order to earn money through her photographic work. Her chances of doing so were probably very slim. A huge number of Jewish businesses were forced to close in the late 1930s because of the government-supported boycott of Jewish economic activity. What Saul Friedlander terms the 'pauperisation' of wide sectors of the Jewish population also accelerated in this period.[1] By 1937–38 Polish professional associations were not accepting Jewish members and the civil service had ceased employing Jews.[2]

There is no doubt that Michaelis's personal circumstances were gravely affected by the momentous political events taking place both in Austria and Poland. A few weeks after she was photographed relaxed and smiling in Vienna, Germany annexed Austria and the aryanisation of Jewish economic assets and the expulsion of Jews from their homes dramatically increased. In late October Jews in the Austrian provinces were advised to either leave the country by 15 December 1938 or to move to Vienna; within six months of the *Anschluss*

45 000 Austrian Jews had emigrated, and by May 1939 more than 50% of the Jewish population had left Austria.[3] The fast-growing wave of anti-Jewish extremism culminated in the infamous *Kristallnacht* (Night of broken glass) of 9–10 November, during which hundreds of synagogues across Germany and Austria were burned down, Jewish businesses and residences were destroyed or vandalised, and Jews were harassed, arrested and killed. By this point the options for Jews wanting to emigrate from the Greater German Reich, whether by legal or illegal means, were becoming extremely limited. In Europe and further afield, countries had grown resistant to increasing the number of Jewish refugees they would accept.

Michaelis was fortunate enough to secure a path to safety. On 12 December she was issued with an employment visa for the United Kingdom by the British Vice Consulate in Katowice, Poland. Exactly a fortnight later – a sure indicator of the urgency of the situation – she arrived in London. The official document in her passport states that she was given leave to land on condition that she register immediately with the police and did 'not enter any employment other than as a resident in service in a private household'.

For seven months Michaelis remained in England, apparently living with an aunt in Chalcot Gardens in northwest London and, like many women in her situation, working as a domestic. It was in this capacity, rather than through

Esperance Bay 1939
5.4 × 5.6 cm

her profession as a photographer, that she became eligible for humanitarian aid organised by the Church of England and subsequently received a visa for travel to Australia. Michaelis regarded this as nothing short of a miracle but, as it happened, her brother succeeded in securing a visa for her at almost exactly the same time. However, instead of joining him and their sister in São Paolo in Brazil, she decided to go to Australia. Sailing on the *Esperance Bay* she arrived in Fremantle on 29 August and in Sydney ten days later.

By the time Margaret Michaelis reached Sydney, Germany had invaded Poland and World War II had been declared. On 4 September in Bielsko, where she had left her parents, German troops destroyed all of the synagogues and Jewish community buildings. Approximately 4000 of the town's 6000 Jewish citizens fled; in 1940 those who had remained were confined to a ghetto. Following the liquidation of the ghetto in 1942 the last surviving Jews were sent to the concentration camp at Auschwitz.

Roanoke flats, Francis
Street, Sydney c. 1939
5.6 × 5.5 cm

I have heard Margaret Michaelis speak about her first few months in Australia in an interview recorded by the Australian Broadcasting Commission in 1979. The program was called *The immigrants* and incorporated first-hand accounts of migrants' early experiences in their new home country. In her interview Margaret explained that shortly after her arrival she took up work as a housekeeper because she wished to gain 'some experience of what it means to live in Australia' (although her domestic service was probably an obligation in accordance with the terms of her visa rather than a matter of personal choice). Between September and November she worked in three different households in Sydney. Her first experience, in a comfortable house with views of Rushcutters Bay, was positive. Though she admitted that her lack of cooking experience was 'a bit of a worry', her employer was supportive, responding to her shortcomings by offering to teach whatever was required. However, Margaret Michaelis's last position came to an abrupt end because of an incident she elaborated on in the interview.

One day I was to do the washing and I was told that there were sausages in the fridge and a piece of bread ... and not to touch the cake – the cake was enormous – and I was not to touch the cake. Now that brushed me up thoroughly and I left a note on the table that I remember my mother when she had a washer woman she cooked particularly good and much for that hard-working woman and I thought that I would be at least as good as my mother's washing woman ... when I came the next day I got a note on the table 'Leave everything'. So I wrote underneath 'Hurray, Hurray'.

As Margaret re-tells her story I can hear her becoming freshly wounded. This is a voice I know, a voice with an impassioned and indignant tone that impresses me. But there is also an excessive quality to Margaret Michaelis's account – evident more in the reading of it than the listening to it – which I find unsettling. It's the amount of detail she provides about an incident that had occurred forty years earlier, and the fact that whatever had transpired between her and her employer had been rankling her all that time.

Margaret Michaelis's dismissal from her housekeeping position was not only unceremonious but also extremely premature. She found herself without work for most of November, though clearly her desire was to resume her photographic career as quickly as possible. She initially approached Russell Roberts who ran the largest studio in Sydney at the time, employing around thirty staff. Roberts responded to the high quality of her portfolio but, according to Margaret's recollections, considered her too talented for the routine work he could offer. Roberts was also reducing his staff numbers as World War II began to have an adverse effect on his business.[1] From late 1939 until March the following year Michaelis worked intermittently as a domestic and took on some casual work in different photographic studios.

Around April 1940 Margaret Michaelis decided to establish her own business. It was an audacious step given the precariousness of her financial situation; she had very little capital, having arrived in Australia with only twelve pounds (by the following April she had accumulated twenty-three pounds, boosted by a birthday present of six pounds from her aunt in London). She rented a darkroom at Grace Studios on the sixth floor of the Grace Brothers Building on Broadway, in inner Sydney, where she processed and printed her negatives, and canvassed for business from door to door. By November that year she had opened her own studio in central Sydney, under what she described as 'great difficulties', but with some financial assistance from the European Emergency Church Committee. Photo-studio, as she named it, was located on the seventh floor at 114 Castlereagh Street, with a display case at street level. The studio was equipped with the precious cameras and enlargers she had used in Berlin and Barcelona fortunately still operable after two years storage in Marseilles and their long sea journey to Australia via London.

In the advertisement for Photo-studio that Michaelis ran during the 1940s, she listed her specialisation in 'Home portraits, Gardens and Interiors'. This, it seems to me, was a sensible strategy, which recognised her previous experience in Europe (principally in the areas of portraiture and architectural photography), as well as the particular character and potential of the local market. However, despite her obvious willingness to diversify, portraiture became Michaelis's primary area of activity. This was not unusual. Exiled European photographers frequently went on to become portrait photographers in their new countries, a phenomenon that says less about the distinctive qualities of European photography and more about portraiture's adaptability and persistence as a mainstay of the photographic industry. Even with the reorganisation of studios that followed the emergence of a flourishing amateur sector in the early twentieth century (led by the introduction of the Kodak box brownie camera), portraiture retained its pre-eminent position in the photographic industry.

While the continued demand for portraits was undoubtedly an attraction for practitioners like Margaret Michaelis, who were starting anew, another desirable factor was the relative ease with which a portrait practice could be established. It was possible to function independently – in Michaelis's case virtually as a one-person operation – without the range of contacts that were a prerequisite for advertising photography, another potentially lucrative area of activity in this period. But I think Michaelis's specialisation in portraiture was also significant for very personal reasons; she had been passionate about portraiture since the earliest days of her career and would remain so throughout her life.

By stint of her own efforts Michaelis slowly built up her business. In the first six months she earned 135 pounds, mainly from portrait photography, with the occasional commercial assignment, and from the retouching she undertook for other photographers in Sydney. In the next twelve-month period, from December 1940 to 1941, her income increased significantly to the substantial sum of 523 pounds and she employed an assistant, a young woman, who was

Unknown photographer
Margaret Michaelis in
Photo-studio, Sydney
1950 9.0 × 8.2 cm

paid twenty-five shillings a week. Michaelis worked long hours, keeping the studio open from nine in the morning until seven at night. As she saw it at the time, the 'studio is still in a developing stage and I feel I have to take every order I can get in order to meet my obligations ... I am here alone and have no relatives or other connections – neither in Australia nor anywhere else – who could support me and provide me with the means for my livelihood.' She lived frugally, claiming that the only item of clothing she was able to purchase in her first two years in Australia was a coat.

The commitment to her profession was evident in her decision to join the Professional Photographers Association of New South Wales in April 1941, where she was the only female member; her membership was the source of some pride, mentioned in one of her letters to Michel in the 1970s and its significance was acknowledged by him. In February 1942 two of her European photographs were reproduced in the journal *Australia*, published by leading publisher Sydney Ure Smith.

For a newspaper story that appeared in 1950 Margaret Michaelis was photographed in her Castlereagh Street studio, the heart of her professional domain. These are house-proud images in which she stands amidst her equipment, inspects some photographic prints and takes a phone call at her desk.

What one sees around her is a small, well-organised space – her space – with a selection of her photographs adorning the walls. By all accounts the set-up was simple. Her equipment comprised five cameras: a Leica, a Rolleiflex, one ICA Reflex quarter-plate fitted with a Zeiss lens, one CHR Tauber studio camera, and an ICA half-plate camera, as well as two Leica enlargers. She generally used her Rolleiflex camera, a standard model without any attachment lenses, and expended two rolls of film on each client.

Even more problematic than her very limited financial resources in the early years of her business were her European origins. These attracted the close scrutiny of government authorities from early 1940 until late 1943 and then intermittently until the late 1940s, even though Michaelis was naturalised as an Australian citizen in 1945. Classified as a refugee alien within a few months of her arrival in Sydney, Michaelis was subject to a host of regulations promulgated under the Defence Act of 1939, governing place of residence and business, personal mobility, and ownership of objects including wirelesses, cameras and binoculars. These regulations had a direct bearing on the conduct of her personal and professional life.

In the first police report on her, carried out in April 1940 and placed on her Australian Security Intelligence Organisation (ASIO) file, Inspector Keefe of the Special Squad gave details of her personal circumstances, employment and associates in Sydney. Indicating that she was under surveillance, he noted that 'According to information received she is visited frequently at her flat by a number of male germans [sic] who call there in two and threes at a time mostly of a Sunday. She also receives numerious [sic] telephone calls from foreigners'.[2] Margaret Michaelis's mail was monitored within a few months of her arrival, with police intercepting a letter written in German (from Kien Mandelbaum). Their report on the matter, in May 1940, stated that Michaelis's correspondent

> writes vaguely in a pro-Russian strain ... The last line cut away contains an allusion just legible, 'comrades who have been sacrificed'. The letter would not appear to be evidence that the writer is pro-Communist, but is held in case further examination is desired.

In July 1940 the shared flat at Francis Street, East Sydney, where Michaelis lived was searched as part of the police investigation into her activities for a dossier being compiled on her as a refugee alien (this was subsequently placed on her ASIO file). The search, in effect a raid, was remembered by one of Michaelis's friends as a gross violation of the residents' privacy and of propriety – the police officers had arrived early in the morning and entered the women's bedrooms while they were in bed, interviewing them while still dressed in their nightwear. According to the police report nothing of interest emerged, 'No literature or other matter found which would indicate that the alien is engaged in any anti-British or subversive activities'. At the same time police interviewed Michaelis's neighbours in the adjacent flats, all of whom responded favourably to questions about 'the alien's general conduct'. Only the manager of the flats was negative; she, the police stated, 'appears prejudiced against aliens generally'. Like others in her situation Margaret Michaelis was required to give police the names of friends of British nationality who could vouch for her character. These people were duly contacted and confirmed that she was 'strictly honest and trustworthy'.

The location of Michaelis's place of residence also caused official concern. In 1941 a security report drew attention to her frequent change of address since her arrival in Sydney; it was noted that in a period of two-and-a-half months she had moved five times which, the report concluded, 'may or may not have some significance'. It was also observed that the places where she lived had all been close to the water.

There was no doubt that by virtue of their European origins, their accents and their 'foreign-ness', Michaelis and her associates were often regarded with suspicion. The possession of a wireless, for example, could become an issue. In 1943, when sharing a house in Victoria Street, Chatswood, with friends and fellow Austrian émigrés Kurt and Suzi Menzer, neighbours reported to the Security Service that Kurt Menzer 'had a wireless set and that a gramophone had been delivered to him clearly labeled "From the 2GB Community Chest"'. This information, included in what the investigating officer described as 'long rambling statements ... [of] little value', was considered significant because the 2GB fund had been established to purchase goods solely for the troops. It was suggested that an investigation could therefore 'be warranted in this instance', although apparently one was not carried out.

Margaret Michaelis was sensitive to the highly charged environment in which she found herself and adapted her behaviour in ways she thought appropriate. Because people who spoke in foreign languages attracted attention and 'stern looks', she later said that she decided to speak only English, which she considered to be the least she could do to adjust to the situation.[3]

Predictably, as an enemy alien, Margaret Michaelis's social activities were tightly circumscribed. They were also monitored; a police report of May 1940 concluded that there was no evidence to suggest she held parties, attended foreigners' parties or kept late hours. Her attendance at a Meeting of the International Youth Committee in 1943 was noted with the minutes to the meeting appearing on her ASIO file. Michaelis mixed mainly with other refugees and was known to be a member of the New Australians Club that met at Sue's Café, 309 George Street in Sydney, on Friday nights. She later said that her 'first important contact' with people was through this club. As with many other European refugees, music was very important to Michaelis as a means of establishing social connections and a sense of community. She associated with people who were musical and loved music; along with her friends Lucy Rofe and Suzi Menzer, she sang German folksongs to raise funds for the war effort. In addition, Michaelis was a member of the Lindfield a cappella choir which, like similar groups elsewhere in Australia, played a vital role in bringing Austrian and German people together, nourishing their love of music and providing crucial social contacts in an environment bereft of a cultured café society. The choir, conducted by Fritz Rice (formerly Reich), eventually disbanded at the height of the war because of the difficulties in obtaining travel permits required to attend practice sessions.

The monitoring of Margaret Michaelis's personal and social life obviously drew inconclusive results, typified more by innuendo than hard facts. Her professional life, however, was a different matter and she struggled with the associated problems throughout the war. By nature her profession was suspect, as it involved the ownership of cameras, which were prohibited for use by both enemy and refugee aliens. Confiscation of her cameras was therefore a very real and urgent prospect that she had to address within a month of opening Photo-studio. In November 1940 she wrote to the Military Intelligence Section of Police Headquarters arguing that 'Even the cancellation of one of these cameras would mean a considerable loss for me and make it practically impossible to carry on the business'. While it was agreed that she could retain her cameras, the Commissioner of Police prohibited her from taking any photographs of naval, military or air-force personnel or establishments. Michaelis contested this decision on the grounds that it would cause financial hardship and enlisted the support of The Right Reverend Bishop C Venn Pilcher, Coadjutor of Sydney. In Bishop Pilcher's letter to the Commissioner he argued that Michaelis was not a security risk:

My personal conviction is that Miss Michaelis is worthy of the removal of this restriction. She is an Austrian citizen and escaped from her country after suffering painful treatment at the hands of the Nazis. I have known her for some time and am fully convinced of her loyalty to the British Empire. Her country was, as you know, Hitler's first victim, while Mr. Winston Churchill has assured us that one of our first war aims is the re-constitution of Austria. One who has suffered as Miss Michaelis has at the hands of the Nazis could never desire their triumph in this war.[4]

As a result of Bishop Pilcher's intervention, Michaelis's permit (issued under Section 3 of the Alien Control Order) was amended on 16 October 1941 to allow her to photograph members of the forces when they were 'included in bona fide wedding groups, parties etc., in the company of civilians and not on or in any defence property or establishment'.

Three months later, when Margaret Michaelis applied for an extension to her permit, new concerns were raised, mainly because of what was perceived as the strategically sensitive location of her studio. In a report, clearly based on a visit to the studio and a close examination of its location, police noted that from the seventh floor window

a view is obtainable of portion of the harbour, and, from a special landing constructed immediately above, which is usable by all tenants, a good view is obtained of Garden Island and the anchorage of large vessels. Furthermore every vessel which rounds Bradley's Head is in view from this position.[5]

Because it was noted that Michaelis could readily observe the movement of troopships, the authorities requested further information about the extent of the 'outside photography' she performed and its necessity in relation to her overall business. In response she estimated that two thirds of her photographs were taken inside the studio, and the remainder outdoors. Perceiving the potential risk to her business the restriction on outdoor photography would pose, she argued that if she were forced to this practice – mainly photographs of weddings and other social functions, and commercial photographs – she would not be able to earn a living and meet her financial obligations. She went further, requesting permission to photograph individual members of the forces, whose numbers were increasing as the war progressed. In support of her argument she wrote that 'Gradually the civilian clients are becoming less, owing to the evacuation of women and children, to more women being in uniform and to many former clients belonging to the forces now'. Her application was unsuccessful, the Director-General of Security rejecting it on the grounds that 'She is already permitted to take photographs of men in uniform as members of wedding groups and this is considered quite reasonable'.[6]

From the Security Service's perspective, it was unfortunate that 'aliens' like Margaret Michaelis, regardless of whether they were refugee aliens, remained in sensitive areas of work. The author of her 1941 security report adopted an extreme position, stating that:

> It is a matter for regret that members of the defence forces and their relatives should find it necessary to visit the studios operated by enemy aliens to have photographs taken and there is little doubt that in some instances, as in the present case, where the name is not obviously foreign, such persons are not aware that they are patronising enemy aliens. In other cases, they do not appear to realize the possibilities of such aliens acquiring information, either by careless conversation or by inference. It is considered that this aspect might well be brought under the notice of all troops by the issue of a military order, in order to discourage members of the services from visiting such studios.[7]

Fortunately for Michaelis no such military order eventuated.

While Margaret Michaelis had to deal with constraints directly related to her status as a refugee alien, there were other difficulties to face. The war years were generally grim for freelance photographers, with the rationing of film and shortage of supplies of photographic equipment (those from Germany were no longer available). And yet, as Barbara Hall and Jenni Mather have observed in their book, *Australian women photographers*, this period saw the 'emergence of a breed of commercial photographers which included several extremely talented women'.[8] A short distance from Photo-studio Olive Cotton's photographic practice was thriving; she managed the Max Dupain Studio from 1942–45 while Dupain was on war service. For Cotton, as for Michaelis and a number of other women photographers, the war years offered professional opportunities that had not previously been available (and that disappeared when the men returned at the end of the war).

Michaelis's own background and position in Australian society did, however, have some advantages, enabling her to attract a particular clientele. These were European and often Jewish people who may have felt more comfortable with an Austrian-born photographer, and who may have also wished to offer her their support. She targeted this sector of the market through an advertisement in the *New Citizen* newspaper that catered for Sydney's émigré community. She also frequently photographed people who were involved in the arts. One of her earliest and most significant clients was the Bodenwieser Viennese Ballet, which she first photographed around 1940 and continued to work with throughout the decade. In this respect Michaelis appears to have been typical of Austrian photographers who, whilst in exile, continued to demonstrate their interest in the arts, music and theatre, with a large number being involved in the portraiture of artists.[9] Margaret Michaelis was also acquainted with Polish painter Maximilien Feuerring, who arrived in Australia in 1950 as a displaced person; she photographed the opening of Feuerring's exhibition at David Jones' Art Gallery in Sydney shortly after his arrival. In collaboration with Feuerring, in May 1950 Michaelis produced a very interesting series of experimental images that she entitled 'Light paintings'. These are small, abstract and fugitive images – their process renders them unstable and they cannot be exposed to light.

Portrait photography is, I think, a notoriously fickle trade that often yields uneven results. Indeed, it is rare to find a portraitist whose works are always exceptional – in part because a successful outcome is so dependent on the chemistry between photographer and subject. Even a photographer as accomplished as contemporary American portraitist Annie Lebovitz moves between two poles: some of her portraits represent consummate performances by both photographer and subject, while others strain for effect. During the twelve years Margaret Michaelis ran Photo-studio she achieved a consistently high standard as a portraitist, but there is no doubt that some portraits are more engaging and interesting than others.

The portraits Michaelis produced fall into two main categories. The first is largely ceremonial and embraces the kind of portraits taken for personal reasons, such as an engagement, a marriage or a significant moment in family

Madeleine c. 1947 30.3 × 36.0 cm

life. In these instances the clients are usually the subjects themselves. The second group comprises portraits taken for public purposes and are therefore generally commissioned by others. They include photographs of the artists H Weaver Hawkins, John Wiltshire and Arthur Murch, commissioned by Sydney Ure Smith and published in the journal *Australia* in 1947.

There are a number of constants in Margaret Michaelis's practice in terms of her approach and the stylistic features of her portraiture. Of the portraits she kept in her own collection the great majority were taken in her studio and, as is typical of this mode of production, a high degree of formality is evident. The studio was used, not as a setting with theatrical backdrops and props, but as a neutral environment with background walls that function only in terms of tone. Michaelis's compositions are generally simple, tending towards the austere. She rarely used environmental detail to convey information about her subjects and their professions, focusing instead on their individuality.

The particular strength of Michaelis's portraiture stems from her commitment to a modernist ethos and her interest in psychology. Her approach was based on a belief in the subject's essence and in photography's ability to capture it. She expected her portraits to go beyond a description of the sitter's physical features and to reveal what could be described as their inner truth. This is borne out by the following description of what she believed to be a particularly successful photographic session:

> One young woman ... came to her studio sporting heavy makeup and looking very unnatural. Margaret persuaded the woman to apply her makeup more sparingly for the photograph. The woman was delighted with the result, 'It was as if she had discovered herself' Margaret said. 'Things like that happened in the studio'.[10]

Michaelis's interest in psychology dated from her early years in Vienna and her own experiences of psychoanalysis. She responded keenly to subjects who displayed a psychological intensity and was sensitive to those experiencing psychic disturbance and pain. I remember hearing, or perhaps she told me herself, that she had recommended her psychoanalyst, Mr Wasserman, to one of her clients who had returned from war service in a tense mental state. Michaelis was delighted when he returned to her studio in a greatly improved state of mind, and subsequently took the wedding photographs for him and his wife.

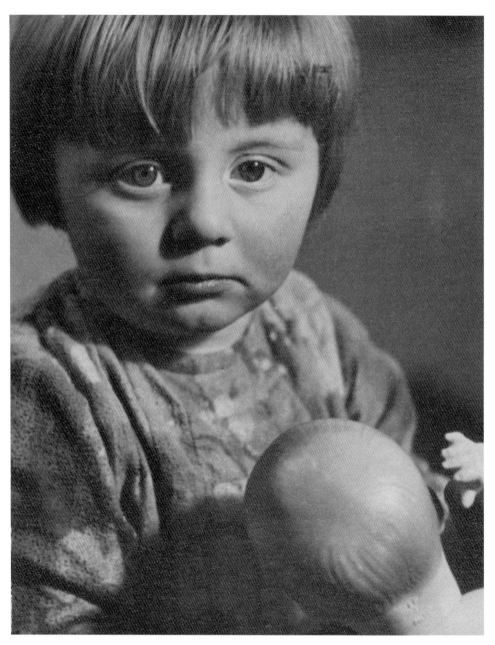

Young girl holding doll 1940s 16.6 × 13.0 cm

Margaret Michaelis introduced psychological and pictorial drama into her portraits through the combination of three primary elements: pose, facial expression and lighting. The energy centres of faces, hands and eyes were especially important, with hands frequently playing a pivotal role; this can be seen in her portraits of actor and producer John Wiltshire, and sculptor Lyndon Dadswell. Wiltshire is depicted engaging in a kind of conversation with his expressively arranged hands, while a pensive Dadswell brings his clasped hands to his chin, thus creating a strong triangular form in the composition, which intersects with the elliptical shape of his head. In another portrait, Viennese actress Elisabeth Bergner is posed with one hand firmly under her chin. The strong, upward movement directs the viewer's gaze to her face and eyes, which look upwards and out of the frame. Like Austrian-born photographer Lotte Meitner-Graf, whose work Michaelis greatly admired, Margaret Michaelis was also particularly responsive to the sculptural qualities of a face, accentuating them through the careful use of lighting.[11]

Michaelis's most successful results depended on the subjects' recognition of the seriousness of the occasion and an appreciation of the art of portraiture. This is certainly the case in an ambitious group portrait of the Bonyhady family, taken around 1943; like Michaelis, they were Austrian Jews who arrived in Sydney in 1939. In a departure from the conventional family portrait, in which family members are usually arranged in horizontal rows, Michaelis creates an unusual diamond-like composition that is fully dependent on the subjects' collaboration. The elder son, Eric, is positioned above his parents, Edward and Edith, while the younger, Fred, appears below them with his mother's hand resting on his shoulder. Rather than facing the camera front on, as in the usual formula, these family members are depicted in three-quarter view, the father and sons looking slightly upwards and into the distance. Interestingly, the mother disrupts the strict order of the grouping by dropping her gaze downwards. Although the composition is unorthodox, it still enables the close study of individual and group physiognomies that remains one of the great prerequisites of family portraiture.

The Bonyhady family portrait is an unusually severe, stripped-down image that forgoes the sentimentality and softness normally associated with family portraiture. Its rhetoric echoes the heroic portraiture of Etta Federn and Emma Goldman that Michaelis had undertaken in Spain, but without the overt propagandist intentions.

Lyndon Dadswell, sculptor c. 1947 50.0 × 39.8 cm

The Bonyhady family c. 1944–45 18.5 × 15.0 cm Private collection

An overview of Margaret Michaelis's work also reveals that she was a better photographer of women than of men. This in itself is not unusual; the same could be argued for Max Dupain and Athol Shmith during the 1930s. But it is the nature of Michaelis's encounter with her female subjects that gives her portraits a distinctive edge. Whereas Dupain's photographs of women in the 1930s are invariably charged with the eroticism of the photographic transaction and his response to his sitter's beauty – consider, for example, his wonderfully seductive portraits of Lelia Roussova, Miss Noleen Woodard and Jean Lorraine – Michaelis's response is of a different order. Her subjects are represented as sensual beings but they are also alert, manifesting a great sense of presence and poise. It is no coincidence that three of Michaelis's most outstanding portraits – of dancer Jean Raymond, actress Elisabeth Bergner and writer Cynthia Nolan – are of independent women, complementing her earlier portraits of *neue Fräu* and revolutionaries Etta Federn and Emma Goldman. The closest contemporary Australian parallels are Olive Cotton's portraits of like-minded women taken during the late 1930s and early 1940s – of her friends Olga Sharp and Jean Lorraine and writer Eleanor Dark.

By Michaelis's own assessment her portrait of Jean Raymond, a dancer with the Bodenwieser Ballet, was one of her best and it was published in the *Australian Photography* annual of 1947 (along with three other portraits of Madeleine, Lyndon Dadswell and a young girl, Frances). I remember her telling me about Jean in one of our early conversations, describing her difficulties in finding a pose that would suit the young woman whose looks she considered very plain. Midway through the session Michaelis was called away to her office to answer the telephone, and looking back towards the studio she saw her subject in profile. This gave her the creative solution she was seeking: a dramatically simplified pose that suited Jean Raymond's features and yet also carried significant historical associations. The young dancer is portrayed with all the dignity of an Italian noblewoman in a painting from the early Renaissance. While the profile pose and the tonal contrasts in the portrait are relatively severe, Michaelis also includes sensuous elements – see, for example, the way the light touches the young woman's lips and the softness of her hair. From the subject's perspective it was a successful exchange; more recently she recalled that when she sat for the portrait Michaelis 'spoke softly, and put me at ease right away ... I could tell she was confident that she was "seeing" ME and was very happy about it.'[12]

Dancer, Jean R 1947 36.5 × 30.3 cm

The portrait of Viennese actress Elisabeth Bergner is representative of Margaret Michaelis's strongest work in its resolution and intensity. It is, however, atypical in a number of ways. Michaelis approached the subject rather than the other way round. Bergner had stated on her tour to Sydney that she would not be photographed by anyone and so it was only after Michaelis had submitted an album of photographs in support of her request to photograph the actress that Bergner agreed to the session. As a prominent Viennese actress, Bergner's past and present circumstances would have been well known to Michaelis; like the Austrian dancer and choreographer Gertrud Bodenwieser, Bergner had been on tour when war broke out and, as a Jew, found herself in exile from her homeland. One can imagine that Michaelis's desire to photograph Bergner stemmed from what they shared as compatriots, Jews, artists and women. For Bergner, too, it was a positive encounter: apparently pleased with the photographs she used some for publicity purposes. Not surprisingly, given the circumstances of its genesis, Bergner's portrait was not taken in Michaelis's studio but on what is probably a stage set.

Margaret Michaelis's clientele may well have been predominantly European, and yet for me the most memorable of all her portraits is that of Australian writer Cynthia Nolan. The one I have in mind belongs to a small group of images taken during a session at Photo-studio some time after March 1948. I say the date with some confidence because a document in Michaelis's ASIO file gives the following cryptic information:

> Violet Cynthia Nolan
> Hansen
> Reed
> Well known to and an associate of Margaret Michaelis.

The existence of this document is in itself very curious. Because the surveillance of Michaelis's activities had all but petered out by the mid-1940s, it is tempting to conclude that Cynthia Nolan, rather than Michaelis, was the centre of this police interest (as for the alleged friendship between the two women, no evidence of this has come to light). What the document does usefully establish, however, is that the widowed Cynthia Hansen, née Reed, has become Cynthia Nolan; her marriage to Australian artist Sidney Nolan took place on 25 March 1948 after what art historian Janine Burke has described as a 'whirlwind ten-week romance'.[13]

Elisabeth Bergner 1952 49.6 × 39.5 cm

Cynthia Reed – writer, Sidney Nolan's wife 1948 29.8 × 23.9 cm

These few details about surveillance and marriage, which allude to Cynthia Nolan's often contradictory role as both a public figure and a private individual, are pertinent for a fuller reading of Michaelis's portrait. After all, what is especially beguiling about this image is its ambiguity: it could as easily be a private portrait – a gift, for example, for Sidney Nolan – or a public commission suitable for promoting Cynthia Nolan's activities as a writer. Cynthia's public persona was formed in the early 1930s when, together with Fred Ward, she ran Modern Furnishings, an interior design shop in Little Collins Street, Melbourne. She was responsible for exhibiting works by modern abstract artists Sam Atyeo and Ian Fairweather, and imported the first Bauhaus chair into Melbourne. An interior designer and a trained psychiatric nurse who worked in Chicago and London, Cynthia was also a writer. Her first novel, *Lucky Alphonse*, was published in 1944 and *Daddy sowed a wind* followed in 1947, just a few months before this portrait was taken. With her marriage to Nolan and the escalation of his fame Cynthia's face was to become increasingly public territory.

In formal terms Michaelis's portrait is a great success. The composition is unusual and unexpected, with Cynthia Nolan's dark-bodied form being represented in a sculptural way. Seated on a chair, one arm bent above her head, one hand resting on her hair and the other touching the side of her face, her forward-leaning pose is charged with energy. There is something mesmerising about the way she tilts forward – outward and into the viewer's space. But it is Cynthia Nolan's face, framed by her arms and set off by the dark jumper she is wearing, that is the centre of attention. Its expression, complementing her pose, is open, signifying an enticing form of complicity. Cynthia presents herself to the camera in a manner that is simultaneously media savvy and intimate, the characteristic austerity of Michaelis's approach providing an alternative to the gloss and superficiality of much standard studio portraiture of the period.

At the time Michaelis photographed her, Cynthia Nolan was very nearly forty; Sidney Nolan was nine years her junior. I mention this fact only because of its bearing on subsequent representations of Cynthia's face. As Margaret E McGuire has observed, in visual and verbal portraits, including self-portraits, Cynthia's face 'is described most often as ravaged' and, furthermore, 'always in contrast to Sidney's boyish appearance'.[14] In his autobiography Patrick White wrote:

> Naturally Cynthia was much hated by those who had designs on Sid. They hated her for her patrician, increasingly ravaged face, her unfailing taste which showed up their own flyblown vulgarity.[15]

For her own part Cynthia, masquerading as a character in her autobiographical novel *Bride for St Thomas*, wished that her face 'was a secret instead of a confession'.[16] In Michaelis's portrait her face appears to be neither one nor the other, but a tantalising amalgam of the two. The overwhelming impression either way is of a self-realised woman, intelligent, knowing and beautiful.

The mainstay of Margaret Michaelis's business, and her primary interest, was portraiture. She was not interested in advertising photography – an increasingly important sector of the market which, according to her assistant Antonia Burgess who worked with her in the late 1940s, she took on rarely and then only for the money. Michaelis did have another passion: dance photography. This grew out of her longstanding love of dancing, and was declared in a newspaper article in 1950, which stated 'Miss Michaelis is now chiefly interested in faces, next to which comes dancing, because she loves movement and tries to get as much of it as she can into her photographs'.[17]

Michaelis's association with dance was confined to her work for the Bodenwieser Viennese Ballet established by Gertrud Bodenwieser, a former professor of choreography and instructor at the State Academy of Music and Dramatic Arts in Vienna. Bodenwieser had left Austria after the *Anschluss* in 1938 and had been on tour in South America when war broke out; her husband, theatre director Friedrich Jacques Rosenthal, had remained in France and was later arrested when attempting to escape into Spain. He was then deported to the Auschwitz concentration camp where he is believed to have died in 1942. Gertrud Bodenwieser arrived in Sydney in August 1939 and re-established her troupe, which presented recitals under the auspices of J&N Tait, the concert division of J.C. Williamson Theatres Limited. She composed over 100 dance works during her Australian years, and through her choreography and teaching was one of the pioneers of modern dance in this country; Czechoslovakian émigré Edouard Borovansky, who also settled in Australia in 1939, was another.

Michaelis was drawn to Bodenwieser for a number of reasons. As Shona Dunlop MacTavish, one of Bodenwieser's Viennese-trained dancers, recalls Michaelis watched a dance class in the Ballet's early days: 'I believe she made this first move as she arrived in Sydney later than Bodenwieser and because she certainly knew of Frau Gerty's standing in the world of art'. It is conceivable that Michaelis was familiar with Bodenwieser's work from their shared time in

Vienna; Bodenwieser had given her first solo performance in 1919 and became increasingly prominent during the 1920s. Moreover, as coincidence would have it, some of the publicity photographs for her troupe were taken by the Viennese Studio d'Ora, with whom Michaelis had briefly worked in 1921. MacTavish also suggested that their common background as Austrian and Jewish-born women, and shared circumstances as refugees in a foreign land, brought them closer together.[18]

Equally significant is the fact that parallels can be seen between Bodenwieser's approach to dance and Michaelis's to photography – in the words of dancer Jean Raymond, the women shared the 'same kind of artistic ambience'.[19] A newspaper review of one of Bodenwieser's first performances in Australia makes this commonality clear:

> There is no scenery, and the costumes are of the simplest. The interest therefore, becomes concentrated on the dancing itself ... There was nothing conventional, or softly sentimental about this. All the performances had vigour, originality, imagination and unfailing discipline.[20]

These were all qualities enshrined in Michaelis's own practice.

The touchstone of Bodenwieser's approach was the use of the body as a means of expression. An article published in the *Sydney Morning Herald* in 1959, shortly after Gertrud Bodenwieser's death, noted that:

> She based the choreography of all her dances on normal human posture and translated dramatic subjects, emotions and thoughts into movement without a stylised code. The dancers' bodies from their hair down to their bare feet had to be their sensitive, fully controlled instruments.[21]

Michaelis's images represent a sensitive engagement with and endorsement of this credo. She emphasised the dancers' physicality – their power and vigour rather than their femininity, as is usually the case in dance photography – choosing to picture them in mid-action rather than in stereotypical static poses. Compared with the photographs of the Bodenwieser dancers taken by Noel Rubie, Max Dupain, Kerry Dundas and other Sydney photographers, Michaelis's are more dynamic, earthier and less glamorous.

Margaret Michaelis's collaboration with the Bodenwieser troupe began around 1940 with *Cain and Abel*, a dance-drama in which Bodenwieser's thesis was that goodness must eventually triumph, despite the 'tragedy of slain youth, of those that mourn'. Other dances Michaelis photographed were *Russian duo*

Encounter (Shona Dunlop and Hilary Napier in *Sea study*) c. 1947 50.0 × 40.2 cm

(1942), *Sea study* and *Exaltation* (both 1947), and *The imaginary invalid* (1950). The dancers regarded her work highly and some attended individual sittings. In MacTavish's estimation, Michaelis

> possessed a keen eye, and unlike so many photographers of dance under whom I suffered much during my performing days, Michaelis possessed that uncanny gift of perceiving a 'moment of truth'. In other words, she had the patience and the sensitivity to catch the picture at its rightful climax. Her aim was faultless.[22]

She was also especially sensitive to the quality of movement. According to Margaret Chapple, one of Bodenwieser's Australian-trained dancers, Michaelis could anticipate the climax of a movement and had 'a lovely feeling' for dance. Vera Goldman, another member of the troupe, described a session in which Michaelis 'made the most beautiful action photographs' of her that 'have remained unsurpassed, her technical skill, her vision – were superb'.[23] Michaelis's photograph of Shona Dunlop in midair was described as a fine action shot when it was published in *Pix* magazine in 1950.[24] As with her portraiture, Michaelis responded to the human form in a sculptural way, representing the dancers' bodies as dynamic accents within the composition.

At a time when much dance photography was shot on stage or in the studio where dancers held fixed poses, Michaelis was inventive about settings. She often photographed the dancers outdoors, in such venues as Centennial Park, the rock plateau above Bondi Beach, the Palm Beach sand hills and the Killara golf course. While this may have been prompted by the Ballet's occasional performances in parks and gardens, it also suggests a desire for greater freedom in the visual representations of sensations associated with dance.

For Margaret Michaelis the immediate postwar years of 1947–48 were good professionally. She produced some of her strongest work and achieved peer recognition, with five of her photographs being selected for the publication *Australian photography*. In the words of Hal Missingham, himself a photographer and later director of the Art Gallery of New South Wales, the prime consideration governing the selection from more than 700 submissions was 'those photographs that unmistakably pronounce themselves as PHOTOGRAPHS, that are not imitative of other graphic methods'.[25] Michaelis was the sole woman to receive recognition and was awarded a bronze plaque (designed by sculptor Lyndon Dadswell) for *In the barnyard*, an image she had taken in Europe. The gold plaque was awarded to Axel Poignant; the silver to Max Dupain, Laurence Le Guay and Hal Missingham; and other winners of the bronze were Geoffrey Powell, SH Lofts, John Lee, Paul Horn and William Buckle. In 1949 Michaelis was represented in an exhibition held by the Institute of Photographic Illustrators at the David Jones' Art Gallery in Sydney, which was also shown in Newcastle. The Institute had formed in 1947 with the aim of raising 'the standard of photography in Australia' and 'encouraging a creative approach in the use of the camera in advertising and illustration'.[26] She was the first and only female member, and exhibited alongside fellow émigré photographer Wolfgang Sievers.

Despite being a member of professional associations, Margaret Michaelis apparently had little to do with the photographic community and was disparaging about the work of Max Dupain and other photographers. In the words of Antonia Burgess, she saw herself as the only 'artistic photographer' in Sydney.[27] Russell Roberts was supportive of Michaelis's work, praising her as 'one for whom photography was not a means to an end, but an end in itself'. Olive Cotton admired the 'very individual, sensitive small portraits' that Michaelis presented in her showcase at street level in Castlereagh Street[28], but never met her.

Working in relative isolation, either on her own or with one assistant at most, Michaelis's circumstances did not lend themselves to proselytising. However, in an article titled 'Camera class', published in *The Australian Monthly* in 1951, she outlined her views on creative photography, which reflected key modernist concerns. She wrote:

> The first problem for you as a photographer is choice of subject. Then, by your decision on angle and lighting, you convey your own impression of the subject before you. In this way you introduce individuality and a quality of imagination essential for the making of a good photograph.

As she saw it, the challenge lay in transforming ordinary, even ugly subjects into a picture, 'not any picture, but one that you personally had the satisfaction of creating' and that would 'stimulate the imagination of the spectator'.[29]

I wouldn't want to argue that Margaret Michaelis transformed Australian photographic practice; I don't think she did. Though she might have desired otherwise, she operated in a very small area of the market – as an émigré, a woman, and a specialist in portraiture and dance photography. The span of Photo-studio from 1940 to 1952 is of itself highly significant: opening within a few months of the outbreak of World War II, when Sydney's leading male photographers had temporarily left the scene, and peaking around 1947 before they returned from war and resumed their professional careers.

Late in life Michaelis explained that the reason for the closure of Photo-studio was her failing eyesight. If this was so, it was contradicted by Russell Roberts's reference letter of that year, which recommended her to 'anyone requiring the services of an intelligent and excellent character with wide experience in the field of art photography'.[30] One-time assistant Antonia Burgess was also surprised by Michaelis's decision to close the studio given the strength and intensity of her commitment to her photographic practice. Other factors may well have been involved, including the small size of Michaelis's operation, and the dramatic and far-reaching reorganisation of the photographic industry that began to occur in the immediate postwar years. By the 1950s portraiture had lost its foothold, and advertising and illustration work had become a major industry; in Sydney, Laurence Le Guay was a dominant force in fashion photography and Max Dupain in architectural photography. Photojournalism was also emerging as a significant new area of practice.

Margaret Michaelis may not have transformed modernist photographic practice in Australia, but she did make an invaluable contribution. Along with other European émigrés and refugees – including Hans Hasenpflug (who initially worked in Sydney), and Helmut Newton, Wolfgang Sievers and Henry Talbot, all of whom were based in Melbourne – Michaelis's work was informed by her own background, training and experiences. It was the inescapable realities of exile and relocation that gave her portraiture and dance photography its particular inflexion. Unlike Max Dupain, Olive Cotton, Athol Shmith and other Australian-born contemporaries, Michaelis's practice did not proceed from a deep-rooted sense of home, place or nation. Instead, her photographs are distinguished by a quality of 'un-homeliness' that has parallels in the work of other émigré photographers, notably Sievers and Newton whose images could have been produced anywhere in the developed world. Margaret Michaelis may never have anticipated it herself, but her contribution is such that it has helped re-shape our notions of modernist photography in Australia, making them richer and far more complex.

15 THE DARK CHAIR

Margaret Michaelis often took personal photographs during the 1940s and early 1950s, printing up the small black-and-white prints in her darkroom at Photo-studio. Her main subjects were her friends and their social gatherings. Those photographed are usually unnamed, and so are now unknown to me. An exception, however, is an image of a smiling, middle-aged couple identified as 'Mr and Mrs Wasserman', whom Michaelis pictured in the sitting room of their home in Wahroonga, probably in the late 1940s. It is a lovely interior view of a room filled with books, works of art and antique furniture, with light pouring in through glass doors opening onto the garden. After his retirement from the Philips company Mr Wasserman, a Dutch émigré, worked from home as a psychoanalyst. Suffering from depression, Michaelis was one of his patients and saw him regularly throughout the years she lived in Sydney.

The companion to this photograph is especially interesting; another interior view, possibly of the same room, it is inscribed on the reverse 'The dark chair'. Michaelis photographed interiors quite often – the flats she shared with Michel in Berlin, rooms in different places in which she lived in Barcelona and Sydney, and a room in her home in Melbourne around 1970 (a close-up view of shelves laden with carefully arranged and treasured things). The reasons for taking these photographs varied – the emphasis could be on the dynamics between the people represented, on objects, or on the room itself and its ambience. In this room in Mr Wasserman's home, which suggests itself as the place where he saw his patients, there are no people and, as Margaret Michaelis's metaphorical title signals, this is no documentary photograph. The focus of attention is two empty chairs – the armchair at the left of the composition presumably being 'the dark chair' in which Margaret sat and at the right Mr Wasserman's chair, positioned strategically next to his desk. What fills the room, however, is not these material objects but something far less tangible: a charged psychic space and the low murmur of voices.

The dark chair, Bundurra Rd, Wahroonga, Sydney c. 1945–48 8.8 × 12.8 cm

Michaelis's use of metaphor in *The dark chair* is extremely unusual, indicative not only of the psychological difficulties she was experiencing at the time (and continued to experience throughout her life) but also of her desire to give visual representation to a particular state of mind. She took this psychological dimension much further in her remarkable self-portrait entitled *14 June 1948, Parramatta River, Sydney (self-portrait)*. In contrast to *The dark chair* this melancholic image was brought to completion as a public statement, enlarged to a scale suitable for exhibition and beautifully printed.

The mouth of the Parramatta River, represented as a godforsaken semi-industrial wasteland, is a most peculiar setting for a self-portrait. Michaelis stands alone at the river's soggy edge, the looming foreground marked with the debris of its tidal wash, footprints and puddles. She does not face the camera, offering herself up for scrutiny as one would expect in a self-portrait, but poses with her back to the camera. Because her face is barely visible in profile it is her body that functions as the main physiognomic marker. Posed very deliberately, she directs her gaze out of the frame towards a view that offers no prospect of beauty, idealisation or escape. The image, resonant with metaphor, is also highly resolved in formal terms, with the positioning of Michaelis's form at the right-hand side of the composition and the effective mirroring of shapes and counterbalancing of light and dark tones.

What Michaelis was thinking about at the time she took this self-portrait – or indeed what she spoke about in *The dark chair* – can never be known (shortly before his death Mr Wasserman confirmed only that he had regularly seen Margaret). But surely it is no coincidence that these images were taken not long after the war had ended, when more information about the Holocaust was becoming public. By then Margaret had begun the excruciatingly slow process of finding out what had happened to members of her family, her friends, and those in her and Michel's circle. Sometimes details were years in coming; Michel's letters in the early 1970s, for instance, finally brought her up to date with information about the lives of friends and acquaintances they had known in Berlin and Barcelona forty years earlier.

In professional terms, in the late 1940s Michaelis was at her peak, having built up her business from scratch, secured a solid clientele and achieved peer recognition. As her personal photographs from this period indicate she did enjoy a social life, albeit limited, joining her mainly émigré friends in their musical activities and spending time outdoors hiking, picnicking and skiing. However, none of this could assuage her deep-seated feelings of loneliness; in a radio interview in 1979 she cited this as her greatest problem during her early

14 June 1948, Parramatta River, Sydney (self-portrait) 29.5 × 36.8 cm

years in Australia. When she arrived in Sydney Michaelis had known only one couple from her home town (they had emigrated before her), whom she saw infrequently; aside from them she was completely on her own. For the first eight or so years she had to deal with unsympathetic rented accommodation that exacerbated her solitariness and her feelings of 'a very, very sharp loneliness'.[1] On Christmas day in 1954, while other people were enjoying festivities with families and loved ones, Margaret Michaelis was on her own, pouring out her feelings in the written piece she titled 'The void'. There she described at some length the loneliness that was engulfing her and her anguish in pretending that 'business was as usual' when, as she described it, the muscles in her jaws were cramped because she had not spoken 'for hours, for months, and in fact for years from the sources of my real being'.

What one sees in Michaelis's work, in a career that spanned Europe and Australia, is the profound sense of loss and dislocation associated with migration. Rather than comprising a single body of work, her European and Australian photographs form two distinct groups that are worlds apart. The main thread tying them together is Michaelis's interest in people – she made very few excursions into other genres, such as landscape or abstract photography – but the ways in which she pictured people and the effects she achieved are significantly different. Her European photographs, particularly those taken for the GATCPAC in the Barrio Chino in Barcelona, have a collective energy. They are social pictures, underpinned by Michaelis's connection to her subject and to a particular community. Taken mostly outdoors and often in the street, they are filled with people and action, the compositions characterised by their spontaneity and fluidity.

Viewed alongside her European work, the majority of Margaret Michaelis's Australian photographs are inward- rather than outward-looking, with states of interiority and introspection being most valued. Invariably taken inside her Castlereagh Street studio, they are tightly controlled pictures in which all individual elements – the subject's pose, gesture and expression, lighting, and background – are attended to. Here life is stilled: it is quietly and conscientiously reined in. This is not to say that the Australian photographs are less successful than their European counterparts, but rather that they are different, the outcomes of two distinct, separate orders of experience.

Within this context Michaelis's dance photography assumes a greater significance because, like the style of Bodenwieser's dance itself, it is more expressionistic. As descriptors of movement, Michaelis's dance photographs engage with flux and a degree of unpredictability that was not available in

Study of Margaret Chapple c. 1947–50 11.8 × 8.8 cm

Study of dancer on cliff top c. 1947–50 20.6 × 16.5 cm

studio portraiture, advertising or her other main areas of professional activity. Her dance photographs were effectively her passage to another world where she could let herself go, revelling in the dancers' extremes of movement and their expressive intensity. This may well explain why some of Michaelis's most memorable dance photographs were taken at the moment when the dancers are airborne, suspended improbably and exuberantly in the sky. Dance photography also offered Michaelis the possibility of dealing with rapture, capturing dancers in a state of self-absorption and full immersion in their extravagant actions.

On the rare occasion when Michaelis's European photographs were published in Australia, in 1942 and 1947, their European origins were made invisible or trivialised. In a double-page spread in the *Australia* journal of 1942, her photograph of a group of children in the Barrio Chino, identified only as *Street children*, was published opposite her image of one of the gargoyles on the Notre Dame Cathedral in Paris. The caption running beneath the images reads 'Ooh ... Isn't he rude? Poking out his tongue at us!'

The split in Margaret Michaelis's pre- and post-emigration photography is especially poignant but is by no means unusual. Many European émigrés who settled in the United States in the wake of World War II faced similar experiences and, as is to be expected, responded in hugely different ways. A pertinent example is Hungarian-born photographer André Kertész, who produced his strongest work in Paris during the late 1920s and 1930s, and who in 1936 moved to New York, originally on a short-term basis. Forced to remain in the United States after the outbreak of war, Kertész suffered a complete breakdown in 1941; this was around the time he was designated an enemy alien and was prevented from taking photographs in the street. The commercial work he produced in the United States after the war – for publishers Condé Nast, *House and Garden* magazine and others – was 'mechanical, impersonal and he hated it all'.[2] Fellow photographer Brassaï summed up Kertész's situation, as he saw it, in 1963: 'Transplanted to a setting which was unfavourable to his nature and forced to earn a living, he did not find his true path but only – and much later – material success'.[3]

While André Kertész was one who never successfully bridged his European and American experiences, remaining acrimonious towards his adopted home to the end of his life, Margaret Michaelis enjoyed a positive relationship with her new home country. As she explained in her letter to Michel in 1974, Australia gave her '35 years of peace and the opportunity to build up a new existence'. Although she found that 'it wasn't easy to understand the Australian mentality, which is so totally different to ours', she was appreciative of the differences, citing as an example the appeals for help made in newspapers or in radio broadcasts during times of personal catastrophe, such as flood and bushfire, and the public's overwhelmingly generous response in such situations. She also remarked to Michel that 'Australians are gradually coming to accept the immigrants. Both the Europeans ... [and] the many Asian people'.

When Margaret Michaelis closed Photo-studio in 1952, at the age of fifty, photography had been at the centre of her life for more than thirty years. Her photographic career was her lifeline, connecting her European and Australian experiences. Though she had spoken of her dream 'to take a caravan, a camera, and a notebook in order to discover Australia ... and especially the life of the Aborigines', retirement was not an option. She had to earn an income and considered herself extremely fortunate to secure a job in the area of social work; her employers were the British-born Richard Hauser, who had arrived in Sydney in 1951 to take up a position with the New South Wales government, and pianist Hephzibah Menuhin, who had recently left her Australian husband, Lindsay Nicholas, for Hauser.[4] For the next two years Michaelis worked with the couple and she was responsible for typing up their research, filing and other administrative duties. It was an environment she found stimulating – 'I spent hours after work reading one report after another and getting [an] insight into their work and their way of thinking' – and she held them in very high esteem. Their way of life was similarly regarded as exemplary by violinist Yehudi Menuhin, Hephzibah's brother, who later wrote of their work in England that 'not only are they devoted to their fellow men, but they express devotion in the most practical, humane and real ways'.[5]

Hephzibah Menuhin, whom Yehudi remarked 'put all her heart and energy' into her social work with Hauser, had the qualities Margaret Michaelis admired in full measure.[6] She was unconventional in her personal life and radical in her political views as an advocate of women's rights and social justice; in 1975 she visited Australia and gave a public address as part of International Women's Year. When Hephzibah Menuhin died in 1981 Michaelis wrote an informal appreciation, which I found amongst her papers; in it she noted that Menuhin's thoughts and views had been a source of 'great delight and an inspiration'.

Michaelis's work with Menuhin and Hauser was fitting because of its socio-political emphasis and her own keen sense of social justice. She later recounted in a letter to Michel that she was involved with a group in Sydney that was active in

> the poor quarter. We invited children from the streets, we played with
> them, and let them work with clay and paint. I had a group where
> we sang and I accompanied them on the guitar. We performed a
> modern opera by Benjamin Britten: 'Let's do an opera.' That was with
> teenagers under 20, who would otherwise be on the streets.

In addition, she worked with Aboriginal children and, as her later letters to Michel demonstrated, remained interested in Aboriginal issues in the decades to come. On a visit to Canberra in 1972 she photographed the newly created Aboriginal Tent Embassy, outside Parliament House, placing the snapshots in one of her photograph albums. She also participated in a demonstration against Australia's involvement in the Vietnam War, telling Michel that 'It was an imposing impression. Around me were students, mothers, even with small children, young people, clergy, and many old people too'. She took heart from the collective action, believing that it contributed directly to the withdrawal of Australian soldiers and the end of the war.

Throughout her life Michaelis remained sympathetic to the position of the outsider and especially the migrant in Australian society. In 1979 she recalled a conversation she had had some twenty years earlier with an Australian man who had labelled Italians 'dagos'. Determined 'to make him aware ... that this is one of those prejudices that can only bring unpleasantness and pain' she spoke to him at some length until he eventually 'got up, stretched out his hand to shake my hand' and assured her that he would no longer use the word dago. From this small victory she anticipated a broader effect, saying that 'I think he goes home and tells a story and tells it probably to a neighbour and then somebody else is aware that the word dago is insulting'.[7]

On 3 March 1960 Margaret Michaelis married Albert George Sachs in the Temple Beth Israel in St Kilda, Melbourne. According to a friend, Michaelis probably met Sachs in Sydney through his brother, and moved to Melbourne to be with him. A Viennese-born émigré and a Jew, Sachs was sixty years old at the time of their marriage and had been recently widowed. Michaelis, who listed her occupation on the marriage certificate as a secretary, was fifty-seven. Sachs was a reasonably successful businessman who owned two businesses in Chapel Street, South Yarra, one selling second-hand furniture, the other a glass and framing shop. Mrs Sachs's friends remembered Albert Sachs as a taciturn man who felt disappointed with life, largely because of his failure to achieve recognition for his considerable intellectual effort. His background was in philosophy and his philosophical text 'Space, time and madness: the philosophy of non-anthropiatic idealism' was copyright registered on 21 December 1948 in Australia, but was apparently never published.

Following their marriage Margaret and Albert Sachs settled in the comfortable suburb of Windsor, Melbourne. She assisted her husband in his work, directing her attention to the framing side of their business. The couple obviously had much in common: they were both Jewish, Austrian-born and had been forced into exile from Europe by the rise of fascism. They also shared an interest in high culture, whether related to philosophical thought, music or the visual arts. And yet Albert Sachs is a shadowy figure in the Archive. Margaret, it seems, took very few photographs either of him or their life together. When he does appear it is his unsmiling, stern demeanour and frailty that are most notable; Margaret is far more robust in the contemporaneous photographs of her.

Five years after they were married, Albert Sachs died from a heart attack. As in the past on a few significant occasions, Margaret turned to a photograph to give her account of what had happened. She chose a photograph taken a few months earlier in which a weary Albert Sachs is seated on a couch between Margaret and an unidentified woman. On the back, in German, she wrote: 'Last and best photo of Albert. He died 30.9.65, 7.30 am. Heart attack – wanted to call the doctor and on the way to the telephone in the next room I found him lying on the carpet'.

16   FORTY-EIGHT PHOTOGRAPHS

From 1967 to 1968 the recently widowed Mrs Sachs embarked on an extensive overseas trip that took her to Europe, Israel and the Middle East, the United States, South America, and various countries in Asia, including India. During her stay in Germany she visited Michel and his wife Marianne in East Berlin – how this came to pass isn't known, as there is a thirty year gap in the correspondence between Grete and Michel in the National Gallery of Australia's Archive. Soon after her visit Grete and Michel began to write to each other again; she sent him letters from Greece and Spain, to which he responded on 28 October 1967. Their re-establishment of contact was, however, fraught with tension. Michel's October letter is terse and belligerent and, not surprisingly given its tone, it was four years before Grete replied.

In his letter Michel took the moral high ground in both personal and political matters, contrasting his own politics and those of the German Democratic Republic with Grete's, which he found sorely wanting. He opened with an indignant outburst against the countries Grete had chosen to visit, writing:

> I am amazed by the consistency of your stamps! The Greek stamps on your airmail letter come from a now suppressed country. If it were only the stamps that were suppressed! In one country, and in the other [Spain], a handful of military people against whom you can do nothing ...

> Also in Israel, where you will be in about three weeks, an imperial system rules which is about to lead the Jewish people into the abyss. You can see that as soon as the winners have tasted the magic of power, even if it is the Jews, they all become the same. Have a good look around when you are there! Maybe then you will better understand the Arabic movement.

Michel's pointed criticism of Grete's lack of political understanding echoes comments he had made decades earlier in one of his letters from Warka, where he took issue with her response to a political lecture she had attended. Then he had regarded her account of the lecture as being suitable only for 'a provincial newspaper, not in a letter. The former is not enough, neither for you nor me', he had written in 1931. In Michel's eyes, it wasn't only that Grete, now middle-aged, had failed to develop 'a healthy class consciousness' but, even worse, that she had made the wrong life choices. He berated her for having 'turned to a false apprenticeship', presumably through her involvement in photography and the arts, and condemned her for having had nothing to do with either philosophy or dialectical materialism. However, what seems to upset him most was a far more recent event: Grete's visit to Spain, which as a resident of the communist East Germany was not an option available to him.

> If I had known that your next journey was to be there I would not have been shy about asking you for a favour. I still have some friends in Barcelona, who during the long years of imprisonment – now I can say it – saved my life ... If the Spanish comrades had not helped me I would not be writing these lines now. Oh well! Since returning to Germany, we have not kept in contact. I have been scared of writing, as a letter from me might only harm them. But a greeting, through you, might have been a possibility to let them know how close I still feel to them.

In a flood of contradictory emotions and memories he grudgingly conceded that he was jealous of Grete's opportunity to see Spain again and 'the beautiful Spanish countryside'. If there was to be any solace for him it was in the German Democratic Republic's 'moral and material solidarity' with 'the fighting Spanish people', which he elaborated on in some detail.

Mid-way through his letter Michel paused for a moment, exclaiming 'Let's stop this lecture, which I would never have believed I would have to give you', but it was not until his closing paragraph that he made any real, though tokenistic acknowledgment of Grete and her contemporary life. He concluded 'I have to say hello from everyone. We have great memories of you. When you are reading these lines in February in Melbourne, the beautiful autumn and nearly the whole winter will have gone. We will have seen what has happened in this world by then!'

However, it is his final line – 'Stay healthy and say hello to your husband' – that is most revealing. On her visit to East Berlin, and in all of her subsequent correspondence, Grete gave Michel every reason to believe that her late husband, Albert Sachs, was still alive. From those who knew Mrs Sachs I have heard two different accounts of her reasons for this: the first was that she did not want to arouse any feelings of jealousy in Michel's wife Marianne, which might have been the case if it was known she was a widow. The second explanation was that Mrs Sachs's own feelings of jealousy would have been the issue because she would have been envious of Michel's familial situation and therefore keen to cover up her own lack in this regard (Michel and Marianne had four children). Perhaps both of these claims are true. They certainly do not preclude the possibility of there being another reason for Mrs Sachs's small deception, which I find more compelling – that is, her own feelings for Michel and her desire to protect herself from them. The continued allusion of being part of a couple may have given her the strength she needed, the mask for her vulnerability.

When Grete eventually responded to Michel's letter four years later, on 2 October 1971, she specifically addressed its contents, obviously writing her letter with his in front of her. She adopted a conciliatory tone, inviting him to give him the addresses of his Spanish friends so that she could attempt to contact them on his behalf and send them a package of food or clothes. She also went to some length to counter his criticism of her and to attempt to bridge their apparent ideological differences by explaining her own philosophy of life. What she wrote, well crafted and honed towards Michel's political concerns, reads like a personal manifesto:

> I have looked ... everywhere in the world with open eyes. As far as possible I try to create an objective picture. One day these periods of history will be absorbed and the real events will become clearer. I would like to talk to you about this and all the other problems of the world, even though prejudice for or against would hardly [enable us to] come to a mature agreement. I have lived here for more than 30 years. The older I get, the more important one thing becomes for me, for a pure and healthy view of the world; an upright way of life, free from prejudice, with tolerance and love for the weak, who are today already in their millions, who suffer and die. I have learnt that the small and the weak countries are toys for the so-called higher political orders that will stop at nothing. We get newspapers, books from all around the world and I read them with all their contradictions, I learn to understand them and interpret them.

> ... Each day it becomes clearer that the entire globe is in danger of
> ending up in an unsalvageable chaos. Overpopulation, millions who
> the world will soon be unable to sustain, and at the same time the
> poisoning of nature ... Scientists all around the world are trying to
> find a solution. If lack of responsibility or stupidity do not lead to the
> outbreak of a nuclear war, I believe that self-preservation will lead to
> the world powers signing a joint non-aggression pact. There are small
> signs appearing, which show that the world powers on both sides are
> beginning to learn that respect for life, and respect for the freedom of
> ordinary people is a much better policy.

Like Michel, Grete adopted a way of writing that is distanced and lacking in
intimacy. While there are obvious differences in their approaches – his is more
spontaneous and hers more considered (the result of having to draft her letter
in English before translating it into German), his tone is more aggressive and
hers more even – the outcome is the same. Their words build up a screen of
self-justification and self-protection that blocks out the possibility of a more
emotional kind of exchange.

In her letter Grete apologised for her delay in replying, explaining that it was
caused by Albert's ill-health. Elaborating on the pretence she gave an extended
description of her late husband's medical problems and his miraculous recovery
following sophisticated surgery overseas. In its immediacy and specificity her
account is convincing, even though Albert had died six years before.

> The grounds for my long silence are due to Albert and I having only
> just gotten over a hard time. Albert had to go through two more eye
> operations. Firstly a detached retina operation on the left eye and a
> couple of months later on his right eye. On both occasions it was a
> worry as to whether the doctor could rescue his sight. After months
> of great concern, something happened which we viewed as a miracle,
> both eyes could see again and were coordinated. Albert had to fly to
> Boston in America for the first operation as the necessary technology
> and knowledge was not available here at that time. There are only,
> as they told us, 4–5 professors who are able to operate on the retina
> successfully. That is – in the whole world.

Towards the end of the letter Grete referred once more to Albert, whom she
said 'has finally given up his business ... and is now working on his philosophical
work'. She also wrote of their common interests – 'We like the same music,
share the same political ideas and hopes' – and of her own interests in the visual

arts – 'I draw and paint and make slow progress, go often to exhibitions, which I cannot let Albert go to! He remained stuck in the Renaissance'. With this accidental and unchecked slip of tense, and on this one occasion only, Albert's death was made evident. In her next letter, however, Grete reported that 'we are now more or less healthy' and sends 'heartfelt greetings from us both'.

In late 1973 the tenor of Grete and Michel's correspondence changed dramatically because of what proved to be a highly significant event in each of their lives: Michel's discovery of Grete's once-buried photographs in the possession of their friend Carl Buttke. This discovery ushered in a new phase in their correspondence and defined the final stage of their relationship. Between 1973 and 1975 Michel wrote four letters that Mrs Sachs kept, along with two, possibly three drafts of her own letters to him written in 1974 after receiving the photographs. Her drafts are in English, suggestive of her loss of fluency with their shared language, and also of her desire to ensure that she expressed herself clearly.

In these last letters the self-defensiveness each had worn like a shield was finally dropped and a different kind of discourse emerged, driven by Michel's desire for redemption, which only Grete could give. In the long, four-page letter that accompanied the package of photographs he abandoned his characteristic recriminations and belligerent tone and wrote with great tenderness. Endearments to Grete, to his 'dear Gretl', run through the letter like a refrain and he signed off with the affectionate phrase 'Your old Michel' in contrast to the cool, distanced 'Greetings, Michel' of his earlier correspondence.

The photographs, whose existence, discovery and effect are so totally unexpected, opened up the past for Michel in a way that nothing else had done. It is not that they picture their shared life – they date from the 1920s, before they had even met – but that they were hers in the fullest sense of the word. As a consequence, Grete materialised in his consciousness as a former partner in a relationship and as an individual with particular strengths. For the first time in his later correspondence Michel praised her for being 'much cleverer than I, you already saw our defeat in 1937', and for making a useful social contribution to society through her volunteer social work. Of this he wrote 'You, who have not been hit by blindness, recognise and change the world too'.

The photographs brought Michel face to face with another dualistic experience; as they released memories of their shared past they reminded him simultaneously of how much he had forgotten. Grete therefore emerged as the repository of memories of their shared experiences, and as such represented the means by which Michel might restore his own, and indeed their own, past.

Young person leaning
against tree trunk
c. 1920–25 5.2 × 8.0 cm

Young woman in long
dress standing in field
1923 7.2 × 5.6 cm

The highly emotional process of recovery and restoration led Michel to a significant realisation. Not only did he want to know the past better, he also wanted to make peace with it. Central to this process was reconciliation with Grete, though the exact form it might have taken was yet to be determined. Michel gently felt his way through the process, outlining their differences (of thoughts, opinions and outlook) and conceding that in part they were the outcome of their divergent experiences and circumstances. At the same time he drew attention to their common ground, signalling what he had come to appreciate as their equality when he wrote that neither of them 'has more emotional strength than the other'. He carefully chose words such as interplay and exchange to underscore his desire for what he termed 'mutual understanding'.

This brought Michel to the emotional crux of his letter. In giving form to his notion of mutual understanding he created a space for genuine reciprocity – at this point he made himself most vulnerable and Grete, now recognised as having agency, became most real. He expressed his hope that they could lay aside their differences and 'the prejudices and judgments remaining from other times [that] make understanding harder'. And he continued:

> I cannot avoid the fact that I am very much to blame. I must have caused you much sorrow during the time of our joint life, due to my egocentric way of looking at things and my actions. Perhaps you have forgiven me a long time ago. But I ask you to once again grant me absolution. Remember the beautiful hours together, and it will be easier.

This is Michel's epiphany. On the simplest level it represents his acceptance of culpability – in relation to the shortcomings in his own behaviour and actions during their relationship, as well as his role in their break-up. But it goes much deeper. His desire for Grete's forgiveness was, in effect, a declaration of her importance in his life. It was also something that I finally came to recognise as a sign of equivalence: if Michel was the love of Grete's life, then she too was the love of his.

48 Photos included

Rudolf Michaelis
1197 Berlin DDR [GDR]
Hagedornstrasse 72

Dear Gretl,

Two years ago you wrote to me in your letter from 2 October 1971: 'It has been more than 3 years since I received your letter upon my return to Melbourne.' So the years pass, and we change with them. When I think back, that already six years have passed since you came over to us, I ask myself whether these lines and the packet I am sending in the same post will also reach you. All the same I am taking up our exchange of letters again. 'Lo que no acaece en un año acaece en un rato', say the Spanish. Which I will Germanise: What doesn't take place in a year happens in the blink of an eye.

As it sometimes is, a word, a song, a letter, a photograph – they wake memories. In my very concrete case, it was words and written material, actually 48 (forty-eight) photos from your earlier workplace. Portraits from – if I have correctly understood it – your time in Vienna as well as your first employment in Berlin. If you like 'excavated' from Carl Buttke's house.

Do you still remember him? Edith, a little rotund, upright and brave Jew, belonged like Jussef and Marianne to the 'Volkerballmannschaft' [Peoples Ball Team], which held games at the Gruenewald Lake. Edith was his wife. Was. As that which the Nazis didn't achieve with her was done by cancer: she died after long suffering a few years ago. She remembered you fondly, and felt that she was bound to you. Today Carl is living with his two daughters in Berlin-Hahnsdorf, in a beautiful house at the edge of the forest. The first-born, Gabriele – in order to sketch some of the details that should show the degree of closeness of our then relationship to this family – is now sleeping with her newly married husband on the same bed that served us in Wilmersdorf. We must have given a whole lot of things to this family when we started our trip to Spain. A few questions concerning this later.

However, I continue: Last weekend Carl Buttke brought your 48 photos to my home. We admired your style of that time in each photo. So for a long time you became the centre of our conversation. The end result on my part was to send you, 'the only woman member of the Institute of Photographic Illustrators', these photos from your youth, which I do herewith.

While on this topic, I think it is important to mention that the packet you mentioned in your letter of 2 October 1971, which should contain 'the promised copies of the poems and the dates of the excavation in Babylon and possibly a book with pictures of our birds and trees', has still not arrived.

And now to the questions, which I would not need to ask you were there not a lot of holes in my memory. For a long time there were whole sections of my life that were totally erased, and it was necessary to have a direct prompt in order to retrieve that which was lost again. I am not referring to the type of memory weakness that is associated with increasing age. No. In my case it is almost certainly related to the five years that I spent in prison in Barcelona, the first three years of which were spent turning me into a skeleton. Additional to the hunger, were the continual beatings that were carried out until consciousness was lost, interrogations with the Falangist police and the Gestapo, in which one would always answer with 'I know nothing' and 'no, no, and once more no'. Over time you really didn't know any more, even the names of your best comrades and fighting companions would be lost. And this has continued up until today. This should explain the situation to you.

So how was it then, at the end of 1933? I came out of the Alex. What a miracle! And so I escaped the concentration camp. Upon my return to Germany I looked up Professor Andrae, who is also long dead, and he said to me that he had tried to get my freedom, through a friend of Goerring's, which then caused him considerable trouble with the Gestapo at the end of the Spanish War. But that doesn't concern me at the moment. So we traveled at the end of 1933 to Spain. During my imprisonment in the Alex you had prepared everything. You had disposed of our possessions. Some of them went to Jussef, others to the Buttkes. Were they given, or were they sold? I know nothing of that. Books, photo collections, the silver eggcups, which I brought for you from Baghdad, and what else was there? Carl Buttke and Marianne are the only ones from our then group of acquaintances who, through some miracle, were able to rescue everything from the Nazi time. In Marianne's case it is not really surprising. She was not in danger for either political or racist reasons. But in Buttke's case: they buried everything that was suspicious, in crate loads buried under the earth. After the annihilation of the Nazis they dug everything up again. This is how Carl is in possession of an enviable book collection, which contains books by Thomas Mann, Siegmund Freud and classic editions, which during the post-war period were gradually republished and some were never republished. Sometimes I borrow a book from this collection. On such a visit Carl's daughter Gabriele spoke of your photographs, which were still in her father's possession. Of course I insisted that they be given back so that I could send them to you.

Perhaps you could remember other things that Carl could possibly have in his protection. He doesn't like to get things out. I already know that! Over his seventy years he has developed, in particular areas a certain stinginess, something that one would really not expect from him. But I was able, with the help of his daughter Gabriele, to tear your photos away from him. This work will surely mean more to you than to the amateur archivist Carl Buttke. Even though I can understand why one would not willingly let such good photos go.

But which things have we not had to part from over the course of our lives. I was able to rescue nothing.

I can see, dear Gretl, that I am giving too much detail, and I am losing myself in the breadth. But when will I write to you again?
The continents in which we live are in reality separated by many oceans and countries. What do we know here, about Australia?
Only very little news comes from there to us. For a while, after your visit with us, I collected everything that came from your chosen home to us through our German press. Actually there was a considerable number of newspaper articles, ethnographic, geographical, political, yes and there are also a number of books that contain information about Australia, both the old and the new. But then I gave up. Europe and South America were more to my taste. Forgive me, I don't in any way want to hurt your feelings of belonging to your new home. Just as you must excuse me: I have only a small connection with 'the famous "Bar of Tenoro"' or the Spanish gypsy camp; neither the classical Greek constructions nor the temperamental dance of the Chilean Huasos, the Chueca, move me. It is then a Luis-Corvalaln-Cueca! It was said at the Xth World festival of the youth and students in Berlin (from 28 July until 5 August of this year) that the General Secretary of the Communist Party of Chile gracefully, mischievously and temperamentally danced this expressive dance as no other had.

Even then. Soon he will, if we are unable to save his life, dance his dance of death, which is being prepared by the murderous Junta. Allende murdered, and Pablo Neruda driven to his death. My entire sympathy to Chile and the Unidad Popular. My sympathy to the students in Greece revolting against the terror of the leaders. If a place in Barcelona comes to mind it is the Café Espanol on the Paralelo, the meeting place of the CNT–FAI, and the best militants, Durruti, Ascaso and Javier among others. When I think of Spain, I think of my friends, who along with me stormed the first position of Franco's Soldiers.

So we follow our own impressions in very different ways to the same object, and neither has more emotional strength than the other. In any case there exists an interplay between emotion and rational search between us. But with the exchange of our thoughts and opinions there appear to be very different outlooks. Different work and fighting places result in different viewpoints. Prejudice and judgements remaining from other times make understanding harder. To exchange experiences and memories does not simply mean representing those that were present as present, rather though conversation and recording, and taking part in saying goodbye to your own past.

In reaching this realisation, I cannot avoid the fact that I am very much to blame. I must have caused you much sorrow during the time of our joint life, due to my egocentric way of looking at things and my actions. Perhaps you have forgiven me a long time ago. But I ask you to once again grant me absolution. Remember the beautiful hours together, and it will be easier.

I can still see us as we left the Barcelona Palace of Justice, and gave our kiss goodbye in the middle of the Paseo de San Juan. You left Spain and I hurried back to the Aragon front. We parted forever as married people. I don't know what you felt then. I ran to the end of the wide street and strode from one side to the other of the brick Arche de Triumph and thought to myself that this was the same number of meters as I was old: 30. T h i r t y! Turning point in human existence. Death, I said to myself, hits you in the back, if you run from it. Forward! To your place in the fight against fascism and for freedom. Then everything seemed so simple to me.

Certainly you were much cleverer than I, you already saw our defeat in 1937, which actually took place two years later. But this defeat was still a victory. Perhaps not for the Spanish people, but for the people of a large part of Europe, for some of the people of Africa and Latin America. Chile too became socialist despite the terror of the fourth Soldeska. The course of history, which we and not the capitalists determine, cannot be held back …

And now to finish off, dear Gretl, a little more about us. We are all pretty healthy. And we are all happy. The children are growing. The 'oldies' are happy. We are nibbling the fruits near to us from the table of our Republic. We are practicing solidarity. What else could we want?

You, you dear Gretl, and your Albert, we wish you beautiful days. Such luck that his sight has held. May he have a clear view and philosophise on the Marxist theory opposing Feurback: 'It is not about interpreting the world in different ways, rather to change it.' You, who have not been hit by blindness, recognise and change the world too. Perhaps through your volunteer social work, the party steps in for the poor, and such is the content of your life.

With lots of love from us all.

Your old Michel.

17   REDEMPTION

Five months after her lost photographs and Michel's long letter arrived out of the blue, Grete wrote to thank Michel. In doing so, she struggled through two, possibly three drafts so that it is not clear exactly which one she eventually sent. What she wrote is relatively open and generous in spirit; she entered into the exchange of fragments from the past initiated by Michel, returning some of his early archaeological reports and poems, photographs of the interior of their flat in Berlin, and her memories of events that he could no longer recall.

In her April letter, for Michel's benefit, Grete also retraced the path her own life had taken after their parting in Spain in 1937. She told him – and this was obviously the first he had heard of it – how it was that she had come to settle in Australia:

> You spoke of my chosen home. Well I came to Australia, as I – through some miracle – was able to get a visa. At this time I was working in London as house help which was very heavy work. At almost the same time my brother wrote to me to say that he was just about to receive my visa. But I decided to go to Australia. Only in 1967, when I was in Brazil, could I see how right it was that I went to Australia. You could say so much, you could even have an opinion about some things. Does it have to remain unsaid what Australia means to me? Among other things it gave me 35 years of peace and the opportunity to build up a new existence.

While Grete's letter conveys a newfound sense of openness towards Michel, her relationship with their past is nevertheless more qualified than his. She wrote carefully, wary of giving away too much, as though she was reluctant to dig too deep. Instead she focused on the present, offering their contemporary lives as a point of connection (a strategy that had apparently failed them during their reunion in 1967). She sent Michel a parcel containing Australian pictorial material and photographs of her life 'with explanatory notes', and asked after his children: 'what they are doing, and what sort of outlook on life they have, and whether they have any special talents or characteristics'. Michel responded fulsomely in subsequent letters, giving details about the activities of his children and grandchildren. In 1975 he sent photographs of he and his wife that had been taken by a young woman photographer; the occasion of being photographed by her, he told Grete, 'reminded me to such an extent of you – she was as old as you were then – that I showed her some of your photographs. She approved of them'.

Michel's last letters also describe his growing interest in Australia, 'your distant land', clearly of significance only because of its association with Grete. In one of the volumes of pictures she had sent him not long before he noted that under the heading 'Australian birds and animals' there was a rosella, and continues that 'A beautiful rosella like that is watching me while I am writing'. His rosella, a sixty-fifth birthday present from his children,

> is sure to be a bird bred in this country who knows nothing of his
> original home. According to Shaw there are three species, one in
> eastern New South Wales, one in Victoria, and one in Tasmania and
> South Australia and eastern New South Wales ... And as if he knew
> that I am writing about him he climbs round his cage and whistles.

Although neither Michel nor Grete may have realised it at the time, her letter of April 1974 also offered some form of closure. It comes in a paragraph on the final page, a carefully considered response to Michel's apposite request for forgiveness. Mindful of what he had written and apparently also wishing to be reconciled with their past, Grete began by saying: 'Even though it wasn't easy, and many years weren't easy, I maintained a positive outlook that helped me in the hard times of life, to overcome sadness and uncertainty'. It may well have been tempting to have stopped there, her feelings well hidden in generalisations, but Grete decided otherwise. She entered into what had become their shared space – a space defined by their mutual desire for redemption – where she addressed Michel and Michel alone. What she told him is this:

> And so I could also make peace with you, and rescue that which
> was positive and beautiful, which still remains deep in my memory.
> And so it is possible for me to, as you wished, grant you absolution.

Grete signed off her letter as if Albert were still alive – 'With heartfelt greetings from us both' – but significantly added the line 'Your Grete', as she had been in their Warka days of the early 1930s. There is no evidence to suggest that she ever wrote to Michel again.

For Michel, however, the process had not yet ended. A few months later he wrote another letter, which is open and relaxed in style. He went further with his confidences and acknowledged his shortcomings. These were now heightened through direct comparisons with Grete. On matters of aesthetics, for example, he conceded that because he understood 'so little ... it may be better to keep silent'. Where he felt his inequality most acutely was in relation to his political beliefs. He concluded that she remained truer to herself than he 'who abandoned this and that or had to cast it off like a worn coat', a probable allusion to his conversion from anarchism – to which he had been so passionately committed in the 1930s – to communism when he began his life in the German Democratic Republic in the postwar years. (This late conversion, my translator suggested, probably made him suspect to communists and was the likely reason for his failure to obtain high-level appointments in East German society.)

Michel kept up his correspondence, writing again in 1974 and 1975, but Grete remained silent. Perhaps from her point of view they had gone as far as they could. Perhaps there was nothing more to say.

A few months ago I had one of those lucky breaks researchers dream about. It was so perfect that it's hard to believe it came about by chance – more fateful, I think, than fortuitous. I was referred to a woman, Mrs Antonia Burgess, who for eighteen months in the late 1940s had worked as Margaret Michaelis's assistant in Photo-studio, in Sydney. I visited her at her home in Glebe, and over afternoon tea we talked about Margaret and looked at copies of the photographs I had brought with me. Antonia's recollections about Margaret's professional practice were invaluable, but even more important for the shape this story has taken were her responses to the photographs I showed her of Michel from the early 1930s. She recognised him immediately, as Margaret Michaelis had shown her exactly the same images more than forty years earlier.

Aged only nineteen when she joined Photo-studio, Antonia had been mainly involved in clerical duties and so was apologetic about failing to recognise examples of Michaelis's commercial work from the late 1940s. From my perspective this hardly mattered; so much time had passed that I was not really expecting to come away with more details about dates and clients. However, what Antonia dismissed as her 'vagueness' had an entirely unanticipated and illuminating effect, for it threw into sharp relief the vividness of her other memories from this time, of Margaret Michaelis herself and of her relationship with Michel.

Even as a young woman Antonia said she recognised that Margaret, though 'a brilliant photographer', was 'not a terribly nice person'. She described her as being 'hard as nails, terribly opinionated, vain and egocentric' and outlined situations in which Margaret had been ungenerous and unfeeling towards her. I was amazed how passionately she still felt; her cheeks flushed as she spoke about one incident where she had fallen ill and Margaret had refused to offer her any assistance.

With great clarity Antonia then went on to tell me what I had not expected but what I really wanted to hear: how Margaret Michaelis had gone 'on and on' about Michel, how he loved and adored her, how theirs was a perfect romance, a great romance, *the* romance of the twentieth century. For Antonia, as for me years later, reconciling these facts with the reality of the couple's separation was difficult (though Margaret had led Antonia to believe that she and Michel were still married and was shocked at my disclosure that they had actually been divorced for ten years by the time she had met her). Perplexed by what she had been told, Antonia eventually asked Margaret to explain why she and Michel weren't together or, more exactly, why she had left Michel, for that was the impression Margaret had given her. Margaret's reply, Antonia told me, had stayed with her all this time – she was no longer with Michel 'because he had been jealous of her work, because he wanted her all for himself and because he suffocated her'.

During the afternoon Antonia made some other remarks that I thought about for many months. She described Margaret as being 'obsessed' with Michel, which particularly troubled me because of its negative connotations, suggesting a state of psychological extremism and emotional rigidity. I knew that Grete's feelings for Michel did not preclude the possibility of other relationships and friendships. Indications are that she did have other lovers; in Sydney, for example, some time between 1945 and 1947 she was involved with an American marine by the name of Jack. I say this on the basis of a small number of items in the National Gallery of Australia's Archive – a few photographs and a postcard of a drawing, Libra the scales, with the cryptic, handwritten inscription 'Why don't you write? A few lines! Just a word! So many months past. I am very much longing for you. I love you so much. So much as ever. If you would know! ... Jack'. The photographs include snapshots taken in Brisbane of a smiling

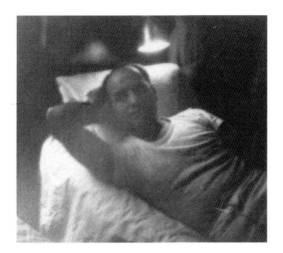

Jack, January 1945,
Brisbane 6.0 × 6.8 cm

Margaret, arm in arm with her dark-haired, uniformed companion. One other tiny photograph stands apart. I recognise it immediately as a photograph of a lover: a close-up of Jack lying on a bed, in a dark room, half lit by the lamp behind him. It is an intimate image in which he gazes into the camera lens and thereby into the eyes of the photographer, his lover.

During our conversation Antonia also made the comment that for Margaret Michel was some kind of 'fantasy'. With its associations of fluidity this appealed to me as a more useful notion than 'obsession' for understanding what Michel might have represented at different times in her life. However, whether he was an obsession, a fantasy, both or indeed neither of these, Margaret Michaelis's preoccupation with him in the late 1940s when Antonia came to know her makes perfect sense. This was when her experiences of trauma and loss were most acute; not only was she dealing with the ongoing loss of home, triggered by her exile in 1939, but she was now forced to face the actual, irrevocable loss of loved ones with the deaths of her parents and possibly other members of her extended family.

In the midst of enormous flux, the woefully incomplete present and a seemingly impossible future, perhaps only the lived-in concrete past offered a fixed point of reference. That the past, signified by Michel and their relationship, assumed so much importance is doubly poignant. Because of their lack of contact for years after the war, Michel himself became a virtual figment of Grete's imagination, an abstraction rather than a reality. All she knew – a snippet of information gleaned from correspondence with their mutual friend Marianne – was that he was alive and in Berlin. As for Grete and Michel's relationship, it was now abundantly clear to me that it was not only tumultuous but brief, lasting four years at best.

As Antonia talked I could hear echoes of my own conversations with Mrs Sachs and realised that what she had told me in the months before she died had been a well-rehearsed story. Antonia had heard it in its early, urgent stages – when a forty-five year old woman was driven to tell it over and over to her impressionable nineteen-year-old assistant – and I had heard it more than forty years later. The fact that the story's basic shape had not changed over the decades did not surprise me but the constancy and strength of the feelings behind it did. Antonia and I had each experienced this directly. I could still hear the tenderness with which Mrs Sachs had spoken to me about Michel; then as now it affected me palpably, like a physical sensation. It was obvious that her feelings for Michel, or rather for her relationship with Michel and whatever it represented, had never been buried deep. These feelings had permeated numerous conversations over the years, affirming with quiet insistence to anyone who was listening, how important Michel was in her life. Those of Mrs Sachs's friends who were familiar with her story described Michel to me as 'the love of her life', and their relationship as her most important, and her 'most intense love relationship'.

While listening to Antonia's recollections I unexpectedly found myself filled with admiration for Mrs Sachs. It came from the realisation that she had been incredibly tenacious and scrupulous in her care, not just of her memories of Michel but of her feelings for him. How closely and how tightly she had held them to her, and for how long.

There was one other significant outcome to our long afternoon conversation. Antonia helped me gain a clearer sense of Margaret's role as the narrator of her own life story, actively shaping her material and weaving lies and subterfuges into it. These lies – that she had left Spain expecting that her 'husband' would join her, that she and Michel were still married and, later, that Albert was alive though seriously ill – had always perplexed me. However, nudged by Luis Buñuel's observation that 'since we are all apt to believe in the reality of our fantasies, we end up transforming our lies into truths'[1], I now began to think about Margaret's lies in a different light. They were deceptions certainly, deliberately so, but they weren't constructed to cause harm. Instead, these lies were fashioned in good faith as a way of dealing with a range of complex psychological and emotional difficulties. It is not only their inventiveness that I have come to admire but I also now see them as necessary. They were the means by which Grete safeguarded her relationship with Michel, intense and flawed in reality, and yet greatly sustaining. Worthy of nourishing, even as fiction.

Circumstances had forced Margaret Michaelis to abandon her photographic career in 1952 but she remained involved in music and the visual arts, developing her skills in painting, drawing and later weaving. She maintained her interests in philosophy and became interested in spiritual matters; a non-observant Jew with many Jewish friends, she also explored the teachings of Buddhism (she visited Kathmandu on her extended travels in 1967 and kept a photograph of the Tibetan leader, the Dalai Lama, amongst her photographs from this trip). Dancer Vera Goldman, a friend of Michaelis's who stayed in contact with her after Albert Sachs's death, remembered 'that she – courageously – always was involved with learning new skills, going to lectures and so on'.[2] Albert Sachs's estate ensured her financial security, enabling her to travel widely in Australia and overseas.

Mrs Sachs was an early member of the Women's Art Register, established in Melbourne to promote the work of women artists and to provide a resource for the community. She submitted two slides of photographs she had taken in 1971 and 1973 and a brief handwritten biography that summarised her career:

> Diploma: Institute of Graphic Arts and Research, Vienna. Worked in studios in Vienna and Berlin, portrait and architecture ... Barcelona own studio. Main work with architects connected with Le Corbusier and Mees [sic] van der Rohe. The Civil War in Spain made work impossible. Reporter photographer Barcelona, Paris. Own studio in Sydney and Melbourne. Portraits, architecture, illustration. Only woman member of Institute of Photographic Illustrators, Sydney. Exhibitions Barcelona, Paris, Sydney, Newcastle, NSW. Bronze medal in connection with exhibition and publication Australian Photography: Ziegler, Gotham publication, Sydney.

This remarkable outline alerted the feminist art historians Barbara Hall and Jenni Mather to Michaelis's potential significance. She was subsequently selected for inclusion in their touring exhibition Australian Women Photographers 1890–1950, held in 1981, and the resultant book, *Australian women photographers 1840–1960*, published in 1986. On the basis of the photographs they had seen Mather and Hall contacted the National Gallery of Australia in Canberra, suggesting that Margaret Michaelis's work might be of interest as an addition to the collection of Australian photographs.

Shelves with books,
photographs and
personal items
c. 1970 8.0 × 11.7 cm

Throughout her life Mrs Sachs struggled with periods of depression. In 1983 she experienced what she described as a complete breakdown in physical and mental health, which precipitated the move from her own home to a retirement home for Jewish people, situated on St Kilda Road in Melbourne. There she spent the last two years of her life in a small, comfortable room with the last of her most valued possessions. Some of these were carefully arranged on her shelves and bench for visitors to see, but most were tucked safely away, hidden from sight.

18   VIENNA

By 1999 I had almost finished retracing Margaret Michaelis's steps in reverse order, a journey that had begun in Melbourne and taken me to Sydney, London, Barcelona and Berlin. The only place left to visit was Vienna, where the young Margarethe Gross had embarked on her photographic career more than eighty years previously. I felt it was important to have kept Vienna until last, to have established a system with an internal logic and consistency and to have followed it through. Going to Vienna before Berlin, or Barcelona before London would have thrown out the order and disrupted the pattern I had hoped to establish.

And there was a pattern. The further back in time I went the less material – photographs, documents, personal papers – there was to hold on to. I arrived in Vienna, therefore, almost empty-handed. A certificate of education, photographic references from Studio d'Ora and Grete Kolliner's Atelier, a few photographs of whose origins I couldn't be sure, and 'Dusk', Mrs Sachs's unfinished reminiscences of her Viennese years. The latter included a description of her favourite area of Vienna that I used to orient myself. It reads:

> It was autumn again. We were to meet in Café Schottentor, not far away from the University. Leo, Gustav and I – Lilli was coming later, directly to the concert-hall. I got there very early. I love to stroll along Schottenring. On the right Votivplatz with its church, the beautiful baroque town-hall with its cool arcades. On the left, Café Schottentor ... through the arcades to the quiet green quadrangle round the corner, back to the ring-boulevard lime-trees and acacias at the foot of the wide University steps.

I followed Mrs Sachs's directions assiduously, walking along the Schottenring towards the University, but what I saw didn't coalesce into the image of which she had written. I took photographs as I went, looking this way and that, constructing what was in effect a cross-section of the area. My anxiety was such that after finishing one roll of film I purchased another at a nearby bar and took the same photographs all over again. Later, when I had the films developed, I almost didn't recognise the images. They are so nondescript – no, more perplexing than that, they seem to be of nothing at all.

In Vienna I felt that any traces of Grete Gross had silvered out and there was virtually nothing left to follow. This situation was hardly surprising given the passing of so much time and the fact that during her Viennese years Gross's life as an independent photographer had not yet taken shape. But there was more to it than that. Gross was a Jew whose residence in Vienna coincided with the beginnings of the mass exodus of Jewish people from Austria. Faced with the growing anti-Semitism in the years leading up to World War II numerous Jewish photographers, including some of Austria's pre-eminent practitioners of the time, chose exile.

The murder and expulsion of Jewish artists and members of the intelligentsia finally began to be publicly acknowledged in Austria in the 1990s and the ramifications for contemporary life became the subject of critical attention. In the field of photography, curator Anna Auer has noted that Austria's emptying out of Jewish photographers left a huge gap and a 'loss for Austrian photographic history' that continues to be all too evident.[1] The major exhibition Exodus from Australia: Emigration of Austrian Photographers 1920–1940, curated by Auer and held in Vienna in 1997, had its roots in what photographic historian Heinz Henisch has described as 'events of unspeakable sadness'. However, for Henisch the exhibition was 'also a record of redemption and great joy'.[2] Various photographers with whom Michaelis had been associated were represented.

Late one afternoon on my way back to the hotel I found myself in Judenplatz, a stone's throw from the original location of Madame d'Ora's studio on Wipplingerstrasse. In the half-light it looked like a bomb had gone off in the rear end of the square. Windows were broken in the surrounding buildings, some of which were boarded up, and sections of the square itself were dug up. In the middle, hidden under protective coverings, was the almost completed Holocaust Memorial by English sculptor Rachel Whiteread. It is a construction of steel and concrete in the form of a cube, with sides that resemble library walls facing outward and floor tiles that contain the names of the locations where Austrian Jews were killed during the Third Reich. The names of some 65 000 people who perished are recorded in a multimedia presentation in a nearby information centre that has since opened (the names of Gross's parents,

Dr Henryk and Fanny Gross, are not listed; perhaps an indication that, unlike their daughter, they were not Austrian nationals).

Judenplatz is the focus of Vienna's program of restitution towards the Jews. It is an area of enormous significance historically and symbolically. It is the heart of the old Jewish quarter, which includes a medieval synagogue destroyed in the pogrom of 1420–21, the remains of which were only recently uncovered. It is also the site of the Misrachi House, a building originally owned by Jews, confiscated in the 1421 pogrom, aryanised after the *Anschluss* and eventually returned to the Jewish community in 1950. Other buildings in the Judenplatz have been used by various government departments; for example, between 1941 and 1945 the senates of the Nazi Administrative Court were housed in the former Bohemian Court Chancellery.

Mrs Sachs didn't live to see the transformation of Judenplatz or, one might add, the continuance of anti-Semitism in Austria. Indeed, after settling in Australia she never went back to Austria, even on her visit to Europe in the late 1960s. This is now recognised as having been a common occurrence – many of the Jewish photographers forced into exile in the 1920s and 1930s chose not to return. Mrs Sachs's compatriot, the dancer and choreographer Gertrud Bodenwieser, was another who refused to go back. The reasons for this phenomenon are complex. They include the government's failure to formally invite its former citizens to return and the pervasiveness of anti-Semitism and other forms of prejudice, which include anxieties about losing 'Aryanised' property and the possibility of dealing with potential competitors.[3]

I couldn't remember if I had visited the Schloss Schonbrunn on my last visit to Vienna nearly twenty years ago, and so on a Sunday morning I took the subway to the station near the palace. From there it was a short walk to the Schloss, which even at the relatively early hour was thronged with people, mainly tourists like me. I wasn't as interested in the palace as in the Schloss's fabulous grounds, and so followed a path that led away from the palace buildings and formal gardens and ran towards the perimeter of the grounds. From there I hoped to get a view of the gardens' overall design. It was a wonderfully atmospheric morning, misty and autumnal, and I shared the path with Viennese of all ages who were out jogging, walking their dogs or strolling with their companions. I remember enjoying the quietness but as the wind came up I was suddenly surrounded by a sound I didn't recognise. It was simple enough – a fast-growing choir of trees shaking down their dry autumn leaves – but hearing it made me suddenly realise I was a stranger with no place there.

Sometimes walking around Vienna I had the peculiar sensation that what I was seeing had slipped out of register and I was experiencing two views simultaneously. One was based on the map of Mrs Sachs's Vienna that I was conscientiously attempting to re-construct, using as its co-ordinates her reminiscences and the few associated addresses I had gathered. The other view, lacking singularity and specificity, was something over which I had no control, flickering tantalisingly into shape when I least expected it. This was the view that became more and more seductive, the one I began to seek out. My walks became wanderings, my map the half-remembered views of a building, a street, a corner, my own hazy memories of a city that I had visited in autumn with my lover many years before.

One thing I did remember clearly was the Kunsthistorisches Museum. I went there with a sense of purpose, to reacquaint myself with paintings I had loved on my first visit – Velázquez's portraits of the Infanta Marie Thérèse and Rubens' portrait of his wife, Hélène Fourment. They were pleasurable enough but this time it was Titian's paintings, especially *Isabella d'Este*, *Danae* and his late work *Nymph and shepherd*, that had me in their thrall. It was as though I had never seen them before and yet I knew of course that I had. What hit me was their eroticism – the way those women, Isabella d'Este, the Danae and the nymph are painted – and the intensity of Titian's vision of his subject. While the paintings seem underwritten with desire, *Nymph and shepherd* also impressed me as an invocation of the impossibility of actually picturing such a thing. Here the wonderfully loose paintwork of Titian's late style functions dualistically: it brings the form and flesh of the nymph to life and yet at the same time conveys a sense of doubt about whether or not such a process is possible. Somehow Titian creates a dynamic relationship between two otherwise seemingly incompatible elements, between something that is solid and something that is not, something that can be named and something that cannot.

In front of Titian's paintings I experienced a sharp, all-pervading sensation that I can only describe as an awareness of loss, though loss of what exactly I couldn't be sure. And so, sitting on a bench in the Titian room of the Kunsthistoriches Museum, I took out my notebook and began to write. It wasn't a story about Margaret Michaelis, as had been the case in every other city I had visited during my research, but a letter to the lover I had travelled with to Vienna twenty years before. I have kept the letter and can't imagine that I will ever send it.

Another section of the Kunsthistorisches was devoted to an exhibition of works on loan from the Miho Museum in Japan. And it is here, with one of the exquisite objects from the Museum's collection, that this story ends. The object, *Seated woman*, which originated in North Afghanistan/South Turkey is a small, ancient stone figure. Her tiny head is perfect with sharp, particularised facial features, and her hair is distinctively parted down the middle. Her eyes are closed. In front of her, lying on the orange silk lining of the display case in which she is enclosed, are two thin white arms. It is not possible to see exactly where these bone-like arms were originally attached and so there is a space of a few centimetres between the figure's solid form and the broken pieces. Although nothing is in this space, it is not empty. It is a space inhabited by secrets that can no longer be spoken or heard, a speculative kind of space perfect for puzzling over and playing in. A space, it seemed to me, filled with possibilities for the telling of stories.

For a very long time I believed that I hadn't properly heard what Mrs Sachs had been telling me in 1985, the year we had met. In my mind I endlessly turned over our few conversations in the hope that something would become clearer. I often cursed myself for having failed to ask her what I had come to see as the 'right' questions – not just about photography but also about love, children, faith and loss. I dreamt up different scenarios of my last visit and hung on to the one that was most resolved, the version in which I agreed to take her photographs and, in acknowledgment that she was dying, kissed her goodbye.

In Vienna, finally, I realised that none of this could have happened. To have spoken about such matters and to have kissed Mrs Sachs as I had imagined would have assumed an intimacy that did not exist. Our relationship, after all, was a professional one based on our shared interest in photography and was always conducted in highly formal terms. It was in Vienna I realised that I did not know Mrs Sachs very well.

Endnotes

2 DUSK

1 Susan Sontag, *On photography*, New York: Delta Publishing, 1976, pp. 19–20.

3 VIENNA

1 Atina Grossmann, 'Elgir professió … un privilegi de les dones burgeses', in *Les dones fotògrafes a la República de Weimar 1919–1933*, exhibition catalogue, Barcelona: Fundació 'La Caixa', 1995, pp. 12–20.

2 Quoted in Val Williams, *The other observers: women photographers in Britain 1900 to the present*, London: Virago, 1991 reprint, p. 90.

3 Monika Faber, 'Amateurs et autres: histoire de la photographie (1887–1936)', in *Vienne 1880–1938: L'Apocalypse Joyeuse*, exhibition catalogue, Paris: Pompidou Centre, 1986, p. 377.

4 Monika Faber, p. 382.

5 Monika Faber, p. 386.

6 Aenne Biermann was one of the few women photographers who had a book on her work published as early as 1930. Ute Eskildsen, 'A chance to participate: a transitional time for women photographers', in Marsha Meskimmon & Shearer West (eds), *Visions of the neue Fräu: women and the visual arts in Weimar Germany*, Aldershot: Scolar Press, 1995, p. 73. (The book was *Aenne Biermann: 60 Fotos*, Berlin: Linkhardt & Biermann, 1930.)

7 Quoted in Ute Eskildsen, *Aenne Biermann photographs 1925–33*, London: Dirk Nishen Publishing, 1988, p. 13. For a full consideration of the work of women photographers of this period see *Les dones fotògrafes a la República de Weimar 1919–1933*, pp. 12–20.

8 Helmut Lehmann, quoted by Heinrich August Winkler, 'Images of revolution and the Weimar Republic', in Klaus Honnef et al., *German photography 1870–1970: power of a medium*, Koln: Dumont Buchverlag, 1997, p. 48.

9 Heinrich August Winkler 1997, p. 48. Winkler continues, 'Semolina, boiled potatoes and bean salad were the typical ingredients of a main meal eaten by the family of an unemployed person. If ever meat happened to be on the table, it was usually cow or horse meat' (p. 48).

10 Quoted by Peter Gay, *Weimar culture: the outside as insider*, New York: Harper & Row, 1963, p. 129.

11 Charles Kessler (trans. and ed.), *The diaries of a cosmopolitan: Count Harry Kessler 1918–1937*, London: Weidenfeld & Nicolson, 1971, p. 399. Harry Kessler (1868–1937) was the son of a German noble and his mother, an Irish woman, was a favourite of Kaiser Wilhelm I. Born in France, Kessler moved in art circles in Berlin during the Weimar years as a patron of the arts and a publisher. He was exiled in Paris in 1933.

4 DEAR GRETL

1 Hans-Jürgen Degen, '"Die Anarchie ist möglich …" Zum Tode von Rudolph "Michel" Michaelis', in *Direkte Aktion*, March/April 1991, no. 86, p. 12.

2 Rudolf Michaelis acknowledged his debt to Rüdiger in his unpublished memoirs, where he wrote that from the 1920s he and Rüdiger were bonded 'by a deep friendship, in which he was the giver and I the recipient', quoted in Hans-Jürgen Degen, p. 12.

3 Hans-Jürgen Degen, p. 12.

4 Marsha Meskimmon, 'Politics, the Neue Sachlichkeit and women artists', in Marsha Meskimmon & Shearer West, p. 16.

5 See Erika Esau, 'The Künstlerehepaar: ideal and reality', in Marsha Meskimmon & Shearer West, p. 30.

6 See Erika Esau, pp. 28–42.

5 LOVERS

1 Roland Barthes, *A lover's discourse*, Richard Howard trans., New York: Hill and Wang, 1978, p. 71.

2 Alfred Stieglitz, *Georgia O'Keeffe: a portrait*, New York: Metropolitan Museum of Art, 1978, n.p.

6 A SORRY STATE

1 See Rolf Sachsse, 'Photography as NS state design: power's abuse of a medium', in Klaus Honnef et al. 1997, p. 87.
2 Harry Kessler, diary entry 12 July 1932, in Charles Kessler, p. 423.
3 Harry Kessler, diary entry 30 January 1933, in Charles Kessler, pp. 443–4.
4 Harry Kessler, diary entry 27 February 1933, in Charles Kessler, p. 448.
5 *I shall bear witness: the diaries of Victor Klemperer 1933–41*, translated by Martin Chalmers, London: Weidenfeld & Nicolson, 1998, p. 5.
6 From Saul Friedländer, *Nazi Germany and the Jews: volume 1 The years of persecution, 1933–1939*, London: Phoenix, 1997, p. 17. Dachau was established on 20 March 1933.
7 Saul Friedländer, p. 17.
8 Rolf Sachsse, p. 93. Sachsse notes that the dismissal, persecution and expulsion of Jewish reporters and photographers who had not specifically identified themselves as opponents of the National Socialist regime was enshrined in the Schriftleitergesetz (editorial act) of November 1933.
9 Harry Kessler, diary entry, 1 April 1933, in Charles Kessler, p. 451.
10 Victor Klemperer, diary entry, 20 April 1933, in *I shall bear witness: the diaries of Victor Klemperer* 1998, p. 13.
11 See Rolf Sachsse, p. 93.
12 Saul Friedländer, p. 50.
13 From a photocopy of documents relating to Gross's arrest, sent to the author by Dieter Nelles. The original is in the Federal Archive in Koblenz R.58, document no. 764.
14 'Personality of the month: Margaret's camera charisma', Montefiore Homes for the Aged newsletter, Melbourne, 1985, p. 5.
15 See Hans-Jürgen Degen 1991. Wartenberg's pseudonym was HW Gerhard.
16 Rudolf Michaelis, 'Encounter with Spain', given to the author by Hans-Jürgen Degen, n.p.
17 Rudolf Michaelis, 'Encounter with Spain', n.p.
18 Hans-Jürgen Degen, p. 12.
19 Hans-Jürgen Degen, p. 12.
20 Sent to the author by Hans-Jürgen Degen in February 1998.
21 Hans-Jürgen Degen, p. 12.
22 'Personality of the month' 1985, p. 5.
23 The other main prison at the time was the Gestapo prison in the Secret State Police building at Prinz-Albrecht-Strasse, which was established in late summer 1933 to hold prisoners required for interrogation by the Gestapo. The number of cells was limited; only fifty prisoners could be accommodated. Reinhard Rürup (ed.), *Topography of terror: Gestapo, SS and Reichssicherheitshauptamt on the Prinz-Albrecht-Terrain, a documentation*, 7th edn, Berlin: Verlag Willmuth Avenhovel, 1989, p. 84.
24 Rudolf Michaelis, 'Rudolf Michaelis in protective custody', in *Der pech-raben schwarze Anarcho Kalender 1994*, Berlin: Karin Kramer Verlag, 1993, pp. 192–201.
25 Hans-Jürgen Degen, p. 12.
26 'Personality of the month' 1985, p. 5.

7 BERLIN

1 Luis Buñuel, *My last breath*, London: Vintage, 1994, pp. 4–5.

8 CRACOW

1 *A vanished world: Roman Vishniac*, London: Allen Lane, 1983, Preface (n.p.).
2 This document is in the Arxiu Històric del Col.legi d'Arquitectes de Catalunya, Barcelona.It is attributed to Michaelis and relates to her photograph of cardsharps published in the GATEPAC's magazine, *A.C. Documentos de Actividad Contemporánea*, no. 6, 1932; the connection was identified by Jordana Mendelson. See 'Incursión en el Barrio Chino, 1932', reproduced in Juan José Lahuerta & Jordana Mendelson, *Margaret Michaelis: Fotografia, Vanguardia i Política a la Barcelona de la República*, Valencia: IVAM and Barcelona: CCCB, 1998, pp. 169–74.
3 *A vanished world*, pl. 97, n.p.

4　See photographs by Albert Cusian and Erhard Josef Knobloch, who worked extensively in the Warsaw Ghetto in 1940, and Zermin who worked in Lodz. Cusian and Knobloch were members of a German Propaganda-kompanie.

5　Elie Wiesel, in *A vanished world*, Foreword (n.p.).

6　Eugene Kinkead, *Roman Vishniac*, New York: Grossman, 1974, p. 17.

7　*A vanished world*, Preface (n.p.).

9　ENCOUNTER WITH SPAIN

1　Raymond Carr, *Images of the Spanish Civil War*, London: Allen and Unwin, 1986, p. 40.

2　Organised on what James Joll has described as 'the best anarchist lines', with minimum administrative arrangements and no permanent officials, the CNT, unlike similar organisations elsewhere in Europe, created an effective alliance between industrial and rural workers. This was of central importance for the success of the spontaneous revolution of July 1936. James Joll, *The anarchists*, 2nd edn, London: Methuen & Co., 1979, pp. 221–2.

3　James Joll, p. 231.

4　Pere Bosch-Gimpera, *Memòries*, Barcelona: Edicions 62, 1980, p. 199.

5　'The back room', *Australian Monthly*, October 1951, p. 63.

6　'Photography is an art for her', *Sydney Morning Herald*, 5 November 1950, p. 13.

7　Joan Fontcuberta, *Idas and chaos: trends in Spanish photography 1920–1945*, New York: International Center of Photography, n.d., p. 30.

8　Antonio Gonzalez & Raquel Lacuesta, *Barcelona architecture guide 1929–1994*, Barcelona: Editorial Gustavo Gili, 1995, p. 25.

10　PARTING

1　Lucia Moholy, wife of László Moholy-Nagy, approached the GATCPAC for work in a letter dated 1933; Walter Gropius wrote her a letter of reference. Documents in Arxiu Històric del Col. legi d'Arquitectes de Catalunya, Barcelona.

2　Sybile von Kastel was a professional photographer who worked in Madrid; see *les avantguardes fotogràfiques a espanya 1925–1945*, Barcelona: Fundació 'la Caixa', 1997. Tina Modotti also visited Spain and attracted considerable attention.

3　Hugh Thomas, *The Spanish Civil War*, London: Hamish Hamilton, 1977, rev. edn, p. 47.

4　In December 1934 the anarcho-syndicalists successfully established libertarian communism in a number of places in Aragon and Catalonia. Durruti led a revolutionary committee at Saragossa, which for several days resisted the police and government troops; see Hugh Thomas, p. 126.

5　Estimates of the number of casualties vary greatly. These figures are derived from James Joll, p. 233.

6　Letter dated 9 August 1935. These letters from Etta Federn to Milly Witkop-Rocker and Rudolf Rocker were kindly brought to my attention by Marianne Kröger. They are in the Rudolf Rocker Archive, International Institute of Social History, Amsterdam.

7　Marianne Kröger, letter to the author, 27 July 1997.

8　Letter from Helmut Rüdiger to Rudolf Rocker and Mollie Steimer, Rudolf Rocker Archive, Flechine-Steimer Archive, International Institute of Social History, Amsterdam, quoted by Ulrich Linse, 'The DAS Group in Barcelona: from Hitler's coming to power in 1933 until the outbreak of the Civil War in 1936', from a manuscript sent to the author by Hans-Jürgen Degen, n.p.

9　Quoted by Ulrich Linse, 'The DAS Group in Barcelona', from a manuscript sent to the author by Hans-Jürgen Degen, n.p.

10　Letter from Karl Brauner to Ulrich Linse, 4 February 1991, quoted by Ulrich Linse, 'The DAS Group in Barcelona', from a manuscript sent to the author by Hans-Jürgen Degen, n.p.

11　Arthur Lehning, diary entry, 8 October 1936, in *Spaans dagboek Aantekeningen over de revolutie in Spanje*, 1996, n.p.

12　Quoted by Ulrich Linse, 'The DAS Group in Barcelona', from a manuscript sent to the author by Hans-Jürgen Degen, n.p.

13　Etta Federn, letter to Milly Witkop-Rocker, 11 October 1934, Rudolf Rocker Archive, International Institute of Social History, Amsterdam.

14　Etta Federn, letter to Milly Witkop-Rocker, letter dated 10 October 1934, Rudolf Rocker Archive, International Institute of Social History, Amsterdam.

11 A NEW SPIRIT

1   Dieter Nelles, correspondence with the author, 1992. Nelles also wrote that Brauner had been a 'young proletarian ... very interested in psychoanalysis, especially its extreme views. He was greatly influenced by Wilhelm Reich'.

2   See Daniel Giralt-Miracle, *A.C.: Les Vanguardias en Cataluña 1906–1939* (Barcelona: Fundació Caixa de Catalunya, 1992) and the chronology in *Homage to Barcelona: the city and its art* (exhibition catalogue, London: Arts Council of Great Britain, 1986). For details of the GATCPAC manifesto see Josep M Rovira, 'The Mediterranean is his cradle', in Antonio Pizza (ed.), *J.L.L. Sert y el Mediterraneo*, Barcelona: Arxiu Històric del Col.legi d'Arquitectes de Catalunya, 1996, p. 60.

3   Antonio Gonzalez & Raquel Lacuesta, p. 25.

4   Daniel Giralt-Miracle, p. 644.

5   Daniel Giralt-Miracle, p. 644.

6   Francesc Roca, 'From Montjuic to the world', in *Homage to Barcelona* 1986, p. 139.

7   Margaret Michaelis, 'Incursión en el Barrio Chino, 1932', reproduced in Jordana Mendelson & Juan José Lahuerta, p. 163.

8   Margaret Michaelis, 'Incursión en el Barrio Chino, 1932', reproduced in Jordana Mendelson & Juan José Lahuerta, p. 163.

9   Jaume Freixa, *Josep Ll. Sert*, Barcelona: Gustavo Gili, 1989, p. 38.

10 Juan José Lahuerta, 'My little Leica', in Jordana Mendelson & Juan José Lahuerta, p. 167.

11 Juan José Lahuerta, in Jordana Mendelson & Juan José Lahuerta, p. 167. 'El barrio Chino de Barcelona (Distrito V)' was published in *A.C.*, number 6.

12 Jordana Mendelson, in Jordana Mendelson & Juan José Lahuerta, p. 171.

13 Jordana Mendelson, in Jordana Mendelson & Juan José Lahuerta, p. 171.

14 Juan José Lahuerta, in Jordana Mendelson & Juan José Lahuerta, p. 167.

15 See Jordana Mendelson, in Jordana Mendelson & Juan José Lahuerta, p. 170. Mendelson notes that the reporter Francisco Madrid renamed the Fifth district the Barrio Chino after San Francisco's China Town. She also points out that the photographic representations of the Barrio Chino from around 1933 range from the scintillating spreads of the weekly mass magazine *Escandalo* to finely executed portraits by French photographer Henri Cartier-Bresson.

16 Josep M Rovira, in Antonio Pizza, p. 66.

17 Jaume Freixa, p. 10.

12 THE STAGE OF HISTORY

1   Graham Kelsey, 'Anarchism in Aragon during the Second Republic: the emergence of a mass movement', in Martin Blinkhorn (ed.), *Spain in conflict 1931–39: democracy and its enemies*, London: Sage Publications, 1986, p. 76.

2   *Berliner Zeitung*, 17 July 1966, quoted by Hans-Jürgen Degen, p. 12.

3   Rudolf Rocker, *Anarcho-syndicalism*, London: Secker & Warburg, 1938, p. 91.

4   James Joll, p. 231.

5   Abel Paz, *Durruti – the people armed*, Quebec: Black Rose Books, 1976, p. 218.

6   George Orwell, *Homage to Catalonia*, London: Penguin Books, 1989, pp. 2–3 (first published by Secker & Warburg in 1938).

7   George Orwell, p. 3.

8   José Peirats, *Anarchists in the Spanish Revolution*, London: Freedom Press, 1990, p. 188.

9   Raymond Carr, p. 129.

10 Paul Thalman, quoted in Hans-Jürgen Degen, p. 13.

11 See *L'art catalan: du xe au xve siècle*, Paris: probably Librairie des Arts Decoratifs, 1937. The Spanish Pavilion featured the work of Spanish avant-garde architects, painters and sculptors (it was here that Pablo Picasso's mural painting *Guernica* made its dramatic debut; the Pavilion also included panels of photographs documenting the daily life of the Spanish people during peace and war).

12 Letter from the GATCPAC Secretary to JLl Sert, 4 November 1936, Arxiu Històric del Col.legi d'Arquitectes de Catalunya, Barcelona.

13 I am most grateful to Jordana Mendelson for her research in this area. See, for example, Margaret Michaelis's story on agriculture published in *Nova Iberia*, no. 2, 1937, which was used in the anti-fascist Civil War magazine *Armas y Letras* in 1938.

14 Hans-Erich Kaminski, *Ceux de Barcelone*, 1937, quoted in Arthur Lehning 1996, p. 36.

15 Lehning was an expert in anarchist history; he was editor of the Archives Bakounine, comprising the complete works of the Russian revolutionary and wrote extensively on political subjects. He founded the avant-garde periodical *i10* in Amsterdam in 1927 and also founded the anarcho-syndicalist journal *Grondslagen*. He was instrumental in the establishment of the International Institute of Social History in Amsterdam in 1935. See Toke van Helmond '*i10* an international review published in Amsterdam', *Dutch Heights*, 3 November 1989, pp. 34–9.

16 Arthur Lehning, p. 35.

17 Candace Falk, *Love, anarchy and Emma Goldman*, New York: Holt, Rinehart and Winston, 1984, p. 482.

18 Raymond Carr, p. 11.

19 Graham Kelsey, p. 78.

20 Hans-Erich Kaminski, quoted by Arthur Lehning, pp. 46–7.

21 Hans-Erich Kaminski, quoted by Arthur Lehning, pp. 45–6.

22 Arthur Lehning, p. 42.

23 Marianne Kröger, *Etta Federn: Revolutionär Auf Ihre Art*, Giefen: Psychosozial, 1997, p. 90.

24 Quoted by Abel Paz, p. 314.

25 Abel Paz, p. 309.

26 Hans-Erich Kaminski, 1937, *Ceux de Barcelone*, quoted by Abel Paz, p. 308.

27 Hans-Erich Kaminski, quoted by Abel Paz, p. 308.

28 Hans-Erich Kaminski, quoted by Abel Paz, p. 308.

29 Hans-Erich Kaminski, quoted by Abel Paz, p. 308.

30 Arthur Lehning, p. 189.

31 Rudolph Michaelis, *Rudolf 'Michel' Michaelis. Mit der Centuria 'Erich Mühsam' vor Huesca*, Berlin: Oppo-Verlag, 1995.

32 Paul Thalmann, quoted in Hans-Jürgen Degen, p. 13.

33 'Personality of the month' 1985, p. 6.

34 Etta Federn letter to Milly Witkop-Rocker and Rudolf Rocker, 9 August 1935, Rudolf Rocker Archive, International Institute of Social History, Amsterdam.

35 Juan Manuel Bonet & Josep Ramoneda, 'Presentation', in Jordana Mendelson & Juan José Lahuerta, p. 157.

36 See Jordana Mendelson, 'Architecture, photography and (gendered) modernities in 1930s Barcelona', in *Modernism/Modernity*, vol. 10, no. 1, January 2003, pp. 141–64.

37 Joan Naranjo, 'Avant-garde photography in Spain (1925–1945)', in *les avantguardes fotogràfiques a espanya*, October, 20, p. 202.

13 EXILE

1 Saul Friedländer, p. 218.

2 Saul Friedländer, p. 219.

3 Saul Friedländer, p. 245.

14 SYDNEY

1 Roberts remained supportive, however, and in 1952 gave her a reference attesting to her skills and reliability.

2 All quotations from the police and government authorities relating to Michaelis's security status are from ASIO file 6119, access gained through the Australian Archives.

3 From the interview *The immigrants*, produced by Richard Brown, ABC Radio, Autumn 1979, transcript in National Gallery of Australia Archives. Dr Helen Light, kindly provided me with a copy of the recording.

4 Letter from the Right Reverend Bishop C Venn Pilcher, Coadjutor of Sydney, to the Commissioner, 2 October 1941, held in ASIO file 6119, on Margaret Michaelis.

5 ASIO file 6119, on Margaret Michaelis.

6 ASIO file 6119, on Margaret Michaelis.

7 ASIO file 6119, on Margaret Michaelis.

8 Barbara Hall & Jenni Mather, *Australian women photographers 1840–1960*, Richmond, Victoria: Greenhouse, 1986, p. 93.

9   Anna Auer, *Übersee: Flucht und Emigration Österreichischer Fotografen 1920–1940*, English translation, Vienna: Kunsthalle Wien, 1997, p. 16.
10   'Personality of the month' 1985, p. 6.
11   Michaelis had purchased some of Lotte Meitner-Graf's prints on her visit to London in August 1967.
12   Jean Raymond Day, letter to the author, June 2002.
13   Janine Burke (ed.), *Dear Sun: the letters of Joy Hester and Sunday Reed*, Port Melbourne: William Heinemann, 1995, p. 27.
14   Margaret E McGuire, *All things opposite: essays on Australian art*, Prahran, Victoria: Champion, 1995, pp. 23, 26.
15   Patrick White, *Flaws in the glass*, London: Jonathon Cape, 1981, p. 236.
16   *Bride for St Thomas*, 1970, quoted in Margaret E McGuire, p. 23.
17   'Photography is an art for her' 1950, p. 13.
18   Shona Dunlop MacTavish, letter to the author, August 1990.
19   Jean Raymond Day, letter to the author, June 2002.
20   Review, *Sydney Morning Herald*, January 1940, quoted by Shona Dunlop MacTavish, *Ecstasy of purpose: the life and art of Gertrud Bodenwieser*, Dunedin: Shona Dunlop MacTavish, Les Humphrey and Associates, 1987, p. 95.
21   'Our debt to Gertrud Bodenwieser's art', *Sydney Morning Herald*, 12 November 1959, quoted by Bettina Vernon-Warren & Charles Warrant (eds), *Gertrud Bodenwieser and Vienna's contribution to Ausdructstanz*, Amsterdam: Harwood Academic Publishers, 1999, p. 172.
22   Shona Dunlop MacTavish, letter to the author, August 1990.
23   Vera Goldman, letter to the author, 10 March 2001.
24   'Camera craft', *Pix*, vol. 25, no. 17, 21 October 1950, p. 33.
25   Oswald L Ziegler (ed.), *Australian photography 1947*, Sydney: Ziegler Gotham, 1947, pp. 6–10.
26   Gael Newton, *Shades of light: photography and Australia 1839–1988*, Sydney: Collins Australia and the Australian National Gallery, 1988, p. 129.
27   Conversation with the author, December 2000.
28   Conversation with the author, December 2000.
29   Margaret Michaelis, 'Camera class', *Australian Monthly*, October 1951, p. 39.
30   Russell Roberts, 28 March 1952, copy in the National Gallery of Australia registry file, 85/298.

15 THE DARK CHAIR
1   *The immigrants* 1979.
2   Ruth Spencer, 'André Kertész', *The British Journal of Photography*, 4 April 1975, no. 122, p. 291.
3   Brassaï, 'My friend André Kertész', in *Camera*, no. 4, 1963, p. 32.
4   Hauser had arrived in Sydney in 1951 where he was engaged to investigate the conditions of workers in the public transport system, see Yehudi Menuhin, *An unfinished journey*, Camberwell, London: Futura, 1978, p. 323.
5   Yehudi Menuhin, p. 324.
6   Yehudi Menuhin, p. 324.
7   *The immigrants* 1979.

17 REDEMPTION
1   Luis Buñuel 1994, p. 5.
2   Vera Goldman, letter to the author, August 1990.

18 VIENNA
1   Anna Auer, 'Exodus from Austria – emigration of Austrian photographers 1920–1940', in Anna Auer, p. 17.
2   Heinz Henisch, Prologue in Anna Auer, p. 12.
3   See Peter Eppel, 'Exiled Austrians in the USA 1938 to 1945: immigration, exile, remigration, no invitation to return', in Frederich Stadler & Peter Weibel (eds), *Vertreibung der Vernunft: the cultural exodus from Austria*, Vienna: Springer-Verlag, 1995, p. 40.

Note on the sources

This book is based primarily on the Margaret Michaelis-Sachs Archive in the collection of the National Gallery of Australia. It includes photographs, letters and personal papers. The photographs reproduced here are gelatin silver unless otherwise stated.

The principal collections of photographs by Margaret Michaelis are held in the National Gallery of Australia; the Arxiu Fotogràfic of the Arxiu Històric de la Ciutat, Barcelona; and the Arxiu Històric of the Col.legi d'Arquitectes de Catalunya, Barcelona.

In Australia further examples of Michaelis's work are in the Mitchell Library, State Library of New South Wales; and in the Pictures collection and Manuscripts collection in the National Library of Australia. Michaelis's photographs are also in private collections in Australia and Spain.

All undocumented quotes in the book are from items in the Margaret Michaelis-Sachs Archive or the registry file 85/298, held by the National Gallery of Australia, Canberra.

Further reading

The principal sources on Margaret Michaelis are as follows:

Helen Ennis, *Margaret Michaelis*, exhibition room brochure, Canberra: National Gallery of Australia, 1987.

Helen Ennis, 'Blue hydrangeas', in Roger Butler (ed.), *The Europeans: émigré artists in Australia*, Canberra: National Gallery of Australia, 1997.

Barbara Hall & Jenni Mather, *Australian women photographers 1850–1960*, Richmond, Victoria: Greenhouse, 1986.

Jordana Mendelson, 'Architecture, photography and (gendered) modernities in 1930s Barcelona', in *Modernism/Modernity*, vol. 10, no. 1, pp. 141–64.

Jordana Mendelson & Juan José Lahuerta, *Margaret Michaelis: Fotografía, Vanguardia y Política en la Barcelona de la República*, Valencia: IVAM & Barcelona: CCCB, 1998.

Author's acknowledgments

This project began as a response to Margaret Michaelis's photographs, one that was framed in conventional art historical terms. Its slow metamorphosis over the years, into a story about photography, politics, love, loss and exile has been facilitated by many people in Australia, Europe and the United States.

I am indebted to the pioneering research of Barbara Hall and Jenni Mather, who originally made contact with Margaret Michaelis and represented her in their Australian Women Photographers Research Project. I would also like to thank James Mollison, Foundation Director of the National Gallery of Australia, who was extremely enthusiastic and supportive about the National Gallery of Australia's acquisition of the Margaret Michaelis-Sachs Archive in 1985–86, shortly after my appointment as Curator of Photography.

Mrs Sachs's lawyers Fraenkel, Kiven & Saubern facilitated negotiations and provided much useful biographical information.

Over the years numerous staff at the National Gallery of Australia have worked on the Archive. The photographs were originally catalogued by Kylie Scroope and Kate Davidson, curatorial assistants in the Department of Photography; Karen Jakubec, an intern in the Australian National

University Museum Studies program in 1997, also provided assistance. More recently Anne O'Hehir, Assistant Curator in the Department of Photography, helped prepare material for the book with great cheerfulness and diligence. Staff in the National Gallery Research Library assisted with my wide-ranging early research queries; in this regard I would particularly like to thank Margaret Shaw and Gillian Currie.

Publication of *Margaret Michaelis: love, loss and photography* was approved under the Directorship of Dr Brian Kennedy and warmly endorsed by Ron Radford, recently appointed Director of the National Gallery of Australia. I am also greatly appreciative of the following for their enthusiastic commitment to the project: Gael Newton, Senior Curator of Photography; Ruth Patterson, Assistant Director, Marketing and Merchandising; and Kirsty Morrison, Publications Manager. National Gallery photographer Eleni Kypridis ably undertook the reproduction photography. Paige Amor was a wonderfully professional and responsive editor, and the designer Sarah Robinson worked with great sensitivity to produce a beautiful book.

Translations of various items in the Michaelis-Sachs Archive were undertaken by many people, including the late Anne Bonyhady, Sasha Debus, Fred and Gerda Kleitsch, Ellen Cordes, Julia Harman, and Dörte Conroy. The Australian Archives and the National Library of Australia enabled me to access significant material; Marianne Dacy at the Archive of Australian Judaica, Fisher Library, University of Sydney, also provided information.

In the early stages of my research Dr Helen Light, Director, Jewish Museum of Australia, Beatrice Faust, and Josephine Phillips referred me to people who had known Margaret Michaelis-Sachs in Australia. Other individuals in Australia who generously offered their recollections were photographers Olive Cotton, David Moore, Wolfgang Sievers, and Mrs Sachs's friends and associates Ruth Benjamin, Antonia Burgess, Margaret Delmer, Mr Heinz Harant, Meaghan Kelly, Wendy Kelly, Erica McGilchrist, Mrs Susi Menzer, Ellen Picker, Anne and Bill Pye, Mrs Lucy Rofe, Ellen Schlesinger, Mrs Waterman, and Erika Wohlwill. In relation to Michaelis's dance photography I am grateful to Paula Boltman, Brian McNamara, Margaret Chapple, Marie Cuckson, Coralie Hinkley, Shona Dunlop MacTavish, Jean Raymond Day, Vera Goldman and dance historian Michelle Potter.

In Germany numerous individuals have helped with information, reminiscences and references. I would particularly like to thank friends of the Michaelises, including the late Karl Brauner. Dieter Nelles, Irme Schaber and Marianne Kröger have all provided useful references, helping me make contact with a community of scholars researching similar areas. Hans-Jürgen Degen gave me much invaluable biographical information on Rudolf Michaelis, which enhanced my understanding of the relationship between Margaret and Rudolf Michaelis. In the Netherlands the late Arthur Lehning and his colleagues responded generously to my requests

The section on Margaret Michaelis's connections to the GATCPAC architects was made possible with the cooperation of the Arxiu Històric del Col.legi d'Arquitectes de Catalunya, especially Andreu Carrascal i Simon, the archivisit, and the Director, David Ferrer. None of the research into the Spanish material could have been completed without the outstanding work undertaken by Jordana Mendelson and Juan José Lahuerta, co-curators of the exhibition Margaret Michaelis: Fotografía, Vanguardia y Política en la Barcelona de la República, held at the IVAM, Julio Gonzalez in Valencia in 1998. Jordana Mendelson combed the Arxiu Històric of the Col.legi d'Arquitectes de Catalunya and other Spanish collections while studying in Barcelona for her doctorate at Yale University, bringing to my attention material that otherwise would not have been possible for me to access. Jordana has been an exemplary colleague, open and generous; her visit to Australia in June 1997 to select loans for the IVAM exhibition enabled a crucial exchange of information and views that has continued.

The following international institutions and organisations have provided information: the International Institute for Social Research, Amsterdam, through Mr Rudolf de Jong, which holds letters written by German anarchists (some of which are quoted in this book); the Bundesarchiv, Koblenz, Germany; the Arbetarrörelsens Arkiv och Bibliotek, Sweden; New York Public Library; and the Jewish Refugees Committee, London.

I received a writer's grant from the Visual Arts and Craft Board of the Australia Council in 1993, which enabled me to first begin the writing process. With small grants from the Australian Research Council and the Australian National University Faculties Research Grants Scheme I undertook critical primary and secondary research in Europe during 1997, 1998 and 1999, visiting Barcelona, Berlin, London and Valencia. This greatly extended the scope of the project. A chance meeting with David Marr on one of the flights to Europe helped me clarify my concepts, especially concerning biographical writing and the construction of Michaelis as a 'character'.

In 1999 I was awarded an artsACT Development Grant from the ACT Government, which gave me much needed time to write drafts of early chapters; my colleagues Professor David Williams, Gordon Bull, Anne Brennan and Chaitanya Sambrani at the Australian National University School of Art have fully supported the project and facilitated my leave to make the writing possible. Many friends have helped me sustain this project over the years and I would especially like to thank Jocelyn Hackforth-Jones in London and Helen Maxwell in Canberra.

My colleague Isobel Crombie, Senior Curator of Photography at the National Gallery of Victoria, read innumerable drafts and, as always, responded with insights and enthusiasm. Tim Bonyhady offered much encouragement during the prolonged writing process and read the manuscript at a crucial stage, as did Ian McLean whose comments on the final draft of the manuscript were invaluable.

Finally, my heartfelt appreciation goes to members of my family, especially my parents, Janet and David Ennis, and my sister Jenny Brown. This book could not have been written without my partner, Roger Butler, who has been extraordinarily attentive to every nuance in Margaret Michaelis's story and in my writing of it. To Roger and our sons, Jack and Ben Ennis Butler, I owe my greatest debt.

Earlier stages of this research have been published in: Helen Ennis, *Margaret Michaelis*, Canberra: National Gallery of Australia, 1987 [exhibition room brochure]; Helen Ennis, 'Blue hydrangeas' in Roger Butler (ed.), *The Europeans: émigré artists in Australia*, Canberra: National Gallery of Australia, 1997; Joan Kerr (ed.), *Heritage: the national women's arts book*, Art and Australia, Roseville: Craftsman House, 1995; Helen Ennis, 'Margaret Michaelis-Sachs', in Anna Gray (ed.), *Australian art in the National Gallery of Australia*, Canberra: National Gallery of Australia, 2002; and Helen Ennis, 'Margaret Michaelis in context', in Juan José Lahuerta & Jordana Mendelson, *Margaret Michaelis: Fotografía, Vanguardia y Política en la Barcelona de la República*, Valencia: IVAM & Barcelona: CCCB, 1998. I also presented an excerpt of 'Lovers' discourse' as a paper at the Art Association of Australia and New Zealand Conference, University of Melbourne, 2001; at the symposium Artists' Biographies at Ian Potter Museum of Art, Melbourne in 2002; and at 'Challenges to Perform' at the Australian National University Centre for Cross Cultural Research in 2004.

The exhibition Margaret Michaelis: Love, Loss and Photography was held at the National Gallery of Australia from 7 May to 14 August 2005.